Financial
Serenity

Financial
Serenity

Successful Financial Planning
and Investment for Women

Lori M. Bamber

PRENTICE HALL CANADA

Canadian Cataloguing in Publication Data

Bamber, Lori M.
    Financial serenity: successful financial and investment planning for women

Includes index.
ISBN 0-13-011611-4

1. Women — Finance, Personal. 2. Investments. I. Title.

HG179.B335 1999   332.024'042   C99-931757-1

Prentice-Hall Canada Inc.
Scarborough, Ontario

Prentice-Hall, Inc., Upper Saddle River, New Jersey
Prentice-Hall International (UK) Limited, London
Prentice-Hall of Australia, Pty. Limited, Sydney
Prentice-Hall Hispanoamericana, S.A., Mexico City
Prentice-Hall of India Private Limited, New Delhi
Prentice-Hall of Japan, Inc., Tokyo
Simon & Schuster Southeast Asia Private Limited, Singapore
Editora Prentice-Hall do Brasil, Ltda., Rio de Janeiro

ISBN 0-13-011611-4

Editorial Director, Trade Group: Andrea Crozier
Acquisitions Editor: Nicole de Montbrun
Copy Editor: Mary Bitti
Production Editor: Jodi Lewchuk
Art Direction: Mary Opper
Interior Design: Lisa LaPointe
Production Coordinator: Barbara Ollerenshaw
Page Layout: Jack Steiner

1 2 3 4 5 F 03 02 01 00 99

Printed and bound in Canada.

Names of some people quoted in this book have been changed to protect privacy.

Visit the Prentice Hall Canada Web site! Send us your comments, browse our catalogues, and more. **www.phcanada.com**.

Contents

1

In Search of One Moment's Peace   1

2

The Inimitable Power of the Human Heart   13
EXERCISE 1: Revealing Our Deepest Beliefs About
Money and Abundance   20

3

Creative Perception: Turning Belief into Power   36
EXERCISE 2: Reframing Old Beliefs   43
EXERCISE 3: Divine Indulgence   49

4

Planting Our Dreams in Rich Soil   54
Growing Abundance: A Case for Order   55

5

The Power of Vision   79
EXERCISE 4: Dreaming a Life   83

6

The Point of Departure: A Thorough Assessment
of Current Reality   89
Financial Net-Worth Statement   91   ◆   Measuring Well-being   95
◆   Cash-flow Statement   100   ◆   Risk Management Needs Analysis   105

7

Unleashing the Creative Power of Vision   110
Revealing the Definitive Dream   113
EXERCISE 5: The Serenity Dream Book   115

8

From Dreams to Action: Becoming the Architect
of Your Financial Destiny   118
EXERCISE 6: My Financial Future—The Vision 122

9

The Stepping Stones of Investment Success   130

The New Investment Landscape   *131*   ◆   What About GICs?   *132*
◆ Getting Started   *134*   ◆   An Equitable Suggestion   *137*   ◆   Bonds and
Diversification   *140*   ◆   Diversification   *143*

IO

Mutual Funds: Pooled Prosperity   145

Stocks or Mutual Funds?   *147*   ◆   In the Years to Come   *156*   ◆   Separating the
Best from the Rest   *158*   ◆   Knowing When to Let Go   *159*   ◆   Fees and
Commissions   *160*   ◆   What You Need to Know About Segregated Funds   *163*
◆ The Bottom Line   *165*

II

Empowerment, Taxation, and RSPs   167

Finding Our Voice   *168*   ◆   The Luxury of Giving   *168*   ◆   The Great RSP
Misunderstanding   *169*   ◆   Qualified RSP Investments and Types of Plans   *170*
◆ Taking Full Advantage of Revenue Canada's Graciousness   *177*

12

Family: Certainties and Dreams   183

EXERCISE 7: Estate-planning Checklist   187
◆ Money As Seen Through the Eyes of Our Children   *187*
◆ Education Planning, Trusts, RESPs, and the CESG   *191*
◆ Home Sweet Home   *194*

13

The Business of Relationships   197

Questions for a Potential Financial Adviser   *201*

Conclusion: The End of the Beginning   204

Recommended Reading

Inspirational   206
Investments   206
Personal Finance   207
Other   208

Glossary

The Language of Investment   209

Acknowledgments

My dear friend Valerie says that "art is a by-product of the artist's process," and the writing of this book has certainly proven her statement true. Every word on these pages is a testament of gratitude to the people who contributed not only to the making of the book, but to the making of its author.

Women tend to meander through life providing for, nurturing, organizing, managing, actively caring, creating something where nothing was before, loving—but rarely pausing to reflect on their gifts to those they touch. I am grateful for this opportunity to offer acknowledgment to the many women whose magic has woven its way into my life and onto these pages. I couldn't imagine who or where I would be without the love and laughter of the women of my family: my mother, Marie; my sisters, Robyn, Debra, and Shari; my daughter, Teryl; my niece, Shari (the younger). Every day of my adult life has been brightened, too, by the love and company of friends—Lisa, Cheryl, Kathy, Shannon, Valerie, Veronica, and Kim. There are others too numerous to name who sweetened my life for a short time in person; they are always in memory, though our paths have taken us in different directions. I am hopelessly indebted to Erika Plessl, whose dedication, kindness, and love for my daughter made my career possible, and to the Reverends Marvin and Katherine Anderson, for immeasurable inspiration.

I am grateful to the many writers who listened to the early versions of this work, and may, I hope, see their ideas brought to life on its pages. Thanks especially to Eileen Kernahagn, who has nurtured and inspired countless writers to do what they thought they could not. My heartfelt thanks go to Teresa Klemm, Dana Petty, Angela Wilson, and Loa Fridfinnson, my first readers; to Kathy Renaud, my first editor; and to Marty Ogilvie, whose artistic vision and belief in this project resulted in one of the most purely beautiful Web sites I have ever seen. I give thanks, as well, to the many women, some of whom are quoted in these pages, whose example of professional accomplishment, balance, and unending feminine competence have inspired me over the years.

I bow with awe and reverence to the divine Joan Whitman, whose wisdom, humour, warmth and imagination saved both me and my potential readers at least a million times. To Roger—any grace to be found here belongs to you. I am grateful to Duff Young, Dean Hannaford, and Robert Harris—the three wise men who first saw the potential in this project and encouraged it forward. To Matthew Shulman, who kept the candle alight in the window no matter how lost I became. To Andrea Crozier, Nicole de Montbrun, Jodi Lewchuk, Mary Bitti, Mary Opper, and all of the other enlightened beings at Prentice Hall Canada, thank you.

Much of this book was written "in my spare time" while juggling the demands of business, life, and livelihood. Every late night, and there were many, was claimed from hours that would have otherwise belonged to our children, Greg, Dereck, and Teryl, and to my husband, Randy. I did not sacrifice alone, and I am deeply grateful for your support, self-reliance, and constant love. No woman has been more blessed by motherhood than I. For restoring my faith in the financial industry and a wealth of professional inspiration, I give deepest thanks to my partner, Rob Potuzak, and to his wife and partner, Donna. To my dad, his family, my brother Dean and his wife, Neesh, my stepfather, George, to Gord, to Marcela—to everyone who warmed my heart, shaped my mind, and filled my days with light, thank you.

The words are mine—the book is yours. You are Beloved.

Lori M. Bamber
1999

In Search of One Moment's Peace

...it was the money that made the

difference.

VIRGINIA WOOLF, WHEN ASKED ABOUT
HAVING HER FIRST BOOK PUBLISHED AT
THE SAME TIME SHE RECEIVED A SMALL
INHERITANCE.

When I began writing this book in early 1996, it had very little to do with money and investment. I had spent the previous eight long years in the financial industry, and I was determined to escape to a world where the bottom line was not measured solely in dollars; a place where "balance" was a noun, not a verb. I was intent on charting new ways of working and creating a livelihood—on finding a way to live while earning a living.

My story wasn't an original one, but I felt a compelling need to tell it. Perhaps precisely because it wasn't original—I heard it over and over in the voices of the women around me and saw it in the eyes of my friends and colleagues. I wasn't alone, but in the corporate world I was determined to escape. Putting a creatively positive spin on the truth was part of the job description.

"Oh, yeah, my husband and I don't see much of each other, but it's just for now. It'll be worth it."

"Who has time for friends? That's the thing you give up first. It's OK. I'll have friends when I'm old."

"You do what you have to do. I'll look after myself when I have the time."

"I'm fine."

Even among our closest friends, we were loath to confess our dark and guilty secrets. We were tired, empty, and unfulfilled—full of longing for something we could not name. For me, it was time to start telling the unvarnished truth. At the very least, I had to ask the question: I was successful; why wasn't I happy?

Like so many of the women of my generation, my Holy Grail had been the impressive title, the executive office, and, of course, the big salary. Oh, and healthy, intelligent, accomplished, well-behaved, loving children. A husband who adored me. A spotless, impeccably decorated home.

Fast forward a decade of early mornings, late nights, and general exhaustion. Juggling the demands of career and motherhood was daunting, and like all working mothers, I was haunted by guilt both at work (my poor family!) and at home. As long as I could see the Grail ahead, however, I never questioned the value of the struggle. Some day, with the right promotion, it would all become worthwhile. My family would be richly rewarded for all the sacrifices they had made while I worked. I would be happy. Things would get better.

This is where my story takes an interesting twist, for in 1995 I got that long-sought promotion. Executive vice-president of one of Canada's fastest-growing investment firms. According to the vision that had guided me since my early twenties, I had it all: a husband I was crazy about, children I was inexpressibly proud of—and there I was. The title, the office, the salary; at long last, everything had come together. Life was pretty stressful with the transition and all, but I deposited those big cheques to my bank account and waited for the contentment to set in. And waited.

There was obviously something wrong with me. I paid $100 an hour, once a week for months, for the privilege of complaining in a safe environment. One hundred dollars an hour to ask my therapist the unspeakable questions I felt ungrateful and petty even thinking. Why wasn't I happy? Why weren't things good? Was I ill? Crazy? In addition to feeling empty, fatigued, and suspicious that there was some cosmic clock winding down somewhere and taking me with it, I was ashamed. I had everything but I wasn't happy. I was a woman-failure. If I ever admitted my real feelings, I would justify every gender-alization I had ever argued against in the workplace. You know—the ones we all hear, all sense, no matter where we work, regardless of what we do.

"Women aren't focused enough for management—you can't run a company and drop things to stay home with a sick kid. Don't get me wrong. It's nothing personal. That's life. That's why guys get promoted first—you don't see them running off when a teacher calls."

"Women are too emotional. You have to be tough as nails in this industry—it's dog eat dog. Swim with the sharks and all that."

It made me feel better to talk about it, particularly to someone paid to listen, but there seemed to be some kind of structural problem. My life was not
working. The signs were clear. Forgetting my six-year-old daughter at school.
Forgetting to feed our lovebird. Colds that came too often and wouldn't go
away. Chronic tension and conflicts in my relationships. When therapy didn't
make it all better, I tried running. I read self-improvement books incessantly,
or rather, listened to the tapes in my car. (Who had time to read?) I meditat-
ed. I went to church. I studied and tried five different time-management
methods, and listened to tapes on ways to manipulate my husband into taking more domestic responsibility.

When we refuse to acknowledge the reality of our lives and to let go of
things that aren't working, a kind of dark serendipity so often seems to lend
a hand. My final crisis began on a Wednesday, an evening I'll never forget. I
was just about to leave my office for one of those obligatory professional events
that look like fun from the outside but so rarely are. I would have done almost
anything to go home. I longed for my bed. I longed for my family. I longed
for some peace. Instead, I faced a previously frozen prawn cocktail and the
press of warm business cards into my reluctant hands. I was an Executive.

The phone rang; never a good sign at this time of night.

"Lori, it's Cynthia. Teryl is not being very nice to me. I'm not going to
be able to baby-sit for you any more."

Damn. Damn. Normally, I would have disregarded the childishness of this
statement, slipped into damage-control mode, and attempted to convince
Cynthia to stay on. My daughter Teryl was, after all, a normal six-year-old
who occasionally hated her sitter and wasn't always nice to her. I was a normal working mother who would say or pay anything to avoid having to look
for new child-care arrangements. Tonight, however, I could hear Teryl wail-
ing in the background, crying as if her heart would break. Something was
definitely wrong.

"Cynthia, what's going on? Where's Randy? I thought he was supposed
to be home at 6:30. Did he call?"

"No, he didn't call, he isn't here, and Teryl is being a little bitch."

OK. I had stepped into the twilight zone. When did the sweet teenager
from across the street, the one caring for my beloved baby girl, start talking
like a prison inmate in a B movie?

"Cynthia, could I speak to Teryl, please?" Silence.

"Moommm, please come home. Please," my daughter said. "She's being
so mean to me, Mom. I told Dereck to move and she said, 'You move,' and

pushed me. They're both swearing at me." (And they were—I could hear them in the background.)

Dereck was my teenage stepson. Next to me, the wicked stepmother, he hated Teryl more than anything in the world. We were at the top of a long list of hated things that included (but was not limited to) school, homework, any food that wasn't available at 7-11 or Pizza Hut, rules, authority and authority figures, helping around the house, and anything that adults liked. A normal teenage boy.

"Teryl, I can't come home, sweetie. Dad should be there any minute. Try to calm down, and go to your room for a while. I'll talk to Dereck and Cynthia. OK?"

After doing my best to remind Cynthia of her responsibilities, and Dereck of the fact that his father would be home any time, I called a girlfriend and begged her to take care of Teryl until my husband showed up. I was 45 minutes away and Randy wasn't answering the $400 cell phone I'd naively bought him in the hopes of staying connected. Missing in action. One of my more competitive colleagues was waiting outside my door to escort me to the seminar. If I cancelled, everyone would know about it in the morning. I had to go. And I couldn't go.

I laid my head on my big executive desk and cried. Fear and frustration and hopelessness, running wet over the stacks of urgent and important memos waiting for my scattered attention. Then I cleaned up my makeup, painted a red lipstick smile on my lips, and went to the seminar.

When I arrived home later, my husband met me at the door. Before I could say anything, he was on the defensive. "Lori, Teryl really is mean to Cynthia sometimes. I've heard her," he said.

Pardon me? I couldn't believe my ears. I was baffled. I turned this statement over in my mind, trying to grasp what I'd heard—and why he thought it was relevant. I couldn't find words to reply. I looked as if for the first time at my husband, this man in whose presence I had once felt wonderful no matter what else was going on. What had happened to us? There he was, handsome, charming, and sweet as ever, and I hated him—for not helping me, for not making it better. My perfect marriage had become one more responsibility that I was failing at.

I made complicated, short-term arrangements for child-care with friends, neighbours, and acquaintances. I ran, confused, repeatedly, through the labyrinth in my mind. What would I do? What could I do? I couldn't continue doing what I was doing. Somehow the night passed, but with little rest, and, too soon, the alarm announced the morning's arrival. I awoke with a flood of dread, dizzy with sleeplessness.

The daily race began: shower, dress, throw something resembling break-fast on the table, wake Teryl, help her dress, gather papers and memos and school notices, and make sandwiches for lunch. *Oh, God, where is the time going? I'm going to be late. Take the dog out. Pee, dammit. What are you waiting for?* Dog won't pee on leash. Remove leash. Dog pees then runs away. Chase dog down street in high heels, gritting teeth with guilty rage while sweetly calling, "Here, Indy. Here, girl." Catch dog. Collect child. Drop child at friend's house for ride to school. Fight rush-hour traffic. Arrive at work 10 minutes late. Ignore pointed looks at watches. Close and lock office door. Set phone on Do Not Disturb. Sit on carpet, cross-legged, hiking narrow skirt up around hips. Gaze at achingly peaceful ocean view. *I will be all right. I will be all right. I will be all right.*

Unable to even think about the stacks of work on my desk, I finally decided to check my e-mail, usually a low-stress diversion with staff birth-day announcements and quotes-du-jour. On this particular day, however, there was a meatier tidbit—a memo from a senior manager I'd fought to hire, addressed to the rest of the management team. I'd been copied. It was about me and my new position. Apparently, a large faction of the staff was unhappy about my latest promotion, and it was further undermining the already poi-sonous staff morale.

It wasn't a malicious attack, or even a personal one. I knew that the manager involved spoke from her conscience and believed she was doing the best thing for the company. The things she wrote were true. In under-capitalized firms that outgrow their resources daily, anxiety is rampant and tends to be directed at the least popular executive or manager of the moment—often, the latest to be promoted. When there isn't enough to go around, a person receiving a disproportionate share is going to be on the receiving end of hostility and resentment. When that person is a woman, particularly a woman with family responsibilities that make it impossible for her to devote herself entirely to the corporation, the dynamics are even more intense.

I knew all that. It was the game. I was good at the game. However, it felt very personal. It felt like a screwdriver had been inserted somewhere between my ribs. It hurt to breathe.

On another day, I would have called a meeting, addressed the concerns of this particular manager and the staff for whom she spoke, and scheduled yet another meeting with the CEO to enlist his support in addressing this latest outbreak of unbridled anxiety. Not that day. On that day, for the sec-ond time in less than 12 hours, I laid my head on my desk and cried. They were right. I couldn't take it.

I have to get tougher, I thought. It is time—either I give up or I get tougher.

A wiser voice spoke from somewhere deep within. Clearly, quietly.

"I don't want to get tougher. I want to be me. I have to quit."

I went home pleading illness (God knows I was sick) and spent most of the next three days in bed with a really big, rapidly depleted box of Kleenex. One thought sustained me.

There had to be a better way.

Jeremy Rifkin had just published *The End of Work*, a book about the disappearance of employment as we know it. According to Rifkin, and the numerous business magazines I had to read every month, micro-entrepreneurs were starting dozens of new, successful endeavours every day. Even the most traditional, patriarchal companies were outsourcing core operations, creating centres of business in homes across North America. It was a revolution, and not only did I want to live it, I wanted to map it. There were millions of yearning souls out there doing the nine-to-five (or more likely, the seven-to-nine) in the corporate wasteland. If I couldn't part the waters, I could certainly chart the path to the ferry terminal.

With my family's tentative blessing ("Does this mean we can have dinner at a normal time?" "How are you going to earn money?" "I guess it'll be OK for three or four months."), I resigned. It was a terrible, wrenching loss, giving up the dreams and illusions of corporate success, but it was also a relief. I did have a career plan—I would write a book about the changing world of work. I would do some consulting.

Consulting was certainly a step in the right direction, offering more of the autonomy, flexibility, and freedom I was longing for. The chance to apply my experience without the hassles I'd come to hate. No more political pools of poison. I arrived, I did a proposal, I implemented, I picked up my cheque. At least part of the time, I worked from my home office and got lots of great tax write-offs. There seemed to be less competitiveness, and if there was anxiety and resentment, I never got to know people well enough to share it. It didn't take long, though, to find that consulting didn't offer the elegant and perfect solution to the working-woman's dilemma, either. It quickly became apparent that it matters little what we are called, how we are paid, or what our contract says. If we are immersed in environments where the bottom line is solely financial, where dedication to the cause is measured by the number of hours worked, our lives will be diminished by it. Intent on "working to live" rather than "living to work," I needed a third alternative.

Without having discovered that third alternative, I started writing. I wasn't entirely sure what I was writing about, but I pressed on, writing and rewriting, four hours or more a day for six months, until I had a credible, 180-page manuscript. Now it was time to broaden my spectrum of research—and, hopefully, find that third alternative. I arranged to participate in a six-week-long government- and commerce-sponsored course for professionals and executives in career transition. Teaching leading-edge skills in entrepreneurial development and enterprise, this program also provided participants with connections to sources of capital and ongoing support. Entrepreneurial heaven. I expected to be surrounded by enthused and optimistic women and men, thrilled with the opportunity to create their own destiny.

Instead, I discovered anxiety and even bitterness. I was shocked to find that the majority of the group looked longingly back on the days when they could sell their souls and most of the hours in their day for a paycheque.

As I absorbed this reality, the term "writer's block" took on new meaning. I was paralyzed by two now obvious truths. The first was that my manuscript, as it was then, was both irresponsible and naive. As Abraham Maslow surmised years ago, self-actualization is a luxury—something we strive to attain *after* the rent has been paid and the bread has been won.

I was among the blessed. I was financially comfortable and had the freedom to make choices about my future. Transition threatened my self-esteem, and perhaps my capital, but I wasn't faced with losing my house, or being unable to support my family. Unfortunately, my situation was too rare. Most of the people in my research group had been downsized or re-engineered, or had been forced off their career path by professional or personal crisis. They had one, overarching, singular concern. They needed a paycheque.

It became clear to me that I was surrounded by "successful" people who had spent 40 to 70 hours a week making a living—and none on making a life; 40 to 70 hours a week creating money, only to spend it on debt and bills, a second sports-utility vehicle and a larger house. The one thing they hadn't invested in was financial well-being.

Freedom wasn't just about finding the right job or the right business or about casting off the patriarchal corporate yoke. It also involved reaching that place where the bread got bought and the mortgage got paid and the dark nights of lying awake worrying about the wolf at the door were behind us.

The fear and anxiety my cohorts were facing brought a powerful and sustaining truth home to me. If I was going to write about freedom, I was going to have to write about the one thing I didn't really want to think about after giving up an absolutely fabulous salary on the quest for fulfillment: money.

Grimly resistant, I decided to scrap the freedom idea and embrace compromise and survival. I would rewrite the book as a self-help guide about carving a life out of the harsh realities of working motherhood on the fast track. If writing about freedom meant writing about money, I wouldn't write about freedom. I'd write about balance.

As I had never actually accomplished this feat in my own life, this second incarnation of the manuscript required extensive second-hand research. I devoured dozens of self-development books for women. Although each offered nuggets of wisdom, I never found the "Aha!" I was looking for. Everybody had an answer—no one had *the* answer. And I knew I certainly didn't. I couldn't get past that singular, unanswerable question: How dare I? How dare I presume to know what that world looked like for other women, and how it worked?

Writing was both my frustration and my solace. It was my conscience and my voice. I was, for the most part, home alone with my computer. I was finding my own path, and I wrote my way. "The book" sat neglected while I wrote poetry and short stories and rants to the editors of local papers.

Despite my struggle to find the right words, it was a wonderful, peaceful interlude in my life. I woke without that strident alarm clock, to a long, slow cup of rich coffee and my meditation journals. I drove my sweet daughter to school, and returned to those creative homecaring projects I'd been planning for a decade or so. I joined a gym and went for long, glorious walks around the lake whenever the sun shone. I was in the best physical condition of my life—strong, muscled, and energized. My husband came home to a hot dinner, an orderly and welcoming home, and a serene wife. I wrote. I attended writing classes and kick-boxing classes and gallery openings. For the first time in 10 years, I had time for friends. It was heavenly.

There was, however, a shadow on my horizon—a storm warning. On other days it was just a tiny, irritating grain of sand in the oyster of my contentment.

Oh, yes. Money.

I was living on our investments—borrowing money from the future. At some point, I would have to think about earning a livelihood. As well, because my husband is a stockbroker, our investment accounts were under his charge. When I wanted or needed money, I had to ask him. I had to justify my purchases. It was humiliating. Demeaning. My independence may have reached an unhealthy intensity, but I had worked hard for it.

Material well-being offered more than freedom—it also bought power. And between my husband and me, the power ratio was now entirely out of balance.

Serendipity intervened again. Bre-X rocked the resource markets. Like so many Canadians, we took a huge hit as the resource market ground to a halt. I was going back to working for a living, ready or not.

It might have been the Bre-X scandal, and its impact on our investment portfolio. It might have simply been the frustration of having to justify each purchase to a man with different values and priorities, or the realization that I, a financial professional, had left all our family investment decisions to someone whose investment philosophy was almost the polar opposite of my own. I'm not sure when, but at some point realization finally dawned. I understood, "with a granite finality," as Leonard Cohen says so beautifully, that the foundation of well-being is financial independence, that place where we can turn our attentions from anxiety to creativity. And I understood, too, that financial well-being was not something that would arrive one day like the proverbial ship sailing into the harbour. This was something I would have to create, if only because there was no one else in the world who knew what it looked like for me. And if my intention was to share my story in a way that enhanced the quality of life of other women, then my calling was clear. I had a responsibility to share my knowledge of and experience in the financial industry and the universal principles of financial well-being, and to do so with respectful recognition of those issues that the financial industry had so far been loath to acknowledge: the context of feminine values, socialization, and realities.

Women buy differently. They think differently. They use language differently. They face different challenges. Life looks different to a woman, and so does money. For the most part, despite the flurry of marketing attention we've received recently, women are not well served by the financial industry. As Andrea Dworkin, one of America's most pre-eminent and outspoken feminists, wrote in 1981, "Money speaks, but it speaks in a male voice." In 1981, this gender bias was an issue that was just floating to the surface of consciousness, though it had shaped our lives for at least 2000 years. It was an accepted fact that men earned the majority of the money and were the natural stewards and controllers of the family assets. As women, our fates were dependent not on making good investment choices, but on choosing the right men.

Things are changing rapidly, and by the time this book is published, women will control a significantly larger portion of the nation's wealth than they do even as I write. They are earning more money, receiving financial settlements as marriages dissolve, and inheriting estates as they outlive their mates. Women are the fastest-growing consumer segment in the financial industry and control 80 cents of every consumer dollar.

Yet we've been taught that women are less competent than men are when it comes to financial issues. Recent studies show that more and more women are again taking up their role as "keeper of the keys." Now as in the days of the round table, it is the women who keep the castle. Now, as then, keeping the castle involves far more than stocking the cupboards. It involves mortgages, investments, wills, estates, powers of attorney. According to Joanne Thomas Yaccato, author of *Balancing Act* and *Raising Your Business*, 95 percent of Canadian women now make joint financial decisions with their partners. Let me say this for the record: if we are capable of balancing chequebooks, filing tax returns, arranging lines of credit, negotiating mortgage rates, and comparison shopping, we are more than capable of making savvy investment decisions.

There is no question, however, that there are challenges to overcome. Most women have been socialized to take direction from professionals (even their doctors) without asking too many questions. We are taught to be nice, to avoid offence. We have watched our fathers and often our husbands make the crucial financial decisions. As much as they love us, we are not always encouraged to participate in the decision-making process. Not realizing that they are often as frightened and uninformed as we are, we are humbled by our inexperience. As one of my friends often says of her horrific experience with a husband who made all the investment decisions until there was absolutely nothing but debt left, "I thought when he read *The Financial Post* from cover to cover that meant he understood it. Boy, was I wrong!"

Our inexperience and lack of confidence make us all potential victims, and every unscrupulous commission-focused financial adviser in the country, and yes, they're out there, wants our business.

It reminds me of something Michael Nairn of the Assante Group once said about limited partnerships. "In the beginning, the general partner [the investment company] has all the experience and the limited partner [the investor] has all the money. In the end, the limited partner has the experience and the general partner has the money."

Well, we unquestionably need the experience but we also need the money. We can choose to learn the hard way, taking advice from professionals who intimidate us and buying investments we don't understand. We can let other people "look after it for us" and hope that it will turn out all right (although I wouldn't recommend it). We can swing to the other side of the material pendulum, turning our backs on all that investment mumbo-jumbo and striving instead for a spiritual, balanced, and peaceful existence. Unfortunately, although some people have managed it quite happily, the frugality movement isn't for everyone. In the real world, lack of money (and lack of financial planning) undermines quality of life, relationships, health, and peace of mind more often than any other factor. Ignoring the need for financial well-being doesn't mean it is going to go away.

Somewhere between the tent trailer and Trump Tower, there is a place of balance, fulfillment, and abundance. I call that place Financial Serenity.

In its final incarnation, this book has become a map of that path, intended to help create a fulfilling, powerful state of being, sustained through a lifetime of personal challenges, market cycles, and LIFE. Financial Serenity is a journey that is as unique as you are, and no one can achieve it for you. Like all journeys, however, it can be enhanced by your companions, provided they are carefully chosen. This book is not meant to substitute for the benefits of professional financial-planning partnerships, but rather to empower them. Seeking professional help from the right person does make sense, and later in the book I'll discuss that further. The reality is that most of us are simply too busy to stay current with the vast amount of information that affects our taxes, our investments, and our future. Even for financial professionals, *knowing* the right thing is not the same as *doing* the right thing. A professional-planning partnership can support you in staying true to your goals when the sundry circumstances of life would lead you astray.

Professional partnerships, however, must be partnerships. That is, open, trusting, respectful relationships, through which competent professionals contribute to the achievement of your dreams. Creating these optimal partnerships requires knowing what you want, knowing what you need, knowing what questions to ask, and knowing what to expect.

Nor is *Financial Serenity* an exhaustive guide to financial planning. The subject is too vast, and the issues too varied. There are literally hundreds of excellent books available on the diverse aspects of financial planning. Somewhere along the path, there will be issues that you wish to study in more depth or with the assistance of a trusted professional. *Financial Serenity* provides a broad understanding of the language, context, and principles of investment and finance, transforming universal, prosaic principles into personal creative power. This book provides the basics and explains many of the financial terms you'll need to know on the journey toward achieving your own place of financial well-being.

At this point, then, let me give you one of the most important investment tips you will find in this entire book: investing in your well-being by committing even an hour a month to reading the books that pertain to your financial situation will pay tax-free, risk-free dividends for a lifetime. Think about how much time you spend earning money. Now think about how much time you spend making your money work for you—and just shift the equation by one hour.

For us (and by "us," I take the liberty of speaking for my gender), everything is truly connected. Our visions, our obstacles, our responsibilities—over the cold, hard numbers of the financial pages run the stories of our lives. The primary challenge, as always, is in coming to understand ourselves.

This is just the beginning of a uniquely personal, powerful, and joyous journey into the depths of your own heart; that place where wisdom, creativity, love, and courage merge together to create everyday miracles. Enjoy. Let's get started.

The Inimitable Power
of the Human Heart

Our greatest fear is not that we are inadequate. Our greatest fear is that we are powerful beyond measure.

NELSON MANDELA

In my own search for financial serenity, it occurred to me that there must have been a time in my life before the existence of money, or at least, before money was an issue. Who was I then?

In an attempt to find my way back, I dug out the old photo albums. There I was at 12, in the awful eyeglasses that "we could afford." There I am at 10, crouched sef-consciously by the chimney in my aunt's hand-me-down pants. Oh, yikes! Pixie haircuts! There I was at six, sweetly innocent of money and most else—with bangs that looked as though they'd been cut with a lawn mower. Suddenly I am back in my mother's warm kitchen, squirming in a vinyl-upholstered chrome chair while she struggles with me and a roll of Scotch tape, a technique purported to ensure straight bangs.

It is an effort for me to recall that little girl, to remember who she was and what she thought about, but I do have a clear memory of her faith. All was right with the world, all needs would be met, everything would turn out for the best. Mom and Dad were, after all, perfect. And their roles were simple—to make everything OK.

As an adult, a full-fledged citizen of the material world, I look back and wish they'd taken me to a real hair stylist, which proves, I guess, that even when we are oblivious to financial issues, we are still affected by them.

It was more then a year later that I remember experiencing my first real moment of anxiety. It began sweetly enough. I was having a sleepover at my friend Debbie's house, a rare and delicious treat, and we were snuggled in bed, giggling quietly under the covers, when her mother came in. My mom was coming to pick me up, she told us, and there was a big surprise.

Even at that age, when a big surprise was always a big delight, I recognized that something was wrong. On the way home, Mom told me that we were going to visit my aunt in the city the next day, and that I wasn't to mention it to my Dad. She would call him when we arrived. Desperate to be grown-up and deserving of this special confidence, I didn't ask the questions that made my stomach feel a little sick and cold and wiggly. Why couldn't I tell Dad? Why wasn't he coming? Why didn't he know? I knew it had something to do with spending money, something I'd recently overheard them speaking of a good deal, their voices hushed and strained.

I went to bed that night, for the first time the possessor of a secret. When I woke up the next morning, however, peace had been restored, and there was a special tenderness in the way my mother laid her hand on my father's shoulder. Later in the day, when Dad was outside, she told me that we would go to the city later in the summer, and Dad would come with us. (I was so relieved that I didn't even ask, nor did I complain, about the loss of my precious sleepover.) The trip, although I remember it well, was a relative non-event. It was that moment, the moment I realized that money could create secrets in my house, that changed the way I saw my parents, and through them, the world.

It was to be the last sweet summer for some time. Over the next seven years, the loving relationship that my parents had enjoyed in their early years together deteriorated dramatically. Like all relationships that come undone, both Mom and Dad (and every relative on either side) have their theories as to why "it didn't work out." From a child's perspective, it seemed quite clear what the battles were about. Money. Too much money spent, too many things needed, not enough money made. Too many children, too many mouths to feed. Too much. Not enough.

Did money destroy my parents' relationship? No. Though money problems can create more than enough stress to erode even the best relationships, they are more often a symptom rather than a cause. Could more money have saved their marriage? Even today, I don't know, and I'm sure they don't either. The only thing I am entirely sure of is that money issues are almost always a central theme in deteriorating relationships. Money is, after all, more than a simple means of exchange. It is a measure of value. To it we attach love, caring, and generosity—and trust. "Does he love me? He did bring me those beautiful roses on my birthday. He is so generous with the kids. Yes, he really does love us." (This statement sounds odd, I know, stilted. We don't think thoughts like this, at least not in the overt verbal way I've presented them. It doesn't take much digging, however, to find these questions just under the surface of our consciousness.) Or, conversely, "She complains about every dollar I spend. She obviously doesn't care about my happiness very much."

Ultimately, freedom and power are bought with money. "I can't leave. How would I support the kids?" "I hate my job, but I just can't afford to quit."

Money buys the power of choice.

Money can purchase influence. If you've ever wondered why it seems to have taken so long to move away from the outdated, patriarchal constructs that govern business, government, and to a large degree, society in general, wonder no more. Those with the most influence are those with the most money. Those who agitate for change do so without the benefit of direct access to the source of power and influence—money.

As a child, through the behaviour of my parents and the community in which I lived, I began to associate money with being accepted, with being liked, with having power and freedom. I also began to associate my life, myself, with "not enough" money. I developed what we now refer to as a poverty mentality. By the time I was about 12, I knew that there was never enough. Life was a struggle. I knew, too, that money was something that dads controlled and moms cried about—a lot.

As I became an adult, had a family, and established a career in the financial industry, those early beliefs were muffled by reams of information. I learned that if I worked really hard, it was possible to earn a reasonable amount of money—not as much, however, as a man of equal competence and ability. I learned about credit, saving, and investing. I became a financial professional. I learned enough, intellectually, to overcome any early debilitating beliefs about financial well-being.

Right. Logically, I understand all the facts, figures, and principles. I've armed myself with knowledge and know-how. I understand complicated financial issues, and I've made financial planning a career, helping other people make the best money choices for themselves. Despite the intelligent and financially astute grown-up I've become on the outside, there is still a 12-year-old within me who believes there won't be enough, no matter what evidence there is to the contrary. That little girl has more power than I care to think about—and she has lots of company.

At one of my workshops, a woman I'll call Joy listened intently to my story of childhood poverty and financial discord, and approached me during a coffee break.

"Lori, I don't mean to sound unsympathetic," she said. "That must have been really awful, but I can't relate at all. My experience was the complete opposite. My parents had a very content marriage and we never wanted for anything. I can't remember money ever being discussed. I'm not sure this is helpful to me, but I always knew there would be enough money."

Joy had come to my workshop because she had a large RRSP that she wanted to manage more actively. For years, she had contributed and her brother had invested the funds for her. She had only recently come to realize that she didn't really know where the money was invested, what the returns were, how secure it was, or if she could access her funds. She felt very uncomfortable about the situation but had no idea how to begin to change it. I thanked her for her honesty and said that I hoped she would find some of the later exercises to be more helpful.

During the lunch break, Joy and I spoke again. "I just wanted you to know it suddenly clicked for me," she said. "My parents gave me everything I ever wanted or needed, but I was a recipient, not a participant. I always assumed everything would be all right because no one ever said that it wouldn't be. But they never said it would be—they never said anything at all. I was protected from money, shielded from it. And I'm still doing that, letting someone else do the worrying, allowing someone else to be in control. I don't want to do that any more."

I couldn't tell Joy how to start taking ownership of her investments, but I knew I didn't have to. Once she understood why and how she gave her power away, taking it back was a process already begun.

At another of my workshops, a lovely lady called me over when she was working through the exercise you'll find at the end of this chapter. "This doesn't apply to me," she said. "You didn't have a childhood?" I asked as innocently as I could manage. "Well, yes, I had a childhood," she said, laughing, "but I never had an allowance, or a job. If my mother thought I should have something, I had it. We lived in the Caribbean, with servants and a big house, and we never wanted for anything."

"It must have been really hard for you to adjust when you married and came to Canada, then," I replied. "How did you feel when you had to pay bills for the first time? Did you ever struggle financially when your children were young?"

Tears sprang to her eyes. "Yes. My first husband died when my kids were all little, and I didn't know anything about money. It was terrible trying to figure out what was going on, what we were going to do."

Sylvia had come to the workshop because she was approaching retirement and felt very anxious about her future. Despite having accumulated a substantial portfolio of assets over a lifetime of frugal living and prudent saving, worry was keeping her awake at night and undermining both her health and her happiness. Together, we were able to connect her current anxiety with the shock of being forced to cope with almost complete ignorance of money matters at a time of terrible loss, confusion, and vulnerability.

For Sylvia, accumulating assets was only part of the solution. Once we understood that the real root of her worry didn't have to do with money but with fear of the unknown and unexpected loss, I suggested creating a comprehensive retirement plan. Sylvia was able to see for the first time, in dollars and cents and on paper, how her material future would unfold. Now, when she feels anxious, she can review her financial plan, and remind herself that her fears are related to past experiences, not premonitions of the future.

All of us approach the world of adult finance with the unique beliefs we acquired as children and young adults. Not all of us have a poverty mentality, obviously. Many of us were raised in relative affluence, or in environments in which material needs and money were simply not talked about. Sometimes too much money burdened us with loneliness, or with dependency. There is no one among us, however, who has not been shaped by early, often unconscious lessons. As adults, we transform these lessons into creation. We build a life using the flawed raw materials of our early perceptions.

As William James wrote almost 100 years ago, "As [we] thinketh, so [we] become." James was talking about something deeper and more powerful than the process we tend to refer to as "thinking." The modern world "thinks" with the conscious mind. Thoughts fly in and out of our heads, and it is these scattered patterns we tend to talk about, the ones we acknowledge. But more important, and perhaps more influential, are the patterns created in the mind that isn't rational—that place we call our "heart," or subconscious—where all memory resides, and all emotions have their birth. It is here that we add power to logic—or subtract it. And it is here that creation begins.

I have watched this truth unfold in my life over and over. It just seems to be one of those lessons I need to keep learning. Never was it revealed more clearly for me, though, than just after my husband and I had reconciled after our separation.

When my husband, Randy, and I separated, there was no Event. There was no earth-shattering, cataclysmic fight. We had problems—serious problems. One day we were working them out, and the next day, we weren't. He was leaving.

For me, this presented an obsessive, unanswerable question. Why?

One of the possibilities that came to mind was another woman. I had faith in my husband and his integrity, but things happen. When he left, and even after we reconciled and he rather inexplicably moved back in, I found myself searching for evidence of the other woman's existence.

A few months after our reconciliation, I was putting some laundry away in his gym bag. Lying right under my probing fingers was a receipt from an expensive, romantic restaurant that I had never been to. Adrenaline rushed through my body, my heart started pounding in my throat. I sat down. This was it. The evidence. I looked at the items on the receipt. Hmmm. Steak. Scotch on the rocks. Dinner for four. Romantic dinner for . . . four? Man food, man drinks. Might be, probably was, a business dinner.

I paused, startled. Not by the receipt, but by my reaction. Although part of me was relieved, I realized that another part of me was . . . *disappointed!* This is a man I adore, love being with, a man I was heartbroken without. What in the world was going on? I sat on our bed and puzzled until it came to me.

I was disappointed because I was wrong. In the world in which I was raised, men betrayed and abandoned you. Men broke your heart.

That was my world view—my heartfelt belief. If someone had asked me about it, I would have absolutely, categorically denied it, even to myself. When I looked at the history of my relationships, however, it was very obvious how this belief had shaped my life. In my early twenties, I was attracted to men who fit neatly into my unconscious expectations. Later, with a man of integrity who cherished me, I was uncomfortable. When the other shoe didn't drop, so to speak, all was not right with my world. Though it would have been devastating to discover another woman, it would also have been comforting; things would have clicked into place and reaffirmed my world view. The discrepancy between the actual realities of my relationship and my paradigm created tension. I would have been relieved to have had that tension lifted, even with heartache.

The good news is that once I was able to understand, I was able to change. Now that those underlying beliefs have been recognized, I can have a dialogue with my anxieties: "Yes, this feels threatening to me, but is it? Why do I feel this way? Oh, OK. These are *old* feelings." Surprisingly, blessedly, it hasn't been much of a problem. It's almost as if, once acknowledged, those buried fears lose their power, leaving me free to see the present as it really is.

This same truth applies to money and well-being. We can view the effects of our belief systems simply by reviewing our circumstances. Beliefs are intangible, but their effects on our lives are not. It is our behaviour, not our intellectual knowledge, that shapes our destiny. Just as not all doctors are healthy, not all financial advisers (believe me) are well off. Until we understand what our beliefs are, and how we came to have them, the creation of financial well-being is a chaotic, uncontrollable process.

We all have a twelve-year-old in us, or a six-year-old—a little girl who carries the burden, or the power, of the beliefs absorbed in our youth. Closest to our hearts, her world view may be far more powerful than the knowledge we carry in our heads.

Many of the prospective clients I see in my professional-planning practice come looking for magic—that fabulous investment that pays such mind-boggling returns that they can spend money with abandon today and continue to do so tomorrow. Oh, and risk is fine—unless there is a possibility that they might lose any money. "Woo me with promises of impressive returns," they say in so many words, "or I will find someone who will."

If there were such investments, believe me, I'd own them, and I wouldn't be working for a living. (There wouldn't be a working financial adviser in all of Canada. We would either be volunteering our services or basking in the sun on our private island.) The magic we seek doesn't reside in an investment. Countless people have managed to lose money on absolutely fabulous investment opportunities. Likewise, although we don't hear their stories as often, many people (and not just insiders) made fortunes in Bre-X before the scandal was revealed. Despite our devotion to investment pundits like Warren Buffet and Peter Lynch, there is no guru who will deliver you to riches without your express co-operation. The bank won't do it for you, and neither will the perfect job, or the perfect husband. The magic resides in us— in me, in you. It is the power that is released when we come to understand our part in the creative process, when we acknowledge our mastery and own our visions. The right financial adviser, the right job, the right bank (maybe even the right husband) will follow—they are effects, not causes.

Investment returns are really only one tiny facet of the creation of financial well-being. Long before we concern ourselves with returns, we must master the art of wealth creation. In order to invest, we must have disposable income (an oxymoron if ever there was one, I know). In order to have disposable income, we must reduce spending, increase income, or both.

It doesn't sound good, does it? Deprivation, delayed gratification, willpower, and self-discipline. Yuck. The past is powerful. Our desire for instant gratification is powerful. Blessedly, there is *nothing* more powerful than a compelling, crystal-clear vision of the future. When we know what we want life to look like, and how to get there, taking the next step becomes supremely satisfying even when it means saying "no" to a passing desire.

The first step in creating that vision is to have a heart-to-heart dialogue

with our inner 12-year-old—the little girl who knows that money is hard
to come by, that there is never enough, that women aren't as good with money
as men are, that women spend and men earn. The little girl who believes that
if we are good, self-sacrificing, "nice," and don't ask for too much, someone
will take care of us. The little girl who thinks that money is something we
shouldn't talk about, or that wanting material well-being is somehow selfish.

"Now wait," says the inner skeptic (first cousin of the inner 12-year-old).
"If what you are saying is true, Lori, why would any of us 'choose' to live in
anything but the utmost comfort?"

The answer, again, is in our belief systems. We are ambivalent, not indif-
ferent, but literally of two minds. We are torn between our intellect and our
heart; between our dreams and disabling, out-of-date beliefs. We envision our
house on the water, and a soft, frightened voice whispers, "No, that isn't what
my home looks like. I could never own a house like that."

Our purpose here, as we move through this guide, is to bring these two
forces together in a powerful, creative partnership. Therefore, as you read, you
will find statements that you wholeheartedly agree with—statements that
resonate with you as being profoundly true. But sometimes you will hear an
inner voice saying, "Wait a minute. I don't think I agree with that."

Wonderful. Write it down. We aren't here to review my beliefs about
money. (I mean, beyond family, friends, clients, and me, who cares?) *It is your
beliefs that will shape your life—and your beliefs that will set you free.* Throughout
the exercises, and while reading the book, keep a pencil handy, and jot down
even the most seemingly irrelevant realizations. Remember, thoughts are
often just fragments of intellectual understanding. It is your *feelings* that we
need to explore, and feelings tend to come up when they want to, not necessarily when we are ready for them. Seize these moments—for it really is
out of moments we shape the day, and out of days we create a life.

Each of us is complex, mysterious, and powerful—our feelings are the
precious map that will guide us to the treasure of our own strength. Like
pirates in search of gold, examine the clues of your feelings with patience
and reverence, and they will set your dreams afire.

● EXERCISE 1 **Revealing Our Deepest Beliefs About Money and
Abundance**

There are no right or wrong answers in this exercise. There is no score. There
are no categories to define us. There is only the recognition that we are
completely, utterly unique in our approach to financial well-being. Patterns
emerge—but they are our patterns, distinct and completely individual.

As children, long before we had the power of discernment, we learned about money. In most cases, we didn't think about it much, and we weren't verbally taught. We felt it. We perceived it on an unconscious level, through the behaviour of the people around us. We need, therefore, to go back there. Let's return to our childhoods.

Just for a few moments, I would like you to close your eyes. Relax. Relax your toes, and then your feet, your ankles . . . work slowly upward, right up to those little frown muscles between your eyebrows. You are far more than the body that carries you around. Let your body rest. Be aware of the thoughts meandering through your mind. Let go of them . . . you are far more than these thoughts. (If your thoughts are you, who is witnessing these thoughts?) Yes, you are more than your thoughts—let that part of your mind rest for the moment. As thoughts stray into your awareness, gently shoo them out. Be aware—be in the wise point of awareness.

How do you feel? Yes, you have feelings. Our feelings feel like us— but where do they come from? We are more than our feelings—we are also the point of divine consciousness that is aware of our feelings.

Be in that point of awareness.

Think about the bedroom you slept in when you were 10. Remember your bedspread, recall the wallpaper or the colour of the paint. Where are your favourite things? Can you see your doll, your crayons, and colouring book? You're lying on your bed, trying to go to sleep. You can hear your parents speaking. (If a single parent or a guardian raised you, imagine hearing that person on the telephone.)

Now, see yourself getting up. Go out into the hallway. You are an invisible witness. Wander through your house. See the hallway, or those awful drapes your mom hung in the living room. Sit at the kitchen table beside your mom or dad. Can you remember what it smelled like? They're talking about money. Listen.

When you're ready, go back to your room. Take your pen and paper, and write:

Did you have an allowance? ☑ Yes   ☐ No

If so, or if you received money as a gift or earned money, did you
☐ save it?   ☑ spend it?   ☐ spend some and save some?

If you spent more than you saved, what were your favourite things to buy?
☐ treats (food and candies)
☐ entertainment (movies, magazines, comic books)
☐ toys   ☐ clothes
☐ whatever your friends were into that week

☑ varied from week to week—no pattern
☐ things for other people   ☐ other (describe below)

_____

_____

_____

_____

_____

_____

If you saved more than you spent, what was your chief pleasure in doing so?
☐ Accumulation of money . . . you loved watching the balance go up in your passbook.
☐ Anticipation of the big buy . . . thinking and dreaming about the day you would get that bike, or go on a trip with a big wad of cash, or turn 16 and buy that car.
☐ The actual pleasure of ownership . . . not the anticipation of waiting to buy the bike, but actually having the bike, riding it . . . taking pride in having saved for it.
☐ Other (describe below)

_____

_____

_____

_____

_____

_____

Was your allowance tied to performing household chores?
☑ Yes   ☐ No

Did you often lose your allowance for bad behaviour, or for forgetting to do your chores?
☐ Yes   ☑ No

Could you increase your allowance or earn money by doing extra chores?
☐ Yes   ☑ No

What was your most creative way of earning money, or of getting something that you wanted that your parents wouldn't buy you?

Didn't do anything. Would usually just go without whatever it was.

Did you
☑ baby-sit? ☐ collect pop or beer bottles? ☐ sell your unwanted stuff to friends?
☐ other (list everything that you ever did to get money prior to becoming an adult)

Did you feel that you had the power to earn money to buy the things you wanted as a child?
☑ Yes ☐ No

If not, what did you do? Did you
☐ tell yourself it was OK—you didn't want it that badly anyway?
☐ keep on asking, perhaps until you got in trouble?
☐ beg, borrow or steal?
☐ hope that it would arrive on Christmas or on your birthday?
☐ dream?

Is there anything that you really wanted as a child that you never got?
☐ Yes ☑ No

Would you ever buy that item or experience for your child if you had/have one?
☐ Yes   ☐ No

If you had extra money, would you buy it for yourself now?
☐ Yes   ☐ No

What lessons do you think you learned as a child from the experience of not getting what you really, really wanted?

_____

_____

_____

_____

_____

_____

Let's explore the larger, emotional money myths that permeated our childhoods.

Do you remember your parents peering over chequebooks, counting pennies, adding up bills?
☑ Yes   ☐ No

Was there a sense of "not enough"? Did you know that "money does not grow on trees" and that "your father is not made of money"?
☑ Yes   ☐ No

Did you sense anxiety about "something bad that might happen" in regard to money?
☐ Yes   ☑ No

Did your parents fight about money?   ☐ Yes   ☑ No

If so, was there a common theme to their arguments (Mom spent too much money, Mom spoiled kids, Dad did not earn enough, Dad spent too much, Dad was cheap, Dad was extravagant, there were too many kids, etc.)? Write down whatever you remember.

_____

_____

_____

_____

_____

_____

_____

Were you ever made to feel shame because you were expensive to raise?
☐ Yes   ☑ No

Were you ever made to feel shame because you asked for too much?
☐ Yes   ☑ No

Were you ever rewarded for not asking for too much?
☑ Yes   ☐ No

Were you ever embarrassed because your parents didn't seem to make enough money?
☐ Yes   ☑ No

Were you ever embarrassed because your parents had more money than other people did?
☐ Yes   ☑ No

Who handled the finances in the family?
☑ Mom   ☐ Dad   ☐ both   ☐ other

_____

_____

_____

Did your mother have a household allowance?   ☐ Yes   ☑ No

If not, did she have to ask your dad for money when she wanted to buy something?
☐ Yes   ☑ No

If your mother controlled the finances, did your dad receive a spending allowance?
☐ Yes   ☑ No

Who made the major buying decisions (the house, the car, the furniture, the vacations, etc.)?
☐ Mom   ☐ Dad   ☑ both   ☐ the whole family

Who bought the gifts?
☑ Mom   ☐ Dad   ☐ both   ☐ the whole family

If your mom was not in charge, or equally in charge, of the family finances, did you ever think about why that was? How did you feel about it then? Now?

_____

_____

_____

_____

_____

_____

_____

Do you think you handle money more like your father, or more like your mother? How and why?

I think I handle $ more like my dad b/c I am quick to spend for the good things, however realize the need to save.

_____

_____

_____

Were you
☐ poorer than most of your friends and neighbours?
☐ about the same as your friends and neighbours?
☑ better off than most of your friends and neighbours?

Did your parents talk to you about money?
☑ Yes   ☐ No

To each other?
☑ Yes   ☐ No

To other people?
☐ Yes   ☑ No

If, and when, money was discussed, was it usually
☑ a calm discussion?
☐ a tense discussion?
☐ an angry discussion?

As a child, did you think of money as something that was

☑ controlled by adults (that is, they could control how much they earned and how much they spent)?

☐ uncontrollable (it seemed to arrive by accident and disappear just as mysteriously)?

What is your worst childhood memory in which money played a role?

_____

_____

_____

_____

_____

_____

_____

What is your best, sweetest childhood memory in which money played a role?

_____

_____

_____

_____

_____

_____

After answering these questions, how do you feel? Do any of these words describe the way you feel right now? Put a check mark beside each word that applies.

Alert	Determined	Curious	Competitive ✓	Excited
Calm	Cheerful	OK	Anxious ✓	Overwhelmed
Less-than	Greater-than	Understanding	Confident	Creative
Nostalgic	Flustered	Relaxed	Responsible ✓	Proud
Optimistic	Pessimistic	Impatient	Great	Reflective
Powerful	Happy	Sad	Nervous	Scared ✓
Sheepish	Self-assured	Sensitive	Strong	Weak
Thoughtful ✓	Vulnerable	Warm	Cold	Embarrassed

Using these feelings as a starting place, write a paragraph about your feelings and impressions. Don't let the pen lift from the page—write as swiftly as you can. Don't stop to edit. Don't stop to think. Just write.

Perhaps you have had a revelation about money and the lessons you learned during your childhood, or perhaps you just don't see the connection. If your belief system is different from the one you learned in childhood, and you find your mind arguing with your heart, let your heart speak first—promise your mind a chance to speak later.

Money was always viewed as a way of measuring achievement. That was how you marked success when I was growing up. Dad particularly wore money as a badge of honour; eager to be able to say that we had this or that - or what we were going to get (ie - new cars, stereo/technology equipment) Mom managed the day-to-day finances and she would usually quietly worry about money - Dad was always more vocal - both about spending & saving. General attitude was that you saved to spend and when you achieved one thing it was time to look forward to the next.

OK. Fast forward to your first job, your first apartment. Think about the shock of really supporting yourself for the first time.

Were you intimidated by the price of essentials like flour, dishwashing soap, TV dinners, and aspirin?
☑ Yes   ☐ No

Was it exciting to be free to make your own choices, or did you find it a wee bit terrifying?
☐ exciting   ☐ terrifying   ☑ both

Did you luxuriate in going a little wild (eating Cocoa Puffs for breakfast, munching pizza in bed, lying in bed on weekends eating chocolates and reading magazines...)?
☑ Yes   ☐ No

Did you save for big purchases or a trip?
☐ Yes   ☑ No

How old were you when you got your first credit card? ____19____

Would you say that you used it responsibly, knowing what you know now?
☑ Yes   ☐ No

Did you balance your chequebook regularly?
☑ Yes   ☐ No

At what moment did you really feel, for the first time, completely independent?

I would have to say that it was when I leased the mazda. my first car. although, I think I knew I got a bad deal it was the fact that I had "achieved" it.

Did you ever end up borrowing money from your parents?
☑ Yes   ☐ No

Moving back home?
☐ Yes   ☑ No

If so, what did that feel like? How did your parents handle it?

I borrowed money, not in the traditional payback "loan" sense or as a result of me specifically asking for it. It came more in the form of gifts of money here and there. They were very subtle in their approach.

Did your parents continue to support you for a time (while you were in university, when you needed a co-signer on your first mortgage, when you ran into a bit of trouble with the rent after that big vacation)?
☑ Yes   ☐ No

If so, do you believe that
☑ they were happy to do it?
☐ they did it grudgingly?

Would you do the same with your children, if you had/have any?
☑ Yes   ☐ No

How would you feel about asking your parents (or another relative) for money now if you ran into problems or if a big opportunity came your way?

I know that my parents would help me in any way, at any time. While I feel a little bad about that it's also extremely comforting to know.

Did you have any financial disasters? Did any of the following ever happen?
☐ I had to move because I couldn't pay the rent on my apartment.
☑ I bounced a cheque.
☐ I bounced cheques regularly.
☑ I didn't pay my bills (telephone, hydro, cable, etc.) on time.
☐ My phone/electricity/cable was disconnected because of late payment.

☐ I had to rely on social assistance/food stamps, etc., to get by at some point.

☐ I developed a bad credit rating.

☐ I defaulted on a loan and left my co-signer responsible for payment.

☐ My car/TV/furniture was repossessed because I couldn't make the payments.

☐ I made a bad investment and lost my money.

☑ Other (describe below).

If you did suffer financial disasters of one sort or another (and believe me, most of us have), what was the turning point? Did you get things together on your own? Were you able to ask for help?

We ran up our credit cards & personal line of credit. We weren't destitute but we definately weren't able to bail ourselves out. It was like being in a hole & just when you start to climb out, the sand gives way & falls back in on you. Mom & dad helped

How did this experience make you feel at the time? How did you feel about yourself as a person?

It made me feel grateful to them, but frustrated that we had let it get so out of control. I didn't feel like I had earned my right to independence. I had been spending independently but paying it off subserviently.

How do you feel thinking about it right now? If you still feel ashamed, or embarrassed, is there anything about the way you handled the situation that makes you feel proud?

Embarrassed, afraid it will happen again. I guess I was proud that I

*didn't give in to panic. always
knew it would eventually be
corrected.*

Did early marriage and/or a live-in relationship rob you of the opportunity to explore financial independence on your own? Or perhaps you found yourself in a situation where you were responsible for both your own financial well-being and your partner's. If you could go back and do it again, is there anything you would do differently?

*Yes, I never experienced true
financial independence - went from
living at home to living w/ Kevin.
But, no I wouldn't do anything
differently.*

Now, let's explore the present. Of the following statements, please check off "absolutely true," "somewhat true," or "not true at all."

People will care more about me if I have lots of money.
☐ Absolutely true   ☑ Somewhat true   ☐ Not true

People will not care about me as much if I am too successful.
☐ Absolutely true   ☐ Somewhat true   ☑ Not true

My friends and/or family will be uncomfortable if I have too much money.
☐ Absolutely true   ☑ Somewhat true   ☐ Not true

My spouse or partner will feel threatened if I have too much money.
☐ Absolutely true   ☑ Somewhat true   ☐ Not true

My spouse or partner will feel threatened if I have or want too much control over our money.
☐ Absolutely true   ☑ Somewhat true   ☐ Not true

People will rely on me too much if I'm economically successful.
☐ Absolutely true   ☐ Somewhat true   ☑ Not true

To be financially successful, you have to be (mark any that you feel apply)
☐ very smart   ☑ well educated
☐ a man   ☑ lucky
☑ aggressive   ☐ greedy
☑ materialistic

I don't deserve to be financially successful.
☐ Absolutely true   ☑ Somewhat true   ☐ Not true

I do deserve to be successful, but I just don't get any of the breaks.
☑ Absolutely true   ☐ Somewhat true   ☐ Not true

I am too old to become financially successful.
☐ Absolutely true   ☐ Somewhat true   ☑ Not true

I am too young to be financially successful.
☐ Absolutely true   ☑ Somewhat true   ☐ Not true

If I put my relationships and family first in my life, I'm not going to be financially successful.
☑ Absolutely true   ☐ Somewhat true   ☐ Not true

I'm not willing to make the sacrifices necessary to be financially successful.
☐ Absolutely true   ☑ Somewhat true   ☐ Not true

Wanting wealth is greedy.
☐ Absolutely true   ☑ Somewhat true   ☐ Not true

If I have everything I want, someone else will have to suffer.
☑ Absolutely true   ☐ Somewhat true   ☐ Not true

There is not enough to go around—look at all the starvation and poverty.
☐ Absolutely true   ☑ Somewhat true   ☐ Not true

Life is hard—we have to count our blessings and not wish for too much.
☐ Absolutely true   ☑ Somewhat true   ☐ Not true

It isn't spiritual to want beautiful things.
☐ Absolutely true   ☑ Somewhat true   ☐ Not true

Wealth just isn't me. I'm not that kind of person.
☐ Absolutely true   ☐ Somewhat true   ☑ Not true

I don't handle money very well—it would be a lot of responsibility to be wealthy.
☐ Absolutely true   ☑ Somewhat true   ☐ Not true

I would be happier if I just had more money.

☑ Absolutely true   ☐ Somewhat true   ☐ Not true

Write a quick summary of your fundamental, feeling-level beliefs about money, abundance, and financial well-being.

I believe that to truly live well you have to have some money. Not necessarily "loaded" but well-off. Everything seems to be dependent on money - as much as I wish it weren't true it all comes back to how much you have. I always have a feeling of never having enough. although it always seems to work itself out in the end... I always have a fear of "now"? I guess I don't know if I'll ever reach that point where I think I've really achieved financial success.

Is there anything that stands between you and the life you envision? Without lifting your pen from the page, write down any belief, attitude, thought or memory that might hinder you.

money! I would love to work as I wished in a job I loved rather than the dictated 40+ hours at something that would pay well. I always get trapped by the responsible approach particularly when it comes to earning money. Not necessarily spending it - but definately earning it! my biggest hold back to pursuing anything else is "how am I going to pay the bills". also, "how dare I consider chucking away such a good level of income?" I have always approached my career as what is the responsible choice & where are the most dollars.

3

Creative Perception: Turning Belief into Power

There can be no greater or lesser
mastery than over oneself.

LEONARDO DA VINCI

One of the most enduring symbols of serenity is the mysterious smile of the Mona Lisa. Oh, to know what she knew.

Da Vinci, creator of that smile, was far more than a brilliant artist. Scientist, artist, mathematician, and philosopher, he is widely credited with designing the first functional flying machines. Many centuries later, scientists studying his drawings have determined that had they been built, the magical machines would have flown. But they weren't built even though the natural resources we have today were also available during the great painter's time. What did the Wright brothers have that daVinci and his patrons did not? What was missing? Design, resources? Ah, yes—belief! Even with daVinci's brilliance and the vast wealth of his patrons, it was hundreds of years before two men finally *believed* we could fly, and hundreds of years before we did.

When we believe, we achieve. It was true of flight, and it is true of financial well-being.

Whatever it is we believe, it is easy enough to find evidence to support it. In a single evening of television, I can watch both a rerun of *Lifestyles of the Rich and Famous* and a two-hour infomercial on the excruciating poverty in Third World nations. Out for an afternoon here in Vancouver, I may rub elbows with celebrities shopping in prestigious Robson Street boutiques, and then drive down Hastings Street on my way home, where this city's poor beg for quarters and sell their bodies for another night's rent or another hour's chemical comfort. Change the street names and similar scenes are repeated throughout cities all over the world.

These seemingly contradictory, even paradoxical experiences are both very real. Poverty exists. And this is a universe of amazing abundance. What we have is not an abundance problem, but a distribution problem. We have a belief problem.

Unfortunately, fear (and Fear's most pampered child, Greed) perverts the natural flow of prosperity. Some have too much to ever enjoy, and yet spend their days in fear and misery, desperately trying to hang on to their bounty. Many more have too little, and live in aching hunger for even the most basic necessities.

We are uncomfortable with too much, starving with too little. What we want and need and are destined to have is *enough*. What we are challenged to figure out is how much is exactly, perfectly, abundantly enough for us. We are challenged to figure out how to make "enough" something we can believe in wholeheartedly, and therefore create.

Exploring your childhood and connecting it to your present has given you a sense of where you are, and how you arrived here. This understanding of your beliefs has delivered you to a station on your path where you get to make an important choice. You must decide to stay on the same belief train or choose a new path. One way or the other, your destination will clearly be a by-product of the route you choose.

Think of it this way. Your mind is a judge, analytical and brimming with information. Your subconscious (the metaphoric "heart") absorbs experience without question, and proceeds to influence your behaviour accordingly. If I am not unhappy with my weight, for instance, my body image must change before my body will change. I can begin this process by verbally affirming my desired reality, actually standing in front of a mirror and repeating, "I am slim and healthy and beautiful," but I'm going to get a strong argument from my conscious mind. "Waddaya mean you're slim and healthy and beautiful? Are you blind? Check out those thighs, Aphrodite."

However, when I also change my behaviour, a synergy develops between the power of the intellect and the power of the heart. After an hour on the treadmill, when I look myself in the eye in that mirror and repeat the same affirmation, I feel slim and beautiful. My subconscious mind absorbs both my affirmation and the feeling attached to it. At the end of the day, it is the volume of positive versus negative affirmations that creates change. If 20 minutes after my workout I'm at the food fair eating a Häagen-Dazs ice-cream bar and berating my gluttonous self, the earlier, positive message is cancelled out. Slim + beautiful + virtuous - gluttonous + fat + weak-willed = right back where I started. This is, therefore, rarely a speedy process. Rather, it requires patience, diligence, and discipline. Eventually, if you keep the faith most of the time, your heart begins to program your body and mind to behave the way a slim, healthy, beautiful being behaves. The behaviour then creates the result.

What doesn't work, clearly, is 5 minutes of "I am slim and healthy and beautiful," followed by 15 hours and 55 waking minutes of "This skirt makes me look fat." "Is my stomach sticking out?" "I wonder if he thinks I'm fat." "Why did I eat that cookie? No wonder I'm so fat."

The same is true of your financial life. Affirmations and affirmative behaviours are the patterns of creation—the seeds of future reality. Imagine, for instance, the power in a single poppy seed—one tiny black mass of cells, small enough to be carried by the wind. Within this minuscule speck is a majestic pattern that will, when rooted in friendly soil, create one of the most vibrant, beautiful blossoms on earth. Those blossoms will bear thousands of seeds, and when the poppies open themselves to the wind, entire landscapes can be carpeted in colour and beauty by that original, almost invisible seed.

The seed analogy also applies because of the fundamental importance of environmental conditions. Unfortunately, there are a lot of poppy seeds whose grandest moment will involve being stuck between someone's teeth. Likewise, you can affirm your belief in new financial realities until the cows come home (as they like to say in Alberta), but nothing will change unless your environment supports growth.

If a poverty mentality is undermining your ability to create financial well-being, for example, you must begin to act as if there is only abundance. This doesn't mean you spend what you don't have, falling deeper into a trap of crippling debt, but rather that you believe that abundance is a possibility, even a probability. If a belief in your financial ineptitude has prevented you from "owning" your own power to create well-being, you must act in ways that are in keeping with financial aptitude.

Caution is in order. Attempting to create an abundance mentality by spending money with abandon doesn't work because remorse and anxiety immediately follow overspending. The secret is in affirming abundance *and* balancing the chequebook.

When I began to acknowledge my own limiting beliefs, I studied the lives of people who had more of what I wanted. How do people behave when they are blessed with an abundance mentality? I read *The Richest Man in*

Babylon and other traditional tomes of wealth creation. Unfortunately, all of those books were about men, and I had a difficult time relating. Frankly, most of the wealthy people I know personally are also men. Not that there aren't self-made millionaires out there fuelled by estrogen, it's just that I'm not blessed with their acquaintance. I realized I had to broaden my research a bit. I had made the assumption, without thinking too deeply about it, that financially successful means wealthy, as in self-made multimillionaire. Since that isn't how I define my own success, I thought of women who have what I want: freedom. The ability to envision a future and turn their dreams into realities. Independence. The means to contribute in some way to the world we inhabit.

The women who come to mind first are not rich in the traditional sense (not that being rich in the traditional sense is a bad thing). They don't fit the patterns that one might expect: none of them came from well-to-do families and there were no large inheritances or lottery winnings. I thought of Judy, who was 25 when we worked together in Edmonton's one and only nightclub (well, the only one that didn't feature exotic dancers.) Judy was a superstar waitress, the kind regular customers asked for by name, and she made far more in tips than the rest of us, which certainly explained part of her success. When we were investing in trendy clothes that would be outdated by the time we got them dry-cleaned, Judy was learning all about the stock market. When I met her, she had already worked her way through a university degree. Later that same year, she made a substantial down payment on her first home. Judy was an ordinary woman with extraordinary belief in her ability to create financial well-being.

Fast forwarding a few years, I thought of my friends Barb and Linda, secretary and bartender respectively, who managed to save enough to spend almost every second summer in Europe. (They were such a mystery to me at the time—this was the same period of my life that a grand vacation was flying from Edmonton to Vancouver to stay with friends for a few days every August.)

There was Lily, a woman I met when she was in her forties. Never married, she had a creative career that she loved, but an unspectacular income. Nevertheless, she had managed to buy two homes, one of which she owned outright, and had compiled an impressive investment portfolio.

Although they didn't initially seem to have a lot in common, the traits these women did share were very interesting to me. First and foremost, they knew what they wanted. For Judy and Lily, the primary goal might have been described as the desire to become "women of substance." They would own property and they would have money. They both had very clear ideas about how much money was enough and they both wanted to own the homes they lived in. I haven't seen Barb and Linda in many years, and I have no idea what their goals may be now that we are all nearer to 40 than 14. I do know that when we were 20, they worked and planned and saved for one reason: to spend their summers in Europe. They had a clear, compelling vision. They believed.

These four women were strikingly similar in another way. They were all directors of their own existence. When I was in my early twenties, my primary activity was looking for the right man—when The Prince came along, everything else, I believed, would fall magically into place. Although time is far too precious to squander in regret, it does make me smile somewhat ruefully to know, in hindsight, that I could have successfully applied the same energy to European summers or developing an investment portfolio.

These women, and many others who welcome abundance into their lives, share some common beliefs about themselves and the nature of the world.

◆ There is more than enough to go around. I don't have to worry or struggle to get what I need. There is enough.

◆ I have the power to shape my life. If I really want something, I have the ability and the resources and the support I need to get it. It won't happen instantly, or without a cost, but it will happen.

◆ I am capable of managing my finances effectively.

◆ When I look after myself well, I have greater ability to look after others and contribute to my world. I care deeply about the world and other people, but it is my responsibility to look after myself first.

◆ I am capable of setting goals and reaching them.

◆ It won't happen for me or to me—I will make it happen.

On some level, to whatever limited degree, these statements are true for most of us, and it might be argued that the strength of your belief is exactly equal to the quality of your financial well-being. For most of us, however, there are dimensions of negative belief that are just as powerful. Unfortunately, because we often think of feelings and beliefs as being less tangible than facts, we choose not to acknowledge, and therefore influence, our belief system. Before we go further on this path, we must acknowledge the reality and the power of these intangible beliefs—and accept our ability to shape them in more creative ways.

Like most valuable endeavours, this process can be a daunting challenge. It is very likely that you found, during the first exercise, that certain money issues were very difficult to articulate because they didn't make sense. "This is true, but that, the opposite, also seems to be true." (The conscious mind calls this hypocrisy, but remember that your heart doesn't judge; it only absorbs—and creates.) For instance, this is one of my favourite paradoxical (goofy!) beliefs: I'm, well, let me put it this way, late thirty-something. I was raised in a farming community in northern Alberta, and I was raised to believe that the way to material well-being was a good marriage. (I can just picture my mom reading this and shrieking, "What? I didn't tell you that!!! That's not what I taught you!" No, Mom, you didn't. And I love you for that.) It wasn't what I was told. It wasn't what I heard. It was what I saw. I knew four kinds of women. Farmer's wives, housewives, teachers, and the women who worked in stores and banks. Bank managers were men. Farmers were men. School principals were men. Store owners were men. It was terribly clear: if you wanted a financially comfortable life, you chose a good man who made a good living.

However, by the time I had my first child in 1978, a woman who didn't work in order to stay home with her children was considered pampered. Real Women managed to supplement their family's income, cook the meals, clean the house, and look after the children—oh, yes, and stay slim, physically fit, and sexually appealing. Shirley Conran's *Superwoman*, a guide to surviving the dual roles of business and home, climbed the best-seller list. With advice on everything from cooking to cleaning to surviving date rape, Ms. Conran sympathetically implied that we could survive—with a little bit of organization and a lot of humour. We lapped it up. Although we didn't dare hope to achieve financial independence on our own, we knew that capturing Mr. Right now depended as much on our ability to make a decent living as on our ability to make a decent meal. By the time I was married, I had completely confused "having it all" (a perfectly acceptable and worthy ambition) with "doing it all" (a self-destructive and impossible-to-achieve ambition).

All of this to say simply: it doesn't have to make sense. Don't try to rationalize your belief system. Acknowledge it. Examine it. Recreate it.

Yes, you are ambivalent. We're all ambivalent. We may have been raised in an environment in which there wasn't enough, or in a world in which women were considered financially inept by nature. However, on some level, we believe—*we* believe that we have the power to change our lives, that there is another, richer way of living, or who would be reading this book? Who, for that matter, would have written it?

Our present confusion may be so profound that our beliefs exert no influence at all—our energies are spent locked in internal struggle and have no external power. Or we create erratic results—we manage to save a substantial down payment on our dream home and then lose most of it in speculative investments while looking for the right house.

Our ambivalence is a blessing. In clarity lies immense power, and we are, for the most part, protected by our impotence. If we weren't, the results could be devastating. That bag lady we are all terrified of becoming, for instance. She has a very powerful belief system. She believes, clearly and without doubt, in poverty, in a universe of "not enough." On the other hand, if we believed, clearly and without doubt, in a universe of abundance and in our ability to create reality, we would be a nation of Oprah Winfreys. Just imagine . . .

I love Oprah. Just the thought of her makes me want to jump up and cheer. A poor, abused, overweight young black woman with lousy taste in men grows up to be the most powerful woman in the world. Not by imposing, controlling, or "winning." Not by manipulating, or maneuvering—but by acting as a model of just how beautiful and enriching a compassionate life can be. Hallelujah!

If we could analyze and duplicate Oprah's belief systems, I have no doubt whatsoever that the world would change so dramatically we would all sit back in awe-filled wonder. Though I'm almost never at home to watch her show, I did have the privilege of catching a recent episode she did on financial well-being.

"I always knew I'd have money," she said, "though what a poor little black girl was doing thinking she'd have money, I'll never know."

It does boggle the mind, but that little girl proved herself right in ways even she probably never imagined. She *believed*. She *created*.

Most of us are somewhere between these two polarities. In between the bag lady and Oprah, there we are, swinging like pendulums. We have days when we believe in our power to create financial well-being as firmly as we believe that the sun will rise tomorrow. The living is easy and the cheque-book balances. Then there are days when we feel out of control, pessimistic, and powerless.

It's OK. Bouncing back and forth is part of the process, as are those dark days. When we feel powerful, we are in mastery—we are creators. On those days we feel out of control, we are growing and learning—preparing for the next cycle of creation. One state cannot exist without the other. They are both essential and follow each other like the seasons (although not always as quickly). It is our challenge to move from financial winter, when our dark nights are long and bleak, to the summer, when the sun shines most of the time.

Fear and doubt are part of the process. Embrace and love the lessons they bring you—let the rest go. (It isn't as hard as it sounds.) Comfort your fear demons as you'd comfort a child assailed by nightmares. If your vision is clear enough, it will prevail, enduring long after the doubts have faded. I don't know for sure, but I would bet that Oprah suffers bleak days, days when she quakes with doubt. I know, too, that she is blessed with a powerful and compelling vision. She overcomes her fears and doubts when they arise. So do I. And so will you.

Do a quick review of the last two pages of the childhood exploration exercise in Chapter 2. Let's use that new wisdom to move into the second exercise. Ask yourself the following questions and let your mind (and heart) wander . . . what is it, my friend, that you want to believe?

EXERCISE 2 **Reframing Old Beliefs**

Of each of the beliefs you identified in Exercise 1, ask yourself the following questions:

1. Although this was true for me once, is it still true?

2. Is this belief serving me well? Do I want this belief system in charge of my future?

3. If I believe this to be true, can I think of exceptions in which it isn't true?

4. If this is true, but I don't like it, what can I do to change it?

5. Does everyone believe this?

6. Do people who live the way I would like to believe this?

Replacing old beliefs was a concept that was initially rather astonishing to me. The things we believe, I thought, were things we knew to be true. To replace these beliefs would be to accept what wasn't true. When I explored my own beliefs more deeply, however, I came to understand how flawed this premise really was. As an example, when I was in my twenties, there were many things I knew to be true, rock-solid reality. I couldn't afford to go to university. (My brother and youngest sister both eventually achieved secondary degrees by applying for student loans and asking my parents for their assistance—options I never even considered.) I couldn't afford to own my own home (but Judy, a waitress, did). I couldn't afford to travel the world (like my friends Barb and Linda). I couldn't afford to save or invest money (like Lily). If I was going to have a good life, it was going to arrive in the arms of a man. (She laughs hysterically.)

Judy, Linda, Barb, Lily, and I all grew up in the same era. We had the same kind of jobs and the same material needs. Some of my truths were true for them, too, but they chose to let another light guide them to their destination. They *chose another truth.*

If you want to create a new reality, you, too, must create a new belief system, one day at a time. It can take longer than you want it to, but hey, time passes faster than you want it to, as well. As the Zen masters teach, water steadily dripping onto the face of a rock will eventually change it in a way that a thousand pounding fists never could. If you are persistent, your life will change.

Even with a number of false starts, my own experience has proven this to be true. At 27, for instance, I was earning about $23 000 a year. That's not a lot, even for a woman in the banking industry, but it was a relatively new field for me, and there was a steep learning curve. I was aware that I was being reimbursed in training as well as money. In addition, I believed that I was limited by some very real disadvantages—no related degree, financial problems of my own, and all the demands of being a single parent.

The man in my life at the time gave me a really hard time about what I thought was a pretty good job. We were both facing difficult times financially, but his were related to a bear market. In his opinion, the root of my financial problems was a tendency to sell myself short. He used to say things like, "With your abilities, you should be making at least $26 000 a year. You're crazy to stay in that job."

Twenty-six thousand dollars a year! Someone else might have seen this as a compliment, but it made me feel very threatened. My job was me, after all—if it wasn't a good job, then what did that say about me as a person? He was implying, too, that I needed to make dangerous changes. I guess, I thought, he doesn't know me very well. He doesn't understand my limitations.

Still, he was very, very cute, so I let him hang around despite the nonsense he spouted. Eventually, like the proverbial water dripping on stone, the surface of my inadequacy started to wear away beneath his persistence.

It was eventually the combination of his nagging and a tense relationship with my supervisor at work that motivated me to look for another job.

I made an appointment to see a well-reputed personnel agent. I will never forget that day. Even now, almost 10 years and a number of great jobs later, I feel queasy when someone mentions her name. She agreed to meet me before work, at 7 a.m. Never a morning person, this meant that I had to get up and get my daughter to the sitter's before six. Naturally, I slept very little the night before, terrified that I wouldn't hear the alarm clock. As I was getting out of the very expensive cab I took to get to her office on time, I caught my pantyhose on a rough piece of metal and ripped the back of one leg completely out. I mean, completely. It was the worst pantyhose wipe-out I've ever seen.

I had timed my arrival precisely, with 10 minutes to primp before my appointment. I used eight minutes and thirty seconds jogging up and down the street in my high heels (in the pouring rain, without an umbrella) looking for an open convenience store. Nada. No store.

With 90 seconds left to go, I dashed up the stairs to her floor, ran into the bathroom, ripped off my pantyhose to reveal red and purple-mottled, shaven-three-days-ago winter legs, and ran to her office. As she opened the door to greet me, a huge drop of water rolled from my sopping hair-sprayed locks into my eye, and before she was back with my coffee, my mascara was smeared over most of one cheekbone and my left eye was an irritated red mass.

She tried not to look. "So? You'd like a new job? Twenty-six thousand a year? Hmmmm." (Five minutes of silence interrupted only by the sound of water dripping from my hair onto the back of my vinyl chair.)

"Do you have your MBA?" *(No, I have an eleven-year-old son and a one-year-old daughter.)* "No. Hmmm. That's too bad. A real disadvantage. Most of the placements I make have their MBA. You can't get much of a position without an MBA these days."

I don't know. Perhaps it was the goose-pimpled bare legs or the hair disaster or even the missing MBA, but I got the feeling she wasn't impressed. By the time I left her office, I was grateful to be employed at all. It was going to be a good long time before I asked for a raise.

Work had never been harder than it was that day. My supervisor had never been more irritating. But I looked forward to the evening, when I could tell Randy exactly what I thought of his harebrained ideas and of the humiliation his flawed encouragement had exposed me to. He didn't let me off the hook. "It sounds as if she wasn't the right person. Maybe she felt threatened—she probably doesn't have a lot of faith in herself, either. You need someone with imagination—someone like yourself—to recognize how valuable you are."

Threatened. Obviously he was incapable of imagining the scene.

I thought that was it for my job-hopping fantasies, but within a few months, divine discontent sent me out looking again. Five interviews—five times the same response (although I did get much better at the interview process—and never scheduled another interview for early morning). "Why would we pay you more in a new position than you were making in your old one?"

Eventually, I accepted a commission sales job. The guaranteed income was slightly less than my salary, but the potential was limited only by my ability and hard work. If no one else would pay me $26K a year, I'd simply have to pay myself. When I gave notice, however, the company I worked for made a counter-offer. A promotion—and a raise. The salary offered? You guessed it.

As uncomfortable as it felt at first, Randy had forced me to see myself as someone worth more, and it was only a matter of time until someone else did, too. Once I had overcome that first hurdle, my life changed rapidly. I knew it was possible—I knew I could do it. In less than six years my income almost quadrupled. You could chalk it up to opportunity, to knowing the right people, to hard work, even to luck. Unquestionably, all of those factors played a part. But I know that my life wouldn't have changed in any way without that fundamental shift in the way I saw myself. As Randy's dream for me influenced my image of myself, my income increased. My beliefs changed—my life changed.

Surrounding yourself with positive people who see your potential (as well, hopefully, as their own) is one very effective way of increasing personal power, but it isn't the only way. Don't wait around for someone else to tell you how great you are—start uncovering the evidence yourself. Ultimately, no one needs to believe in your potential except you.

When I resigned from the position of executive vice-president, some of my friends were wonderfully supportive. There were others, with equally excellent intentions, who were afraid for me. When I spoke of my dreams (writing a book, presenting workshops, working in more balanced ways), I heard the equivalent of "Well, yeah, that would be great, but how will you make a living?"

"Well, yes, everybody would love to take a year off and write a book, but you know it's impossible to get a first book published, don't you?"

"You learn to appreciate a salary when you don't have one, Lori."

One lunch was enough to send me into a spiral of depression, but I had a vision, and the vision pulled me onward, upward. Eventually I came to understand that these friends spoke from their own fear. If I wanted to go further, in new directions, than the people around me, I couldn't rely on their advice to guide me. The faith of others had brought me this far, but the next leg of the journey was something I had to undertake on my own.

On my own, but not alone. A new friend became dear as she dragged me to creative-writing classes, and challenged me to move beyond my comfort zone with golf and horseback-riding lessons. She gave me a copy of *The Artist's Way,* and *Simple Abundance*—books that would become maps as I moved through a new life-scape. I went to the library and took out a dozen books at a time, on downshifting, on simplicity, on developing an abundance consciousness. I found sites on the Internet. I continued to meet new people, friends who were making leaps of courage and choosing alternative ways of living well.

Following these different paths to their destinations took some time, and not a little bit of courage. If I hadn't been in so much discomfort at the time, I might not have bothered, but what I found was amazing. More importantly, it was transforming.

Here is a scientific process to enhance your belief system so that it serves you in powerfully positive ways:

1. Know yourself, and where you are now. Once you understand what you believe, and which of these beliefs are hindering you, you are on your way.

2. If possible, surround yourself with powerful, positive people. (Remember, positive people make those around them feel wonderful because they find so much joy in enhancing the well-being of others. You know that it makes you feel great to help someone else—it isn't an imposition to lend a hand, but a privilege. Remember this when it is time to invite someone else's help.)

   If you can't find these people in your life initially, you will find them in the library, in the biography and autobiography sections. Finding an individual mentor can be life changing; if you can't, consider joining service organizations that interest you—they are often full of like-minded individuals.

3. When you have the privilege of meeting people you admire, ask them to recommend a book, or simply to spend a few minutes talking about what's meaningful to them, about what beliefs have shaped their lives.

4. Limit the time you spend in the company of negative people. No, don't stop calling your mother. Love your family and those doom-saying friends with all your heart—but limit your visits to whatever length of time you know you can be a positive influence in their lives as opposed to them being a negative one in yours. (Remember, too, that those dire warnings of your imminent failure come from love and a need to protect you. They aren't always rational and are almost never helpful, but they are well intentioned.)

5. Decide what you want to believe, and begin to act as if it were true. Choose your truths and repeat them verbally, in writing, in symbols, in action, until they manifest themselves in your life.

One last thing. Whatever the obstacle between us and well-being, we have created and nursed that obstacle because of some gratification it brings us.

In order to let go of the obstacle, we have to identify the gratification and find another way to get it. Financial serenity is not about suffering or deprivation.

Let's consider power-shopping as an example. In a magazine I perused in my doctor's office some years ago I found an interesting article about a study conducted on male and female shopping behaviours. Not surprisingly, these scientists concluded that the way we shop today is a barely evolved version of the way we brought home the goodies at the dawn of (Wo)Man. Women were gatherers and the first agriculturists, working in union and creating relationships with nature. Men hunted—find an animal, kill it, and drag it home.

Today, we see less blood but much the same behaviour. My husband runs into a mall, grabs the closest pair of black socks, pays, and dashes. Eight minutes, give or take five for parking. I might meander for hours, searching for just the right shade in just the right fabric at just the right price. I buy from businesspeople with whom I've formed warm relationships, enjoying the process of interaction as much as the thrill of the purchase.

This research also provides a theory on why shopping feels so good for women—even those of us who profess to hate shopping are prone to at least occasional bouts of mall therapy, often followed by spending hangovers. We seek the pleasure of acquisition—we feed the hunger of our genetic programming. Shopping, for us, is a way of supplying the needs of our families in the same way that gathering was—we haven't changed a great deal, but the world has. In this New World, because we pay for the things we buy, we are no longer asset-gathering, but exchanging units of value. Therefore, the pleasure we feel when we make that perfect purchase is too often followed by "buyer's remorse"—the realization that we have not improved our lot, only changed it.

It's a little like the guy who gets in a fight in a bar "protecting" his girlfriend—it is a million miles from appropriate, completely unnecessary, but it feels great to gratify those Neanderthal instincts. Until the morning after. I'm happy to say that never once have I woken up in the morning with a black eye, sore knuckles, or a hangover (well, only one of the three). I have, however, spent $3000 on my Eaton's card in one Christmas season.

There is hope for me, and for anyone who has ever suffered a money hangover. Once you understand the pattern, you can achieve the same gratification without the remorse. You can cultivate the art of waiting for the truly perfect purchase (that is, perfect for your needs *and* your bank account), the art of thrift, consignment, and garage-sale shopping. Actually, this is one of the fun parts. You can improve the well-being of your family while spending less. The joy of finding a beautiful designer suit or the perfect end table is magnified a thousand-fold when you lay down $20 or less at the cash register, believe me.

Perhaps you have either wrestled the mall-therapy monster to the ground, or have never even met the beast. You are at the opposite end of the pendulum's swing, tending to endure rather ascetic and extreme self-deprivation. Your budget is in order, but you have developed an ironclad poverty mentality through the self-denial of life's luxuries. Your challenge, then, is to maintain financial health while inviting richness into your life.

EXERCISE 3 Divine Indulgence

Whether we spend too much or spend too little, our souls are hungry for divine indulgence. Just for fun, make a list of as many things as possible that would give you real joy. Any kind of joy—thrills, comfort, sinful pleasures, silly luxuries. One caveat: your thrill must be available, somewhere, for $25 or less.

To prime the pump a bit, this is my list:

- a successful shopping spree at Value Village, the local thrift shop, or a serendipitous garage sale that finds its way onto my daily path

- a copy of *Architectural Digest*, a vanilla latte and an hour at Starbucks

- a manicure

- a bottle of sparkling non-alcoholic wine, bath salts, and a great paperback book to accompany a two-hour retreat in my soaker tub

- *The English Patient* (or *Out of Africa*), a big bowl of buttered popcorn, a bottle of chilled Fruitopia

- a day on the beach, followed by a great, once-a-summer dinner at the fish-and-chip stand

- a really good movie in a really big theatre (NO talking, please)

- a faux gold compact

- fresh flowers, anytime, any place, any kind

- a flat of new annuals to plant in my much neglected flower beds

- really excellent ground coffee (brewed in a French press with steamed milk, cinnamon, and raw brown sugar) and an hour of meditative affirmation and writing—every morning!

- a garage-sale frame for a beautiful art postcard

- fabulous new underwear

- great Body Shop body scrubs for the shower (yes, please support women-owned and compassion-centred businesses)

- one truly divine Belgium chocolate

- sushi (nothing exotic, though!)

- a wonderful hard-cover edition of a favourite poet—from the bargain rack, of course!

- a bike ride around Deer Lake with my daughter followed by hot cocoa at the Art Centre

- an hour-long walk with my dog, followed by a big mint-chocolate-chip ice cream in a waffle cone, the sun on my face

- a lobster cocktail with sparkling grape juice for lunch by myself in a stunningly silent house

- a Sunday brunch under a blue sky with a dear friend

Now, your list:

- a manicure
- a copy of "O" magazine & a cup of tea
- antiquing & enjoying a leisurely lunch
- renting classic movies & spending the afternoon on my couch
- going for a walk w/ Kevin & getting ice cream.
- shopping in courtenay w/ my mom.
- new underwear
- spending a quiet evening at home alone w/ classical music & yoga.

"Plus: Everything on Lori's list!"

Now, you may be asking where do we get the money to indulge in these extravagances? (Aren't we supposed to be *saving* money?)

When I took a good look at my own spending patterns, I found I was devoting a fair amount of money to things that gave me no pleasure whatsoever. The most obvious was probably lunch at work—I paid more than $6 for a sandwich with soup or a drink. By taking lunch, I could eat well and save about $4 a day, about $80 a month. That $80 created a rich Divine Indulgence fund.

There were other ways I found I could exchange pleasurable indulgences for non-pleasurable expenses—a big one was simplifying our eating. An ardent food fan, I never even considered the possibility until I read Elaine St. James' *Simplify Your Life*, which makes a compelling case for all kinds of radical and life-enhancing behaviour modification. (The book's suggested retail price, as I write, is $10.95. It is available almost everywhere books are sold. I highly recommend putting it on your DI list.)

I digress. In the old days, I bought a lot of food, and threw out a lot. My great intentions were not matched by my energy at the end of the workday. In addition to the myriad packages of expensive bags of washed and precut salad makings that eventually went into the garbage while we ate takeout, I spent an unconscionable amount of money on not particularly tasty frozen meals.

Now our dinners are very simple: an omelette with toast and sliced apples, grilled-cheese sandwiches and tomato soup, pasta in tomato sauce with a green salad. If it can't go from idea to table in half an hour or less, we don't eat it. I save on groceries, I don't buy overprocessed food, and we eat out less because preparing dinner is less daunting. Prepared tomato sauce and cheese on a pita is just as fast and much less expensive than frozen pizza—and it tastes fabulous. By leaving more room in our diet for fresh fruits and vegetables, we save on nutritional supplements as well.

Then there was my wardrobe. I have always been frugal, but after an early six-month employment stint at Holt Renfrew, during which I learned the true meaning of "mark-up," I swore I'd never pay retail again. To maintain a suitable business wardrobe, I buy one new piece at the end of each January when the real sales are on, never paying more than 50 percent of the original price. Many of the classic items in my closet are years old—some have been worn by three members of my family. Trendy, fun additions come from consignment and thrift stores (also a wonderful way to spend a few hours on a rainy weekend). When I say frugal, I mean Frugal.

My Achilles' heel, and I did have one, was the EVENT. My husband would announce a dinner or party and my mind would start spinning. Out I'd go to the mall, often with just an hour or two to buy the new outfit. (And, of course, I never had the right shoes, either.) Only then would I ever, out of sheer desperation, consider paying full price. Only then would I buy something that didn't complement the rest of my wardrobe. Only then would I consider using my credit cards for clothing purchases. And only then would I invariably buy something I hated as soon as I left the store.

No more. I am proud to say (only after finally reaching my maximum pain-tolerance level) I have sworn off the "I don't have anything to wear" shopping trip forever—by preparing, in advance, for any eventuality. I have a dinner-with-the-boss outfit, dinner-by-the-colleague's-pool outfits, and barbecue-on-the-boat outfits. I have wedding outfits and shower outfits and camping outfits and après-ski outfits. I am not a fashion diva, of course, but neither am I a fashion victim. And I have learned that no one really cares if I show up in the same outfit more than once. As a matter of fact, if people do notice, they generally like it—because it makes them feel a bit better about the new event-wear now steaming up their credit cards.

There are many, many ways to convince our inner 12-year-old that this is a universe of abundance. Some of them are fun. Some are less fun—and even more powerful. Check out your feelings as you read through the list. Generally, we feel the greatest aversion to the steps that will change our lives the most.

If you don't keep a journal, now is a good time to start. Splurge on the most beautiful lined book you can afford and start working on a few lists of your own.

Things That Are Working in My Life Right Now

What gives you joy? What makes life easier, smoother, sweeter? Off the top of my head, these are some of the things that are working for me today:

◆ Commuting—taking the train to work gives me a period of respite, morning and night, in which I can read and think and be at peace.

◆ My relationship with my daughter.

◆ Work.

◆ My wardrobe.

◆ My fitness program (which, coincidentally, is the simplest fitness program I've every practised, consisting of two 20-minute hill and stair sessions with my dogs morning and night, thirty push-ups, and a hundred crunches two or three times a week)—no stress, no gym membership dues, no good excuses about not enough time.

Things That Are Not Working in My Life Right Now

What ticks you off? Irritates you? Causes you stress? Detracts from your happiness? For me, today, it's the following:

- Not having enough time with my son and husband.
- Letting myself become immersed in stock-market hysteria.
- Not having enough time with my friends and extended family.
- Worrying about things I cannot change.

At the moment, there aren't any money issues on my list. There are things that I could certainly do better, but they aren't at issue for me at the moment—largely because I've been on the Financial Serenity path for three years now and have worked through many of my most disabling money issues. You might look at my list, and your own, and wonder what it has to do with material well-being. We'll get to that in the next chapter, as we overcome the obstacles that hinder us and as we create channels of order in which joy and abundance can flow. For now, it is enough to simply consider our days and the ways in which they unfold.

4

Planting Our Dreams in Rich Soil

'Speak to me of God, sister,'

she said to the apricot tree, and

the apricot tree blossomed.

AUTHOR UNKNOWN

Gardening is a wonderful metaphor for the creation of a financially serene life. In this era of instant gratification and quick fixes, the natural world teaches us that there is a season for everything under the heavens, and that no amount of worry and toil can make a poppy blossom faster than it wants to. Weeds, harmless and often even pretty, become destructive when allowed to overwhelm—just as excessive indulgence or frugality repels well-being.

The most glorious gardens illustrate, too, that even the wildest beauty requires order. In nature, order is imposed by the seasons—the fecundity of spring and summer, the rich harvest of the fall, the dark, cold dormancy of winter. In our financial lives, we must create order through our actions.

On the following pages, you will find a plethora of suggestions for creating order in your own gardens. Not everything will apply to your situation, but as you read, be aware—it is often the things we need most that we feel the strongest resistance to. If you find yourself making excuses ("I'm just not that kind of person." "I like mess." "I thrive on crisis." "Who has time?"), ask yourself these questions:

"Am I happy?"

"Do I feel content?"

"Am I fulfilled?"

"Is my life as serene as I'd like it to be?"

There is a reason you're reading this book, and it is likely that there is something in your financial life that isn't working as well as you'd like it to. Just for the sake of living deep, try the things that don't feel comfortable. Don't make the age-old mistake of doing everything the same way and expecting new results. Information alone will not change your life. Action is required.

Growing Abundance: A Case for Order

The Daily Stuff

Order creates channels through which creative energy can flow. Without order, energy is blocked, diverted, or diluted. Whether we are at-home moms, career women, or a combination of the two, we are so often overwhelmed by the many details that we have to take care of. In order to make the most of our precious time and energy, we must streamline, simplify. Those endless "little things" begin to take care of themselves when we invite order into our lives, and we are free to commit our energies to more important issues. Order gives us peace of mind—everything becomes clearer. We stop worrying about what might have been overlooked, and start planning for what may be achieved.

For too much of my life, my creative energy was squandered on anxiety and reactivity. I wish I could say I'm completely cured, but I'm a good example of "progress rather than perfection." If I thought I was alone, believe me, I'd keep my own shortcomings in this department secret, but I know that I'm not. So often, when women share their stories with me, part of the tale is about the dark place where energy drains away: overdue bills that haunt us; bank accounts that consume our money (because where else could it be going?); and destructive relationships, personal or professional, that undermine our confidence and distract us from our goals.

I unfortunately didn't realize it at the time, but I learned much of what I needed to about creating order in my very first garden. I was a proud member of the 4H Garden Club in Beaver Crossing, Alberta. I joined for two noble reasons: it got me away from the farm (and farm work) and because cake was almost always served after our meetings. I was ten years old and it was Northern Alberta, which meant that our fragile, little plants had about five weeks between spring thaw and autumn frost. Our spring garden plans were modest. I don't remember much about the vegetables we grew, although

I do have a vague recollection of peas that appeared, proliferated, and then turned bitter before I could manage to eat them all—raw, out of the shell, with muddy hands, standing in the garden with one eye out for my mom. My favourites were the flowers, marigolds, and sweet peas.

I remember marvelling at the dry, hard seeds. How could life grow out of something that felt so solid and lifeless? What a thrill it was to have my own small plot of earth. My mother unobtrusively supervised as I raked and moved the rocks away, and then she showed me how to run a string on two sticks planted at each end, hoeing row after astonishingly straight row. Perfectionists, we planted, and every seed was a measured distance from its siblings. Then we waited.

Each morning I ran out to check for the green sprouts, and for what seemed an infinitely long time, there was no sign of life. Barren earth. With my mother's encouragement, I kept the faith and watered even when it seemed I was just pouring the water away. Then one day, magic occurred— the tiniest green shoot poked through the crumbly soil. By afternoon, there were a dozen shoots. Soon there were too many to count and my garden was born, the rows I had so carefully hoed reappearing in green.

I felt like a magician! And when the delicate, fragrant sweet peas began to bloom, I was Merlin, an artist of creation. By midsummer, however, the enchantment was dimming. If I didn't water one day, what difference could it make? And those weeds—how could they grow so fast? Where did they all come from? Surely I couldn't be expected to keep up?

When the day came that the 4H Club was to arrive en masse for an inspection, I knew I had failed. In a little, insignificant bit at a time, I had lost control, and the magic had faded. Even in their glorious red and orangeness, my marigolds were limp, my peas were dull and rippled, and my corn was so immature it was plain there would be no butter-dripping cobs at table that year. Oh, but that moment our leader pulled a carrot from that hard soil and remarked on its plumpness and its deep colour, how I swelled with pride. And in that simple, little garden, I learned many lessons that are just as applicable and effective in my life today.

◆ The simplest things, done well, will bear rich fruit (or vegetables) eventually.

◆ It is not that grandiose, perspiration-drenched final effort that makes the difference, but the little things done (or not done) every day.

◆ There are times it all comes down to faith. If we take care of the details (straight rows, weeds, and watering; bank accounts, credit cards, putting some money aside), miracles will occur—in their own good time.

I am very grateful for my mom's gentle direction on those warm summer days, and in her honour, I offer these suggestions in the same hopeful spirit.

Are Your Chequing/Savings Accounts in Order?

1. How much time do you spend balancing those accounts? And yes, you must balance them. If this is a huge chore, try simplification. Save your cheques for those rare situations where cash, credit, or debit aren't practical. (I thought I was addicted until I stopped carrying a chequebook. Withdrawal was amazingly pain-free.) If you are adept at using credit cards responsibly, make as many purchases as you can on either debit or credit cards. Warning: if you do not pay off your credit cards monthly, do not use your credit card for daily expenses. Use debit or cash.

2. Do you really need more than one chequing account? If there isn't a good reason for having more than one, think about closing the rest. (If it works best for you, maintain a savings account within your main account for savings, household expenses, etc. You will have only one statement to balance to, one institution to deal with, and one fee.)

3. Unless you have an inordinately low level of activity (do the math with a representative at your bank or credit union), choose an account with a monthly fee that includes free withdrawals, free debit purchases, free chequing, and free bill payments.

4. If you have a computer, choose an institution that provides online banking.

5. Compare fees. It isn't worth changing institutions for three or four dollars a month, but if you find yourself paying dozens of one- and two-dollar withdrawal or phone-transfer fees because your bank's branch locations aren't convenient, make the shift. A lot of us end up with a particular institution because it's "convenient"—that is, there happened to be a branch on the corner of the street that we lived on 12 years ago and we've been dealing with them ever since. If you have a good rapport or history, there is incentive to continue the relationship, but at least negotiate the best type of account package for your needs within that institution. That being said, I dealt with the same bank for years without ever speaking to anyone who knew my name. When I made the switch to a local credit union, it was only weeks before I knew all of the staff in the branch where my account was held and felt entirely comfortable calling my financial adviser for advice or help.

Do You Really Need More Than One Credit Card?

Yes, I know, credit feels like money—but baby, it isn't. As my friend Loa so aptly described it, credit-card debt is "no money minus!" If you must have more than one credit card (and remember, once credit is granted, it is usually included in any debt calculations even if you don't have a balance on that card), at least try to use only one. Think about the ease of one statement, one payment. Now, which one? First of all, check out the interest rates on the cards you have. Check out the annual fees. Don't get starry-eyed about air miles or new-car credits. If you do the calculations, you will find that you often spend far more accumulating those "benefits" than you will eventually save. If you are carrying a large balance, it makes sense to use a low-interest account even though it probably means paying an annual fee until you can pay it off. Switch to a no-fee account when you are able to pay off your balance monthly.

Before you do anything else, before you even think about investing, **create a monthly plan to pay off all high-interest credit balances.** If you have department-store or gas-card balances, you are probably paying 28.8 percent interest, compounded monthly. Paying off your balance monthly may save thousands of dollars in interest over a lifetime, providing you with some of that "disposable income" that is so difficult to find. Think of it this way: if you have a department-store credit card with a balance of only $1500, you will be charged over $36 per month in interest. In one year, you will have made a phantom purchase of about $432. I don't know about you, but I can think of a million things to do with $432 that don't involve giving it to a credit provider.

On the other hand, if you don't have a credit card in your own name, it is time to get one. A spousal card is not the same thing—ex-husbands are notorious for cancelling these just when you need them most. Establishing individual credit is a fundamentally important step for all women, not just single women.

If you have a poor credit history, speak to a representative at your credit union about applying for a "secured" credit card—you will be asked to purchase a locked-in GIC, usually worth twice the amount of the credit limit you've applied for. Or you can start with the department-store cards, but since they are issued to almost anyone, they don't give you much credit credibility, and you risk falling into the high-interest trap (see above).

More on Credit and Credibility

According to Cara Savage, a financial adviser at VanCity, Canada's largest credit union, these are some of the most important and often-overlooked credit-management concerns for women:

1. Establishing an individual credit history. If you are separated, divorced, or widowed, a credit card and/or line of credit in your name can become tremendously important—and may not be easy to get after the fact. Don't make the mistake of assuming that the good credit rating you enjoyed as a couple will be extended to you as an individual. It won't. It isn't fair, but it is reality.

2. Establishing a relationship with a loan officer at the financial institution you deal with. Some day, when you decide it's time to start your own business, or need emergency funds to tide you over in a difficult time, this relationship can make the difference between having your loan approved or not.

3. Understanding how credit works. If you are a right-brain thinker (creative, intuitive, and imaginative) versus a left-brain thinker (logical, rational, and analytical), the idea of making three $20 minimum monthly payments simply doesn't make as much sense as ignoring the overdue notices for three months and sending one cheque for $60. Unfortunately, computers are not right brain, and will award you two demerit points for two late payments—enough, in itself, to create a problem for you down the road.

When I was having financial difficulties in my late twenties, a Mr. Glasgow in The Bay's credit department was so shockingly nasty to me, that after writing to the president of The Bay and receiving a nonchalant form letter back, I still won't shop there. However, for a couple of years afterwards, whenever I went by their storefront open-a-Bay-account-and-get-a free-cheap-pen display, I filled out an application. I knew I would never get approved because of my history with the company, and I didn't really need the pens, but it vented some of my resentment to put them through the trouble and expense of doing a credit check, etc. As it turns out, the joke was on me—Cara later advised me that each application created a black mark on my credit history. Think of it as "negative desperation points." Who would have thought? Another example of revenge never paying.

    Managing credit effectively is fundamental to well-being. People with abundance mentalities use credit cards for convenience, not as a loan facility or an extension of their chequing accounts. If you need to carry a monthly balance, it makes far more sense to arrange an actual loan or line of credit than it does to continue to pay exorbitant interest charges on your credit card. Are you paying off your balance monthly? If you aren't, think about why. As a friend once said, there is nothing more depressing than paying off a credit card balance when the vacation is just a memory and the tan has faded. And who has time for depression these days?

One of the most dangerous traps you can fall into is mistaking credit for income. If you can't pay off your balance monthly, you are spending more money than you are making. It doesn't matter what else you do. A raise will not save you. A genius financial adviser will not save you. You must save yourself, and you can do it by digging deep and identifying the patterns that drive you.

Where Does It All Go?

Unless you've been through this exercise before, **record all expenditures for at least six months**. I know, it sounds like a spend-hours-to-save-pennies endeavour, but after numerous creative attempts, I haven't found another way to achieve the same beneficial effect. You don't have to do it forever, but you do have to do it. Until you know where your money is going, you will never have complete peace of mind.

I try to purchase almost everything with either a debit card (personal) or a credit card (business), so I can record each purchase when I get my statement. I use Microsoft Money, which sorts everything into spending categories for me and provides a wonderful tax report at the end of the year. I've never used Quicken, but it looks great. If you don't have a computer, or you'd rather not use it, you can buy an accounting notebook at any stationery store.

When you set up your categories, be detailed. Work clothes are not in the same category as leisure clothes. Under Food, for instance, I have groceries, fast food/takeout, dining out/work related, dining out/pleasure, entertaining, luxury items, and coffee (those vanilla lattes). I also have a food category under Business Expenses—dining out, entertainment—which appears on my tax reports for deduction purposes.

Use whatever method works for you—but please, please, do it. Knowing where your money goes, and how much time you are sacrificing for those purchases, is absolutely fundamental to peace of mind and future planning. You can argue with the theory—but you can't deny the experience. Just try it, faithfully, for six months, and I guarantee your life will change.

Bill Paying 101

Budgeting is like dieting. With enough pain, angst, and self-sacrifice, it will work for a while, but as soon as you relax, you start your way back to square one. For most people, dieting doesn't work, and neither does budgeting. Instead, put modern banking technology to work for you. After all, whether you realize it or not, you're paying for it. **Wherever possible, have your bills debited directly from your account, or pay by postdated cheque.** I'll talk more about this later, but your pay-yourself-first program debit should be set up to occur automatically, as well.

Try to have monthly expenses debited directly from your account on the same days your paycheques go in. Even if it costs slightly more, you might find it more manageable to set up annual costs, like insurance, on monthly debits. If you have annual expenses that can't be paid monthly, such as car maintenance, chimney cleaning, and your annual pilgrimage to the lake, set up a subaccount and transfer the required amount monthly. In addition, because it's those unforeseen expenses that make everyone truly crazy, start putting a few dollars aside every paycheque into a subaccount just for the day your dishwasher spews froth onto the kitchen floor and expires. You won't miss $10 or $20 or $50, and it's nice not to have to worry about where the money will come from when something goes wrong.

For monthly payments you don't know about in advance, such as your long-distance bill, **designate a day each month to sit down and pay up**. I do this on the 16th. I'm not sure why, but paying at the end of the month stresses me out. Find a day that works for you, and mark it on your appointment calendar. As bills come in, put them in an attractive basket, and when the day arrives, sit down with a glass of wine or a cup of tea, play your favourite CD, and feel abundant. The experience can actually be pleasurable when you take the time to pamper yourself.

Always pay bills before they are due. For many years, I paid my bills late. At first, I didn't have enough money. Payday was the desperate day I sat down and decided who was most likely to cut off service or harass me at work. Later, it was out of some rebellious and deluded idea that I was beating the system by paying when I got the overdue notice. Then it was simple procrastination.

Once again, I speak from the voice of experience. You will never, ever, beat the system. You will be charged interest penalties and ridiculous administration fees. Your credit rating may be affected. And most importantly, unpaid bills destroy peace of mind. It isn't worth it. Pay on time.

There is nothing in this book that is more important than these steps. Before graduating to the next level of financial planning, please complete the following checklist:

◆ I have not bounced a cheque or received an overdue notice in the last 12 months.

  ☑ Yes   ☐ No

◆ I save/invest at least 10 percent of my net income on a monthly basis.

  ☑ Yes   ☐ No

◆ I pay off my credit-card balances every month.

  ☐ Yes   ☑ No

◆ I have no problem keeping up with all my financial statements.

  ☑ Yes   ☐ No

◆ I know where my money goes.

  ☑ Yes   ☐ No

◆ I am confident I'm paying the lowest interest rates available on any credit balances or loans.

  ☐ Yes   ☑ No

◆ I balance my accounts every month.

  ☑ Yes   ☐ No

◆ I know what I owe and I know what I own—and what it's all worth.

  ☑ Yes   ☐ No

If you responded with a Yes to each of these statements, you are a STAR and you graduate with flying colours and my admiration. If you didn't, join the majority of Canadians who would have to answer the same way you did. It isn't something to be ashamed of—just a cue to take control, to create order.

It is time to stop worrying and start changing. One thing—take control of one thing. Just for today. You can do it. Yes, you may find that you are making too little money and spending too much. Change. Oh, you can do it. And at first it may hurt a bit—even a lot—and then it is going to feel *so* good.

Making Time Sacred

So often at this point, women tell me that they don't have enough time. Listen, as a mother, financial adviser, wife, spiritual-being-in-progress, writer, student, companion of two dogs, friend, commuter, and fitness enthusiast, *I* don't have enough time. But I have learned that I always, always have time for my first priority. I write this with tears in my eyes, because I *know* what a struggle it is to write one's own needs at the top of a priority list filled with important, heartrending demands. Everyone (don't you *hate* to hear this?) has the same 24-hour day. The truly terrifying thing is that we get to make both our schedules and our priority lists. If we don't have enough time for the things that are most important in our lives, who has stolen that time from us? Who will give it back?

The truth is that when we say we don't have enough time, what we are really saying is that we don't have enough time for "this." If "this" is our well-being, our happiness, then a crime is being committed. We are robbing ourselves. We are robbing those we love of the company and example of our greatest potential self.

Creating order has a lovely side effect—we find more time. I clean my desk, I no longer have to search 10 minutes for each piece of paper I need. I get my expenses in order, I don't have to worry for 20 minutes when I lie down to sleep, and I can get up 20 minutes earlier and still feel rested.

When you find yourself using "not enough time" as the reason for not doing something that needs to be done, explore your feelings. If you don't feel that "it," whatever "it" is, is important, then that's the essence of good time management. If you don't think you, and your happiness and well-being, are important, then take a long, hard look at your priority list.

When Optimism Alone Isn't Working

Back to money issues. If you are struggling with unmanageable debt, speak to a professional credit counsellor. Most provinces sponsor a debt counselling service—try the blue pages under "debt problems" and call for an appointment. Beware of private "debt counsellors" who charge a fee to negotiate "a deal" with your creditors. There should be no fees for consultations, and unless you actually declare bankruptcy or enter a debt-repayment program, no money should change hands. As always, if things don't feel right, they probably aren't. Just telling your story to another human being can be the healing experience that sets you on the road to freedom.

If your expenses are too high, and your income too low, make a plan. What are you going to change? The one thing you can't do is continue to do what you are doing. Would a second job help? Do you want to make the sacrifice? Are you earning too little money to meet basic life necessities, or do you have a spending problem? If you do, what hunger are you trying to feed? Is there another way to achieve that satisfaction?

Adam and Eve at the Bank

Ideally, "How will we handle our money, Honey?" is the beginning of a deep and fruitful discussion that happens early in a relationship, somewhere between "Is that your toothbrush in the bathroom?" and "How many children would you like to have?" Unfortunately, because money is such an emotionally charged issue, we too often don't discuss it at all, or we come up with a cerebrally acceptable plan that causes violent storms on the emotional front for years after. We compromise more than we want to and fight about it later.

As my editor-goddess, Joan, reminded me last week, there are a thousand different and effective ways for couples to manage their money. To be entirely honest, I haven't had much luck handling joint finances, and I'm perhaps a little overcautious. If whatever you're doing is working for you, for heaven's sake, don't change it on my account. On the other hand, if you are in a partnership and are concerned about how things are working financially, you might consider the following suggestions.

The ideal time to discuss finances is in the early stages of a relationship, but, as is said about investment itself, the second best time is the present. Nick Murray, author of *The Excellent Advisor*, says, very simply, that "money is love." His statement stopped me in my tracks. It had the ring of truth to it, but his declaration sounded too simple. And too threatening. If money is love, I've seen some very unloving behaviour in my life, both personally and professionally. In the end, though, I had to agree. The heart of the reason that money issues cause such turmoil in relationships is because they are symptoms of even larger disorders.

If I could go back and do it again, I'd manage my relationships and my joint financial arrangements a lot differently, and I would do it much earlier.

My dream conversation would go something like this:

"Honey, there is something I need to talk to you about. I really love you, and I love the fact that we're together, but there are some things that concern me. I'm sure you have concerns, too, and I thought it would be good to discuss them."

My affianced, who looks amazingly like a first cousin of both my husband and Kevin Costner, has the intellectual brilliance of Stephen Hawking, the charisma and eloquence of Pierre Trudeau, and the devoted loyalty and affectionate nature of my puppy, replies: "Yes, my love. What a good idea. Now that we are living together and plan to get married, I think we should work out a plan for our future. I want to know that you and our kids are going to be all right, and that we both feel good about where our money is going. Can I get you a glass of sparkling water? Why don't I rub your back while we talk? Here, I'll put a blanket in front of the fireplace for you. Now, where would you like to start?"

"Well, dear, I guess we should talk about expenses first. You make more money than I do, which is lovely, but it bothers me a bit that I'm disadvantaged. Canadian women still earn only about 73 cents for every dollar a man makes when comparing equivalent work in full-time jobs. I'd like to think that we are going to share our lives and lifestyle—anything else could cause problems. Yet, if I'm expected to pay half our expenses, I'll have to work 22 percent more than you do, or almost nine hours a week more. Even if we reduce our lifestyle so that I don't have to work those extra hours, I still won't enjoy the same quality of life because I'll be spending a lot more of my income than you on necessities, without a lot left over for discretionary spending. I'm so grateful that you insist on doing half of the housework, cooking, and caring for the kids, but I still don't feel good about an 'equal' division of expenses."

"Yes, you're right. That isn't fair. I have an idea," says Kevin. "Why don't we figure out how much all our expenses add up to, and then we will both contribute a percentage of our earnings to a household expense account? Then we'll have a fair division in place when you become rich and famous, too. While we're at it, we can have a financial plan prepared. Perhaps we can also discuss applying a percentage of our incomes to investments, vacation spending, and discretionary spending, so we both have spending money that we can do what we want with. Then there is no chance of friction when I want to buy you a ridiculously expensive gift, or you want to go away on a seven-day spa vacation with your girlfriends."

"Oh, Kevin, you are so sweet. Mmmmm, yes, oh, harder right there, please. I like that idea. It sounds very fair. But listen, what are we going to do if we are short of money, for instance? What if one of us loses our job?"

"That's a good question. We'll make that appointment with a financial planner tomorrow. Let's make sure that we both have enough disability insurance, first of all, in case something happens, and that we have enough life insurance. I would die twice if I thought that I was leaving you and the kids in financial hardship. Let's make an appointment to update both our wills with the lawyer, too. When we meet with our planner, we should probably ask for recommendations on creating an emergency fund. We'll both contribute a set percentage now while things *are going well, and then if something happens, we'll withdraw whatever portion is needed. It will be like our private unemployment fund. Hey, I know we haven't decided on whether we will have kids together yet, but if we do, we can use our unemployment fund for your maternity leaves, too."*

I sit up, banging my head on the lamp. "Maternity leaves!"

"Don't get excited, my love." (He covers the palm of my hand with kisses.) "Whatever you want—if you want more kids, great! If you don't, that's fine with me, too. I don't mean to pressure you. Whatever happens, I'm the luckiest man in the world. I just want to know that if that's what you want, it doesn't have to mean financial hardship." (Passionate kissing.) "As a matter of fact, that is something we should probably talk about, just to be clear. When and if you are on maternity leave, I'll make my RSP contributions into a spousal account for you. My planner tells me that, with compound returns, this will somewhat make up for the income you'll lose by being out of the workforce during that time. She says that maternity and child-care leaves diminish a woman's CPP contributions, and can make a dramatic difference in both her government and private pension payouts. My spousal contributions won't make up for the raises or promotions you might miss on the 'Mommy track,' but I'll do everything I can to make that up to you in happiness, OK? We'll make sure to talk to her about it when we meet. We want to make sure that looking after our current and perhaps future kids doesn't create further financial disadvantages for you. And, of course, if we do have babies together, you know I'll be an equal partner in everything, including staying up all night and leaving work to pick them up from school when they're sick. I know that employers just assume that mothers aren't completely committed to their careers, but if your employer sees that we divide the emergencies equally, you'll get that next promotion a lot faster. Mmmmm. Your skin is so soft." (Lingering, gentle kisses along my neck.)

"No. You know what, honey? I don't want to make you feel pressured to have sex—I know how tired you are. Let me just massage your feet a while longer— or would you rather take a hot bath while I finish up those dinner dishes?"

OK. All a bit farfetched, I know, but this fictional conversation brings to light many of the fundamentally important aspects of joint money management that almost never get discussed. How do two people who love each other handle the fact that one of them may belong to a subspecies that is paid less for work of equal value? How are they going to compensate for the fact that most women still perform a substantially larger portion of home and child care, leaving less energy and time for personal and career development?

Then there are the issues of values. Hopefully, you and your mate share similar views and agree on the fundamentals. For instance:

◆ How much money you will give to charity, where, and when? What to do if you are short of funds? Do you give to charity first or make your RSP contribution first? Do you replace the hard drive in the computer that you play games on or make your charitable donation? In other words, how important is charitable giving to each of you?

◆ If you're lucky enough to receive a windfall of some sort or another, will you put a down payment on a home or buy a sports car? Again, what's important? If you disagree, how do you plan to handle that?

◆ Would you choose a job that paid twice as much money but kept you out of town most of the time? What happens if one of you gets a big promotion that requires moving to another city?

◆ If you have a financial emergency, will you borrow from your in-laws? Under what conditions?

If you have or plan to have children, it is important to come to terms with issues like whether teenagers should be required to work for spending money while they're in high school, and if you plan to pay for your children's university tuition. Should your children receive an allowance? Do household chores for spending money? What is an appropriate spending limit for their Christmas and birthday gifts?

If either of you has children from a previous marriage, this can be a minefield. What about your wills? Is there any property that you wish to pass directly to the children of the previous marriage? How are you going to handle child-support payments? What if his child-support payments put a burden on your new family—are you both prepared for that? What if the ex-spouse is supposed to pay child support and doesn't? How will you handle that? Do your children's allowances come out of the family budget or out of your discretionary spending money? What about daycare? Because this is such a complex issue, I strongly advise that if you are thinking about blending families, you should start by reading some of the excellent self-help books out there on the subject. If at all possible, get some counselling before you even think about moving in together. And whatever you do, do not make the mistake I did—do not think that it will be easy, and then blame yourself when you discover that it isn't. I don't think there is another relationship more fraught with peril than this one, unless it's polygamy.

Be prepared for some tense discussions. Even asking the questions can sometimes be perceived as an indication of mistrust, but the reality is that different people have different money-management styles, and opposites attract. It is not just possible, but likely, that you will have a different style than your mate, and although it may very well have been one of the things that attracted your affection in the first place, it may also cause some friction later on. The more open and comprehensive the initial discussions, the more smooth the financial sailing later.

All right, then. You are like most of the rest of us, firmly entrenched in a relationship in which your pre-cohabitation discussions around the issue of money were limited to how much you could afford to spend on rent. Things are not going well. What to do? The following is a desperate plan for desperate people (meaning, it worked for me).

1. Set a date and time, make some tea, and sit down together to figure out exactly what it costs to maintain your household, how expenses will be divided, who is going to pay what, and when the individual contributions will be deposited to the joint household account. You might want to start this process on your own, and when you've come up with a rough draft, ask your mate to go over it with you. If you anticipate a tense discussion, you may want to use my fantasy conversation topics as a guideline. I find it always helps to be reading something out of a book.

2. Arrange to set up individual personal accounts and a joint account for household expenses.

3. Arrange to have as many bills as possible either debited from the household account or paid by postdated cheque.

4. If at all possible, arrange to alternate bill-paying duties for anything that can't be paid automatically, so that you both have a solid understanding of what is going where and when. So much resentment is created in relationships because partner *A* can't understand why partner *B* spends so much on groceries, or because partner *B* isn't aware that leaving the little light on in the bathroom all night because partner *A* is afraid of the dark actually costs only 35 cents extra per month.

If the above method doesn't work because one partner is not prompt in making a deposit, for instance, you might try this alternative:

5. Arrange to divide expenses by partner. For instance, you pay the telephone bill, which is in your name; your partner pays the hydro, which is in his/her name. You buy the groceries; your partner pays the condo fees.

Whatever method you use, if expenses don't conveniently split according to your agreement, do an equalization payment at the end of the month. If you have decided to split expenses 50/50, for instance, and your expense payments equal $1800 while your partner's are $2000, you should split the difference and write out a cheque for $100 at the end of the month.

Assuming there is money left over after the necessities of life are met, aim for complete individual control of discretionary spending and investment. Nothing can smooth the edges of a relationship more sweetly than never having to argue about money again.

Once more, I will graciously use myself and my long-suffering husband as an example of what to avoid. Randy works solely on commission, so we never know what his income is going to be from month to month. Until the last few years, my salary was predictable. Therefore, we paid all the household expenses first out of my salary. Any shortfall came out of his commission and investment earnings. His income also paid for larger-ticket purchases and for our investments. It sounds sensible, doesn't it?

Unfortunately, because we were never sure what he would earn, we didn't make a financial plan. We had a general "we will put as much money into the market as possible," "invest in equities rather than real estate," and "minimize our expenses" kind of plan. We didn't actually have a Plan.

All kinds of trouble ensued. Without a cash-flow statement, the money I earned seemed invisible. It was spent on groceries (three kids, two of them teenagers, loads of convenience food because no one had time to cook—we had one formidable grocery budget), the myriad of stuff a household requires, gas, hydro, daycare, carpet cleaning, art classes, insurance . . . ad infinitum. Thus, even when I earned a very substantial salary, I was forced to ask my husband for supplemental funds at the end of the month, and he was never really happy about having to write that cheque. It was demeaning to ask for it, and it felt as if I was working for nothing. Certainly, my earnings were not giving me satisfaction. And when I actually spent money on myself, I felt even worse, explaining apologetically that I needed extra money for household bills because it was time for my annual new jacket or shoes or contact lenses.

Isn't it amazing? Even with a salary that most people would have given their right arm for, I managed to create a situation in which I would be in the same demeaning position my mother had been in when I was growing up—justifying my spending to someone with entirely different priorities.

When we made large purchases or investments, my husband paid. Therefore, without giving it much thought, I deferred to his preferences. The result was a much more aggressive investment portfolio than I would have chosen, a 51-inch television set, hundreds of dollars worth of computer games, a Corvette ZR1, a race car—I could go on and on. Even more insidiously, we both thought of everything purchased with his income as his. When he moved out, it was very painful for him to come to terms with dividing our assets because he really wasn't cognizant of my financial contribution. My contributions were spent on everyday living expenses, the consumables that leave little trace and little gratification behind. Everything we had, he had paid for.

I was doing the financial housework. And having never shopped for consumables, it was difficult for him to make a comparative analysis, but "it sure seemed like a lot!"

When I began creating financial plans for my clients, I realized that it was just crazy not to have one for myself. I completed a draft for our family, using estimates of my husband's income. He flipped through it briefly, made some "hmmm, ummm" noises and put it in the drawer he uses to save things he doesn't feel comfortable throwing out and plans never to look at again.

What I needed was a strategy that would allow me to be independent within my relationship.

Over the next couple of days, I prepared a financial plan for myself. I itemized each expense, totalled each category, and presented it to my husband. I asked him to let me know if he was uncomfortable with any of the items or amounts. When he didn't get back to me with any requests for discussion, I let him know what his half would be on a biweekly basis.

I then created an investment plan for myself. Though it was a financial sacrifice, we hired a nanny to take care of all domestic and homecaring duties, and we each pay half of her salary. This allows me to focus more of my energy on my career and on creating income without the conflict of negotiating duties.

For the first time in my life, I'm in control of my finances, and I can't tell you how wonderful that feels. Whatever happens, I have a Plan.

It took me a long time to wake up from my raised-in-the-'60s trance and realize that it is not my partner's job to create financial well-being for me. It is my job. Sometimes, doing this job requires being pragmatic, not "nice," about handling finances when a partner is irresponsible, incompetent, or just uninterested. I once ended up in dire financial straits because of a poor partnership choice—but I made that choice. Later, I'm happy to say, I unmade it and started making better choices. There is a solution to every problem, and it's us. *We* are all we really need.

Keeping More of the Money We Earn

You've heard it a million times. Pay yourself first. People who achieve financial well-being rarely do so through employment income—they do it by sending their money out to work for them. If you save whatever is left over at the end of the month . . . well, is there ever anything left over at the end of the month?

Too often, we use this very fact to justify not setting up a pay-yourself-first program, but it doesn't wash. How many of us can "afford" to pay taxes? And yet, when our employer deducts 30 percent or more of our income at source, we manage to do without it. We have done it for years—and between 1961 and 1997, taxes increased more than 1100 percent. No, that isn't a typo. If we can do this for the Government of Canada, isn't it possible we could do it for our own future well-being?

Yes, 10 percent of net income is the magic number, and there is something truly magical about it. When you are able to save 10 percent of your net income, your financial affairs will begin falling into place in ways you can't even imagine. This is one of the fundamental principles of prosperity.

However, the concept of "all or nothing" has kept too many of us from making progress. If you are living on a tight budget already, taking an additional 10 percent off the top may seem a ridiculously daunting feat—so don't start there.

Start somewhere.

Things turned around for me when I started taking RSP loans. It was a way of getting my hands on a tax refund and, more importantly, putting money aside that I couldn't access for everyday "emergencies." It doesn't work for everyone, but it really worked for me. The monthly payments are debited from my chequing account, and the loan is paid down by the refund and is off by the end of the year. Unfortunately, I do pay interest on the loan balance, but this year, 1998, that interest was only 6 percent, and the returns on my investments more than covered that. At the end of the year, I've saved a substantial amount of money that otherwise would have found its way into daily expenses. Do I miss it? Not a bit. Not for a second.

Let me put it this way—don't wait until you feel that you can afford to put 10 percent of your net pay away. Start today with whatever amount makes sense to you. Five dollars a day, fifty dollars a month. When you realize you don't miss it, and you will, increase the amount. And so on.

I'm on my metaphoric knees now—I'm begging. Do it now. It will change your life in ways you haven't yet dreamed. It will bring you peace and abundance.

We Reap the Seeds We Sow

Does the way you spend reflect your values? If it doesn't, you suffer from discordance-conflict due to lack of harmony. Another energy drain.

We have been blessed with 24 miraculous hours a day. Most of us spend eight of those hours in dreamland, replenishing the mind and body. (Or at least we should.) That leaves 16 hours with which to build a life.

The demands of the body (food, shelter, an occasional trip to the Caribbean) generally require that we exchange at least another eight for money. This is where it gets exciting. I don't know about you, but I wasn't taught an awareness of the time/money correlation. That is, I didn't realize that I worked a year for my Jeep Cherokee. Now, I love my Jeep Cherokee, but I don't know if I love it a year's worth of work.

"Wait a minute," you might be thinking. "A Jeep Cherokee is what, $40 000?" (And mine wasn't—I bought it secondhand for a lot less.) "Surely you make more than $40 000 a year?"

Well, yes. But that is in pre-expense dollars. **Start thinking of yourself as a business. The profit of a business isn't the amount of money that comes in the door—it is what is left over after the expenses are paid**.

Let's use Jane as an example. She is a buyer for a retail clothing chain and at age 32, makes a very nice salary of $65 000 a year. However, because Jane doesn't do any financial planning at all, she pays approximately 50 percent of her earnings in taxes. At the end of the year, for the sake of simplicity, let's say she nets out at about $32 500. Jane's workday is generally between eight (rare) and ten hours, but she commutes an hour either way and travels on business at least five days a month, keeping her away from home, hearth, and husband for at least one weekend. On average, she estimates that work (including travel and commuting) consumes an average of 60 hours a week. She has three weeks' paid vacation per year, so we'll base our calculations on a forty-nine-week year. That is, $32 500 divided by 49 divided by 60. Jane earns $11.05 per hour.

However, before we get all excited, this is a quick list of items that Jane feels she buys (on a monthly basis) solely for work, to unwind from work, or because working leaves her with too little time.

JANE'S PURCHASES FOR WORK (MONTHLY)	
Clothes for work	$100
Pantyhose	$ 32
Dry cleaning	$ 35
Fast food	$150
Commuting	$176
Coffee and treats	$ 50
Total	$543

That's $6516 per year on work-related expenses. Therefore, Jane's net salary is now $25 984—divided by 49 weeks divided by 60 hours equals $8.84 per hour. That still doesn't sound too bad, until we start analyzing where that hard-earned money goes. For instance, Jane and her husband really, really needed a vacation last year—too much time apart had unravelled their relationship, and they were both exhausted. Throwing caution to the wind, they took a two-week sojourn to paradise, courtesy of Visa. However, by the time they had paid off the vacation in American dollars and interest on the credit-card bill, they had spent well over $5000. Let's assume that Jane paid half—she worked 565 hours to pay for that vacation. That is almost two full months of 10-hour days. Was it worth it? Only Jane and her spouse can decide, but it bears thinking about, doesn't it?

This is important to think about when we have kids, too. Do they really want that new Nintendo game, or would they be happier with the 20 hours (of our labour) that is required to pay for it?

Now, let's leave Jane in peace and try this exercise for ourselves. What do you earn per hour? What do you buy solely as a result of having to work?

Once you have the figure, go back to your monthly spending records. Yes, this is really why we need to do them, and this is where life changes. Did you know that you were working 40 hours a month just to wear those designer clothes to *work*? How about 10 hours a month for your magazine subscriptions and the gym-club membership you never use?

Once you start to understand where your money (and time!) is being spent, you can make informed spending decisions. After doing this calculation for myself, I have absolutely sworn off buying any clothing items at full price. Never—not ever! I rarely buy magazines any more, and I reserve lattes for a special once-a-week treat instead of the twice-a-day purchases they used to be. (I was working three hours a week for latte!)

Keeping Track

Create a receipt filing system that works for you. I have four envelopes in a hanging file in my desk labelled "personal," "business," "statements and confirmations," and "gas and car-related." One of my girlfriends has two four-drawer filing cabinets. (My husband has half a sock drawer and three Safeway bags.) I have found that the best systems are the simplest, but experiment a bit until you find something that feels comfortable to maintain.

I keep an envelope in my Daytimer and transfer receipts out of my purse into it every morning. Once a week, or when it gets too full to cram anything else in, I move the contents in the receipt envelopes in my desk.

At tax time, I separate those receipts into specific piles, add them up with an adding machine, attach the adding machine tape, match the totals to my Microsoft Money report—*voilà!* Those receipts that don't get filed with my taxes go into an envelope with a copy of my tax return with the year written on the outside, and into an old filing cabinet in my basement.

Use whatever system works for you—but try to keep it as simple as possible, and attend to it regularly. (Remember the weeding—don't let receipts stack up for six months. They turn into little monsters that keep you awake at night and make tiny worry lines on your forehead!)

Now we've covered the basics of daily money management. It is time to look at personal obstacles to financial well-being—and to take action.

If you chronically deprive yourself of luxury, put a copy of your list of divine indulgences on your fridge, and start rewarding yourself for meeting your life goals—or just for being the wonderful person you are.

Are you really proud of that report you just completed? Reward yourself with that vintage silk scarf you've been coveting. You made it to the gym three times this week? No question—you've earned that scented candle to enjoy while you soak in a hot bath.

Remember, be generous and be gentle. There are times when your greatest achievement will be just making it through one particularly hard day, or speaking softly to your children when you would like to shriek.

If a tendency to overspend (particularly credit card spending) is your personal stumbling block, try "distracting your material girl," as Sarah Ban Breathnach suggests. The next time you are overwhelmed by a desire to hit the mall, take a deep breath and find a thrift store instead. Take $5 or $10, and make it your mission to find just one treasure. Don't set your heart on finding the perfect suit, or a fabulous pair of red shoes—it is likely you will be disappointed. Instead, search for the glorious "something" that is meant just for you. One treasure.

If you tend to let others take charge of your financial well-being, take just one thing back. Open a personal chequing account, or apply for your own credit card. Offer to pay the household bills. Read a book on mutual-fund investment, or review your mortgage documents. Introduce yourself to the loan officer at your bank or credit union. Sign up for a workshop or attend a seminar. One thing—just one thing.

How is the weather where you live? No, I don't mean outside—how is your inner environment? Serene and warm? Or stormy and turbulent? Gardens don't do very well in hurricanes, and neither do financial plans. Luckily, this is your universe and you get to make your own weather. Here's an exercise that can bring those halcyon days inside.

As soon as possible, preferably next weekend, devote Saturday afternoon to your own fulfillment. Play your favourite music, make your favourite lunch. If you have kids, you'll need a sitter, or at least a box of treats and the video they've been begging you for. If you have a partner, schedule this for a day he or she will be out of the house—preferably with the kids. You'll need some boxes or a package of big, black garbage bags. You must be ruthless and determined. Start in any room. Take your time. Breathe deep. Listen to that inspiring music.

Examine each article. Does this article serve a functional purpose? Is it beautiful? Does it make you feel good and prosperous? If it isn't beautiful or functional, is it beloved by a member of your family? If the article is not functional, beautiful or beloved, why is it cluttering up your sanctuary?

Take a deep breath. Now, you must decide whether it is irredeemable, in which case the trash is the obvious recipient. If it no longer serves a purpose in your life, but might in someone else's, donate it to a charitable organization—there are a number that will pick up useful clothes and household items at the curb. If it is useless and graceless, but you can't bear to part with it, at least hide it in a storage room. You will just have to throw it away or give it away later, but sometimes this just has to be a multistep process. We're human, after all.

Go through each and every room, reducing clutter, creating beautiful order. Do you feel that space? Into order flows creative energy—can you feel it?

Before you lose your courage, tackle your wardrobe. Here you will need a few more piles—garbage, charity, storage, and tailor. If any item hasn't been worn in the last year, it really must go. However, if the problem is fit, or a fallen hemline, or a ripped shoulder seam, now is the time to have it repaired. No, you will never do it yourself.

You will be amazed at the wonderful effects of clearing clutter from your life. And as you clear away the old and the tattered and the simply ugly, you will begin to see new grace and possibility. Enjoy.

Now for our master's degree in abundance creation.

Give.

I am humbled when it comes to addressing this issue. Every spiritual and material philosophy in the world recognizes the value in giving back to the universe a portion of what one receives, but if we all embraced these philosophies as dearly as we purport to, the world would be a very different place.

Some people give naturally, with joy, because they know how rich and wonderful it makes them feel. Some people don't know, and give because it is the right thing to do. Some people don't give—they don't feel that they have enough, or they rationalize that no one needs it more than they do.

Tithing and charitable giving are profoundly personal issues, and I'm not sure if it is productive to give out of a sense of guilt or "should." I, therefore, can't tell you that you should do this. It isn't any of my business, and even if I could insert myself in your heart and influence your behaviour, I am not sure if the rewards of giving back are in the action or in the wanting and needing to.

What I will tell you is this. My life changes dramatically when I commit 10 percent of my income to the universe that sustains me. When I stop, for whatever reason, the flow of abundance seems to diminish.

Among my clients and friends, those who give generously live richer, more fulfilling, and more prosperous lives than those who don't. They are unquestionably, undeniably happier.

You decide.

The Pretzel Mentality (or, In Praise of Pretzels)

Before we go on, I have to make a sweeping gender-alization. Because we are women, we are biologically aware of something that seems to come harder to men. We know that *everything is connected.*

It is a scientifically proven fact that men, at any given time, are thinking either with their right brain or their left brain. They are thinking creatively or they are thinking logically. They are thinking objectively or subjectively. Women, on the other hand, have more efficient synapses (neurological con-nectors) between the right- and left-brain hemispheres. We think both creatively and logically, objectively and subjectively. As you may have expe-rienced, this difference in brain structure can create some significant communication obstacles.

One of the reasons our society views life and time as linear is that most men think in a linear fashion. Point *B* follows Point *A*, therefore *C* is the obvious, rational, unavoidable conclusion. Most women, on the other hand, have what I like to call a pretzel mentality. Nothing is separate—we group events and facts in patterns and draw conclusions from the patterns rather than the events themselves.

Let me demonstrate with an example.

Joe comes home 25 minutes late from work. He walks in the door with a "Hi, Honey!" and Honey wings a freshly baked but slightly scorched roll at his head, screams in frustration and locks herself in the bedroom, crying.

Joe stands outside the locked door, perplexed and frustrated.

"All this because I am 25 minutes late from work? Twenty-five minutes?"

To Joe, Honey's behaviour is illogical, overemotional, and maybe even neurotic. Perhaps it is. But what Joe doesn't understand is that, for Honey, there is no such thing as an isolated incident.

For her, the fact that Joe is 25 minutes late is simply the straw that pushed weeks of accumulated "data" beyond her point of tolerance. In her mind, Joe is not just 25 minutes late. He is 25 minutes late after being late at least three times a week for months. He is 25 minutes late after she calmly and sincerely told him that it was a problem for her when she made dinner and he wasn't home when it was ready. He is 25 minutes late after giving her his word that he would call her when he was going to be late. He is 25 minutes late after forgetting their anniversary a month ago.

"What does this have to do with money?" you might ask.

It's this. During my years in the financial industry, I have known many men whose financial situation was fabulous but whose lives were a mess. Marriages on the rocks, businesses in trouble, haven't talked to their kids for years. But they were OK financially.

I haven't met any women in this situation. Not one. If our lives are in disarray, our finances are in disarray. (Or they are about to be in disarray.) So, having said everything I've said about creating order in your daily financial affairs, I have to add that unless you have created some degree of order in your life, you won't achieve serenity simply by following these steps.

You know where disorder breeds in your life. It might be in regard to your health—not taking care of yourself physically. Or in your relationships. I think the most recurrent theme I see in my planning practice is that of being overcommitted. We simply take on too much, until we have so many balls in the air that it is only a matter of time before something hits the ground with an ugly splat.

Over the last two years, I have read perhaps a dozen books on simplifying your life. All of them have been tremendously helpful; all have changed my life for the better. I would be misleading you, however, if I didn't admit that it continues to be a daily struggle for me.

I'll still spend an occasional precious Saturday cleaning my house from top to bottom, seething with anger because my spouse is lying in front of the TV watching sports. I still feel guilty and somehow insufficient leaving my office after an eight-hour day. Until I absolutely couldn't, I continued to schedule too many after-school activities for my daughter, beefing up my good-parenting points.

The challenge, however, is one I will always rise to meet because nothing creates more fruitful results in my life. I am so far ahead of where I was three years ago. I insist on getting at least seven hours sleep—even if that means cancelling work on the morning after I've been up with a sick child in the night. I insist on having at least four hours of restorative time for myself on weekends, although that has often meant bowing out of extended-family activities I'm expected to attend. Most of the time, I don't do anything domestic unless I can do it with enjoyment and without resentment. I ask for my husband's support—not as often as I should, but sometimes. I've let go of a lot of the things I thought I never could. My house is not spotless. I will not make $100 000 this year. Instead, I have moments of silent, clear happiness, and I almost always know that everything will be OK.

As a woman, I find that the bottom line for me is this:

I can only achieve lasting order and serenity in one area of my life if I have also achieved at least a degree of order and serenity in all areas of my life.

This may not be true for you. If not, count your blessings. If it is, I recommend scheduling five hours off next week to do nothing but examine the imbalances in your life. If you had unlimited power to change your situation, what would that look like? Please don't place limitations on yourself. When I told friends what I wanted from my life two years ago, they laughed at me. I wanted to make how much and work when? I wanted to go into the office when? I wanted to do what for a living?

My life is a miracle—and I am here to tell you that yours can be, too. It takes courage, and it takes work—and it takes more courage. But you can have order and serenity in your life—in every area of your life. And when you do, your financial serenity will be deeper and richer than you ever dreamed. Your relationships will be deeper and richer than you ever dreamed. Your physical well-being will be deeper and richer than you ever dreamed.

5

The Power of Vision

Courage is the price that life exacts

for granting peace.

AMELIA EARHART

During my late teens, I was a passenger in three car accidents. None of them was terribly serious, thankfully, and in the first two, there were no injuries beyond bruises, teenage hysteria, and the loss of my husband's beloved 1970 Barracuda. When my son was just seven months old, though, I was with my sister-in-law when she turned left into the path of a speeding car. Then seat belts were still rather a novel concept, and baby seats a rare luxury for the paranoid. Greg was nestled in my lap, and if I thought about it at all, I guess I believed that I could hold him should something happen.

I couldn't. On impact, he flew from my helpless arms, hit the passenger window, and was flung across the car to land at my sister-in-law's feet. There he lay, completely limp, quiet. After a long moment of eerie silence as the car came to a stop, we looked at each other in horror. My son wasn't moving, not whimpering, not crying. I screamed.

Only then, at the sound of my grief and terror, did he begin to wail. A practical sort, my sister-in-law picked him up, brushed the dust off his chubby little legs, and handed him back to me. I checked him over for broken bones and general soundness, and my heart eventually resumed its normal rhythm. Beyond a few nasty bruises, he was fine—I fared less well, with a concussion and a sprained ankle that would prove sorely inconvenient while carrying a baby about. We were delivered by ambulance to a hospital, and after we were all examined, treated and released, my father-in-law collected us and drove us home.

Then the strangest thing happened. I had planned to go shopping with my mother-in-law the following day, but as I was about to get in her car, I realized that I couldn't make myself do it. I was terrified. Frozen. I had lost my faith. I saw every vehicle as a lethal weapon, every driver as a potential killer. For six months, my phobia continued to escalate. We lived on a farm at the time, so I was virtually housebound, unable to shop for groceries or take my son for his medical checkup. When a friend of ours was killed in a car accident, I rode to his funeral slumped in my seat, crying, my hands over my eyes—not just because he had died, but because my husband and I were risking the same fate. I would leave my sweet baby an orphan.

Eventually, my isolation and the unhappiness it caused became a greater force than my phobia. In desperation, I decided to take driver training—perhaps if I couldn't be a passenger, I could be a driver. My poor driving instructor got far more than he bargained for. I was a shaking, sweating, teary-eyed nightmare of a student. Before we even began our first lesson, I asked him to explain one of the mysteries that had frightened me the most. "How do you keep the car between the lines when you're driving so fast?"

"Look ahead," he responded. "If your eyes are far enough ahead on the road, the car will follow."

It really worked, by keeping my primary focus about 200 metres ahead of my car, I found that it followed the road without my conscious help. I could stop obsessing about keeping the car between the lines and start thinking about things like braking and signalling. I was aware, too, of the events occurring closer to my car, but I was able to respond without overreacting.

It was much more than a simple driving tip. It has always been my metaphor for the power of vision, and one of the secrets, I'd like to believe, of a life thus far well lived. Driving, gardening, or investing, if we focus our energy on our vision of the future, the issues of today begin to unfold in creative, miraculous ways. Fear, distraction, and reactivity falls away and we are drawn forward on the clear path before us.

It was many years later that the work of Robert Fritz, author of *Path of Least Resistance*, taught me how to apply this concept to my life in a remarkably powerful way.

According to Fritz, the tension that is created by the discordance between the life we want and the life we have can be turned into creative energy. Like an elastic band stretched to its full capacity, this tension will find a way to resolve itself. Too often, this resolution takes place when we give up—when we start saying things like "Well, it was silly of me to think I wanted my own business. Who can afford to take that kind of risk with a family?"

When we start telling ourselves how impractical we've been, the tension drains away—and so does the power. We do it because tension feels uncomfortable, but there is another way. We can begin to move ever closer to our dreams.

Turning tension into creative power is a three-step process. We've already touched on all three, but let's take some time now to put it into a format.

First, we need to have a vision. Oh, yes, this is tricky for most of us. My friend Shannon and I went for a long walk in the rain last week, and she spoke of how difficult it was to actually write down the things she wanted in her life—her perfect job, her perfect home, her perfect mate. Shannon and I have been friends for close to 10 years now, so I suspected immediately what it was that might be getting in her way. She is the most practical, efficient person I know. If you have something to do, and you need it done perfectly, call Shannon. She is the "ways and means" committee. Her first question, always, is something like "Well, how are you planning to do that?"

To create a powerful vision, you have to learn to put the cart before the horse. Yes, that is what I meant to say. There is nothing more destructive to the visioning process than worrying about *how*. *How* has no place here. Before you start working on your vision, always spend a few minutes meditating on a world without limits. What if you had all the money in the world? All the time in the world? All the options in the world? What if you could have it all and more?

The power of a vision is in the clarity of the details, and you can't work out the details if you are thinking about the limitations. You have to know exactly where you wish to go. This is goal-setting as an art form, the transformation of specific, scintillating dreams into reality. Not "I'd like to have a new home." Not "I'd like to have a new house with four bedrooms and a nice backyard." What does that house look like? What colour is it? What kind of trim does it have? Does it have a big white soaker tub or a cream-coloured jacuzzi? What is the yard like? What kinds of flowers grow there? What do you see from your bedroom window? Is there carpet or hardwood? What colour is the carpet? How many rooms are there? Are the light fixtures modern and elegant, or whimsical and country? Where is it?

Until you see that new home in your mind, it does not exist. You are missing a pattern, and without a pattern, your image shifts and fades, losing its power—the creative tension is diluted.

There are a number of exercises later in the book that will help add further clarity to the vision. Don't expect your dream life to appear in a blinding flash before you and stay the same until you eventually make it happen. That is one of the most wonderful aspects of dreaming—you can change your mind without having to renovate, and as you grow, you will find that your heart's desire will make itself known to you in ever greater clarity.

Once you have a scintillatingly clear vision, it is time to chart what Fritz calls "current reality." Oh, yes. You must have a clear understanding of where you are today. No spin-doctoring, looking at the bright side, or pessimism. No judgment attached. Just reality as it is—today.

A financial plan really consists of three parts: the vision, or objectives; current reality, which includes current net-worth statements and cash-flow forecasts based on current income and expenditures; and action steps, or the recommendations. Because, for most women, all things are connected, I have broadened this structure to include everything that gives life meaning. Money is a fundamentally important tool in a life well lived, but it is a grave error to think that enough money ensures happiness, security, or even contentment. It is *only* a tool. To measure material wealth without an integrated understanding of how you will apply it in the creation of your vision is like collecting a library of books without ever reading them.

This next exercise, therefore, will help create that powerful and compelling vision. This isn't as easy as it sounds, particularly for the feminine gender. We have been socialized to believe that our worth increases each time we compromise, each time we put someone else's needs ahead of our own. As mothers, daughters, friends, wives, we place our needs at the bottom of a long list. The voice of our soul's hunger has been silenced so often it is just the faintest whisper. We've tried to muffle it with food, with alcohol, with work, and with ceaseless activity. We distract it by attempting to improve those around us, or through perfectionism. Still, it speaks.

A number of years ago, Dr. Lee Pulos, a pioneer in the power of vision in athletics and business, spoke at a sales seminar I attended with a group of more than 100 investment advisers. Astonishingly, he guided this dark-suited crowd of left-brain businesspeople through one of the most joyous meditation sessions I have ever experienced. Since then, I've adapted the technique he used that day to include all my most beloved meditation images. It is my pleasure to share it with you—and please feel free to adapt it to your own needs. Meditation, like financial planning, is an intimately personal process. There isn't one right way. Experiment until you find the way that works best for you.

If you still find the whole meditation thing a bit intimidating, remember this definition: prayer is speaking to Spirit; meditation is listening to Spirit. We tend to make it complicated, but there is nothing simpler, and nothing, perhaps, more rewarding. As the Bible says, "be still, and know..." Be still and let your heart be heard.

EXERCISE 4 **Dreaming a Life**

Note: you may want to record yourself reading this next session and use your voice as a meditation guide.

Find a quiet room, and a comfortable chair. Place your feet flat on the floor and your arms at rest.

Breathe. Breathing in, envision peace, drawing it into your lungs, and through your lungs to your bloodstream. Exhale ... gently expelling fear. Breathe in ... peace. Exhale ... fear.

Do this as many times as you need to.

When you start to feel a sense of calm, start at your toes, tightening your muscles and then relaxing them. Using the same method, relax your feet and your calves. Your thighs and your abdomen. Your diaphragm and your chest. Your shoulders, arms, fingers. Relax your neck, and then focus on those tiny muscles around your eyes. Relax your lips.

When your body is completely relaxed, envision yourself in a place of calm. It might be a garden, or a white-sand beach. Wherever it is, you are comfortable, you are safe, and the sun warms your shoulders. A breeze plays lightly in your hair.

My place is a garden, a forest really, on a mountainside overlooking the Georgia Strait and the Gulf Islands. From where I sit, I can see the tranquil bay, the sun painting mirrors and light on the water. It is warm. I can feel the sun on my shoulders and bare arms. Where are you?

Now, let's awaken all of our senses.

See the sun, the ocean, the lake, the mountains. Wherever you are, feast your eyes on the beauty of this place. See your paradise.

Feel ... feel the sun on your shoulders. Are your feet bare? Feel the grass, or the sand.

Listen ... can you hear the waves? Or the songs of birds? Or just the sound of stillness?

Touch ... pick up a leaf, and run your fingers over its etchings. Imagine running your hands over the bark of a tree.

Taste ... open your mouth to taste the tang of salt air. Pick a peach from the tree near your hand and bite into it, feeling its juice on your lips.

Smell ... inhale the aroma of the peach, the smell of the sun on your skin.

Breathe.

Next, envision a geographical field of granite about 9 metres below the earth at your feet. This granite is a powerful magnet and has the power to absorb and neutralize all negativity. Feel any anxiety, resentment, or residual fear draining from your mind, your chest, your diaphragm, down through your legs and out the bottom of your feet.

Now, as if you were to rise above your body and view yourself from above, see yourself in this place.

Envision yourself being as brilliant as you have ever been. Envision the synapses of your brain alighting with wisdom and power. Think back to a time in your life when you felt smart, creative, and expressive.

Aloud, say: "I am now at my most creative. I am a channel of wisdom."

Remember a time when your body was at its best: fit, healthy, and beautifully energetic and vital. Envision each cell vigorously alive, receptive to creative healing and renewal.

Say: "I am healthy and full of energy—mind and body."

Think back to a time when you were filled with unconditional love for someone or something, overwhelmed with feelings of kindness and warmth. Envision a time when a relationship was particularly rewarding and meaningful to you.

Say: "I am loving and loved, and fulfilled in my relationships."
Think of a time when you felt richly abundant, when all of your material needs were met. Envision the tiny sparrow in the field, flitting, without a care or anxiety, from the tree with its multitude of fruit and their seeds to the meadow with its lush grass and grains.

Say: "This is a universe of abundance, and all my needs are met abundantly. My ways are prosperous."

Now, in your mind's eye, look up. See the sun. From where you are in the garden, imagine where you want to go next.

Where would you like it to be?

You are leaving this peaceful place, and you are going into the world you have created. What do you do for a living? Where? Whom do you work with? What are they like? What do they value? What does your home look like? How much time do you spend there? What do you eat? What restores you? Who are the people who support you in your endeavours?

Think about it with your heart. Think about it until it comes into focus ... full colour.

Now, I'm going to bring you back. Imagine that you are the architect of this world you wish to live in and you are drafting plans for the builders. Remember that money is no object—there are no limits, and you can create anything you desire.

Who is there? Whom do you spend time with? What interests do you share? Who are your friends and colleagues? What kind of relationships do you enjoy with your family?

What are you doing? What do you do to create a livelihood? How do you spend your workday? What skills are required? Perhaps you don't work for pay—you might volunteer your time, or devote your life to gardening, or reading, or philosophy. What are your activities?

Where are you doing it? What does your work environment look like? Are you in an office or an artist's loft? Where do you live? From your windows, what do you see? Are you in a rustic cottage on a lake or in a high-rise condo downtown? What kind of furniture do you have? Is there art on the walls?

When do you work? When do you play? When do you sleep? Do you get up and leave for work at the crack of dawn, or do you saunter in at about 10 a.m.? Do you have a nap each afternoon or burn the candle at both ends?

My Vision

_____

_____

_____

_____

_____

_____

_____

_____

_____

_____

_____

_____

_____

_____

_____

I feel obligated to attach a warning sticker to this exercise.

I first did this a little over two years ago, just before I left my corporate position. I wasn't happy, but I wasn't yet planning to make any changes in my life, either. I had a fabulous position—and to repeat my father's famous line, "How *do* you quit a job like that?"

How, indeed? It was a question many of my friends would echo, and I certainly didn't have the answers. As I saw it, the problem was not my job, but something else I couldn't quite define. Dissatisfaction, perhaps, or old-fashioned burnout. If only my husband would help more, or my kids would be quieter . . .

Within a few weeks of clarifying my vision by practising this meditation process, all hell broke loose. It wasn't enlightened decision making that changed my life—it was a series of disasters that brought me to my knees. And while I was down there, I realized I had no choice but to resign.

So I did. I resigned my place in the women's march to corporate success and committed to becoming the wife and mother my family dreamed of having. I would give up my dreams of having it all for freshly baked peanut-butter cookies after school, a hot gourmet dinner on the table at the crack of five. I would be Laura Petrie, or June Cleaver: a relaxed, contented wife, greeting her man at the door after his hard day at the office. I'd join the parent advisory committee and do some volunteer work.

My marriage needed some work, but I was ready. I was blessed among women. My husband was gorgeous, intelligent, funny, kind, and successful—and we had enough money to allow me to take a sabbatical. Who could ask for more?

Two weeks after I left my career, my husband left me. He said it was just too late for him, and that he didn't want to be married any more. Our relationship wasn't working. It was heartbreaking for me to admit, but he was right. I was crazy about him, and he loved me, but our relationship had stopped "working" a long time before.

Be careful what you pray for, say the wise. And, based on the early results, one might well wonder what on earth I had prayed for.

This was the life I dreamed:

Who *is there?*

The people in my life are multidimensional and measure success by a series of bottom lines, including their contributions to society, and the health and happiness of their families and themselves. They are warm and thoughtful. They bring passion, laughter, energy, and a need to give back to life. They are dreamers and explorers. They are tolerant and open-minded. They have strong opinions but respect the beliefs of others. They are courageous and innovative. Together, we enjoy relationships that are caring, honest, open, respectful, and nurturing. Together, we grow as individuals, testing our limitations with the support of a community of kindred spirits.

What *am I doing?*

I write and give workshops. My day includes a series of activities, starting with morning meditations and ending with replenishing, loving time with my family. My daily work is creative (writing) and includes service to like-minded people (meeting and listening), presenting (workshops), and constant learning.

Where *do I live and work?*

I see trees, grass, flowers, water, and mountains from my window.

I write in an office overlooking the sea. It is warm and bright, filled with natural light. I drive into the city for business and drive out of it at the end of the day, leaving work behind and embracing my home.

When? *What is the pattern of my days?*

My work is flexible and allows me to spend time with my family when I'm most needed. I have time to meditate in the morning and to create balance in my life—exercise, time in nature, time to learn and grow. Time to write. Time to replenish my energies, and to honour my humanness through rest and recreation. I travel about four or five days each month, often taking my family with me.

Simple. Short. Uncomplicated.

I dreamed my life, and I resigned from my career. The job I had was a million miles from the job I wanted and needed. I wasn't ready to let it go, but I did. I loved my husband very much, and though I knew our relationship wasn't working, I wasn't ready to let go. He did.

I guess I just hadn't thought about everything I would have to give up in order to build the life I was dreaming of.

I was lost. If I was not Lori, executive vice-president, or Lori, wife of Randy, who was I? It was as if the universe took a brush and wiped the slate clean. I found myself recovering from the loss of my career, the loss of my marriage—the loss of my identity. There were many false starts and disappointments, many days when I wondered if I had been completely out of my mind to undertake such a radical change. There were hours, even days, of despair.

Only one thing sustained me—the clear, sweet dream of the life I wanted to live. I returned, over and over, to my written vision statement, seeing myself writing in an office overlooking the water, presenting workshops, spending time with friends over lattes and enlightened conversation. When I simply couldn't cope with the emptiness for one more minute, a miracle would occur. A friend would drop by with a book I must read, or call to say she'd signed us up for a walking club. I found the little house of my dreams, with hardwood floors, a marble fireplace, and an 18-metre-high pine tree in the backyard. I discovered a creative-writing class full of inspired and inspiring fellow writers. My poetry received honourable mention in a literary contest. Each miracle confirmed that I was on the right path and allowed me to stay on track for another day.

Looking back over the years that have passed, I am inexpressibly grateful. The life I dreamed is the life I live. Things aren't perfect—the house of my dreams is a little untidy at the moment, and we had to let our beloved nanny go when the stock market went its own way. I don't yet have the balance in my life I dreamed of, and I still spend too many hours working and not nearly enough time playing.

This path has given me something greater than perfection, however. It has given me faith. Today I know that I have to let go in order to receive. I know that things will not arrive according to my schedule, and that the time between the moment I express my desire to change and the fruition of my dreams may be marked by pain, angst, even hopelessness.

Whether you are dreaming about relationships, health, or a comfortable retirement, this principle applies:

It is your vision that will sustain you.

6

The Point of Departure: A Thorough Assessment of Current Reality

Life shrinks or expands in proportion to one's courage.

ANAÏS NIN

I have no sense of direction. I was born without an internal compass, which is a real disability for a girl from the farm. In familiar territory, I find my way around quite effectively by using landmarks, but I can always count on getting lost when I go somewhere for the first time. I've come to plan on it, and even enjoy it. Getting lost is now my method of familiarizing myself with landmarks.

When I was a child, however, it was a different matter. Once, when I was about 10, my sisters and I had been helping my father in a field a few kilometres away from our home, and I decided to walk home. It was late afternoon, a September Sunday, and my mom was to pick us up. We finished early, or she was late, and I became impatient. Unfortunately, my dad owned a lot of land, and I was confused about which field we were in. I headed off in sort of the right direction, so he didn't question me, and for the first hour, the hour that it should have taken to get home, I didn't question myself. It was when it grew dark and I realized I was walking through the swampy muskeg that my heart began to beat a little faster. The muskeg covered a large area, but I knew that the closest section was at least a kilometre from our house. I didn't know where I was, but I knew I wasn't supposed to be there. The problem with muskeg, too, is that in some places the vegetation is so thick that you can walk on its surface while the next step can lead into a sink-hole of leech-infested water a metre deep or more. Then there's the wildlife: coyotes, black bears, the occasional cougar. I've always been pretty brave, so I just stayed on the ground that seemed most solid, moved in the direction I thought would bring me home, and refused to think about the noises in the darkness.

After another hour had passed, my pulse had become a river of noise in my ears, and I was thinking of the stories I'd heard of lost people dying in the bush because they'd panicked. I decided to find a tree I could climb in the event of a bear visit and stay there until morning or until my family found me.

The story has a happy ending, obviously. After I'd sat under my tree for a few minutes, I heard a familiar sound, not a bear, thankfully, but a car. Then I saw the reflection of its headlights as they illuminated a huge checkerboard sign that I immediately recognized as the one on the corner a few hundred metres from my parents' house. I jumped up and ran home as fast as my quivering little legs could carry me—and was terribly hurt and irritated to find my family enjoying Walt Disney and Sunday dinner without one iota of concern.

I did indeed learn my lesson. Sometimes it's better to wait until mom picks you up. And even more importantly, no matter how clear your vision of the destination is, you had better know where you are before you start off. Because if you don't know where you are, you're lost before you take the first step.

In financial planning, we map our point of departure by preparing net-worth and cash-flow statements. Unfortunately, traditional financial statements give us a rather limited picture of the true quality of our lives. Money is awfully nice, but it really is only a tool with which we create our larger dreams. On the path to financial serenity, we need to broaden the spectrum. We will begin by measuring our financial health, and then explore each of the integral aspects of well-being, eventually comparing our current list of assets to the life we have dreamed.

Begin by collecting your statements and records, making yourself a cup of tea, lighting a candle, and putting on your most inspirational music. Spend a few minutes meditating on your vision. Remember, there are no evil secrets to be uncovered here. Even the things we tend to see as liabilities can be viewed as assets if we see them within a broader context. Unhappy with your current job? What a wonderful motivation to look for something better. Dissatisfied with your physical appearance? What better inspiration to work toward greater physical health and vitality. Try to silence the judge/critic/anxiety committee in your mind. (There's no point arguing with them; just send them to their rooms for a while.)

It isn't as if we are going to stay here forever—we just need to chart the terrain as preparation for departure.

FINANCIAL NET-WORTH STATEMENT

Assets

Description   Approximate Value

Personal Assets

Residence (as of last tax assessment) _____

Jewellery, rare coins, art _____

Collectibles _____

Furnishings (resale value)_____

Automobile (approx. resale value)_____

Other_____

Total Personal Assets: _____

Liquid Assets

Non-RRSP savings accounts, chequing accounts,
money market funds, Canada Savings Bonds, T-Bills

_____

_____

_____

Term deposits and GICs under one year

_____

_____

_____

Total Liquid Assets:_____

Investment Assets

RRSP investment accounts

_____

_____

_____

Non-RRSP investment accounts

_____
_____
_____

Commercial or non-residential real estate

_____
_____
_____

Cash value of insurance policies

_____
_____
_____

Small business assets, or outstanding loans to individuals or small businesses

_____
_____
_____

Total Investment Assets: _____

Total Assets:_____

Liabilities

Description   **Approximate Balance Owing**

Credit cards and personal debt (short-term loans, car loans, lines of credit, loans to family members). Include interest rates and payment terms in description.

_____
_____
_____
_____

Total Short-term, Non-deductible Personal Debt: _____

RRSP loans

_____
_____
_____

Total RRSP Loans: _____

Mortgage(s) on primary residence

_____

_____

_____

Total Mortgages on Primary Residence:_____

Tax deductible investment loans or mortgages

_____

_____

_____

Total Tax Deductible Investment Loans or Mortgages: _____

Total Liabilities: _____

Total Assets Minus Total Liabilities = _____

Financial Net Worth _____

Measuring material wealth is relatively easy. Value judgments are simple: in terms of assets, more is almost always better. In terms of liabilities, less is almost always better.

Measuring quality of life is more challenging. Ultimately, there is only one judge, and we are she.

That being the case, I'm going to ask you to assign your own values. This exercise requires a challenging degree of self-honesty, I know. It is threatening to admit that a situation is less than satisfying, because to do so is to admit the need for change. To admit the need for change itself invites a challenge. Still, this is only one small step. You have dreamed your glorious life. Now it's time to ascertain where you are. Later, you will determine what action steps are needed to move from here to there—and it is only at that point that you will have to decide whether or not to incur the cost of creation. This is a safe place, as threatening as it may feel.

Some of the categories may not be relevant to you at all in the present stage of your life. If this is the case, feel free to skip over them. There is no total score.

Rate the 33 aspects of well-being beginning on page 95. Using the scale of one to ten illustrated on pgae 94, think about your life and the way you feel about it now. It doesn't matter what other people think, or what you think you're supposed to feel. This is just another way of listening to your heart, and there are no right or wrong answers.

I'm going to make a statement or statements that represent the "ideal." If you feel that you are living your ideal in that area, you would assign a rating in the six to ten range. If you feel there is something you need to change, something you don't feel good about right now, assign a rating somewhere between one and five. Spend a few minutes thinking about each issue, and pay attention to your body. How does your stomach feel? Do you feel physically comfortable? Is there a temptation to move on and not think about some of the statements? Do you feel your neck and shoulders becoming tense?

DEFINING THE SCALE OF ONE TO TEN

I feel discouraged and powerless. I've given up. ①2 3 4 5 6 7 8 9 10

This has always been a problem in my life, and I continue to struggle with it. 1②3 4 5 6 7 8 9 10

This is not something that works very well in my life, but some days are better than others. 1 2③4 5 6 7 8 9 10

This is something I struggle with, but I'm winning, slowly but surely. 1 2 3④5 6 7 8 9 10

I think I'm probably as successful as most people in this area. 1 2 3 4⑤6 7 8 9 10

I think that I'm as successful as most people in this area, but I continue to work for and see regular improvement. 1 2 3 4 5⑥7 8 9 10

I am proud of my accomplishments in this area. 1 2 3 4 5 6⑦8 9 10

I know there is more work to be done, but I'm content. 1 2 3 4 5 6 7⑧9 10

This is an area of deep satisfaction for me. I'm not a master, but this area of my life really works. I have what I need. 1 2 3 4 5 6 7 8⑨10

This area of my life is rich, joyful and fulfilling. I feel I bring a degree of mastery to the process; I enjoy sharing my abilities with others. 1 2 3 4 5 6 7 8 9⑩

MEASURING WELL-BEING

1. General health

"I feel good. I'm almost never sick."   4

2. Vitality

"I hop out of bed in the morning and have lots of energy all day."   3

3. Strength and resilience

"I am physically strong and able to meet life's demands."   3

4. Concern about health

"I know I am healthy, and I don't worry about serious illness."   5

5. Body image

"I'm very happy with my physical appearance. I am content with my weight and don't struggle with being 'too fat' or 'too thin.'"   9

6. Sleep

"I wake well rested and ready for the day."   2

7. Emotional well-being

"I feel calm and centred almost all of the time. I'm in control of my moods; they're not in control of me."   2

8. Physical activity

"I get more than thirty minutes of physical activity at least three times a week."   2

9. Nutrition

"I eat lots of fruits, vegetables, and unprocessed food, and feel that my diet contributes to my well-being."   4

Subtotal Physical and Emotional Well-being   34

10. Primary relationship

"My relationship with my significant other is fulfilling, growth enhancing, and supportive." **Or,** "I'm not in a relationship right now and I'm really happy about that."   10

11. Parenting

"My relationship with my children is a source of joy and fulfillment in my life. I feel really good about the time we spend together and the way our family interacts." **Or,** "I don't have children and I'm content with that choice, certainly for now."   4

12. Friendships

"I am blessed with close friends, and our relationships are supportive, connected, respectful, and caring." **Or,** "I don't have the time I'd like to maintain close friendships right now, but I am content and feel supported by my life partner and family."

9

13. Extended family

"My relationships with extended family members (parents, in-laws, grandparents, siblings, etc.) are a source of joy and fulfillment in my life."

10

14. Professional relationships

"My relationships with my professional colleagues are a source of support and pleasure in my life."

5

15. A sense of community

"I am surrounded and supported by like-minded individuals who share in and support my life's endeavours."

5

16. Growth in relationship skills

"I grow daily in my ability to enjoy supportive, open, respectful, growth-enhancing relationships."

8

Subtotal Relationships   51

17. Home sweet home

"My home is a place of refuge, order, and peace. Whatever the trials of my day, I look forward to unwinding at home."

10

18. Working environment

"The environment in which I work is joyful and conducive to creativity and productivity."

2

19. Larger living environment

"I am in the right place—I live in the city and love the city." **Or,** "I live in the country and love the country."

3

20. Connection with nature

"I am able to regularly enjoy time in the outdoors and feel a real sense of restoration when I do."

2

Subtotal Environment   17

21. A sense of meaningful contribution

"I feel that I am contributing to the world in unique and meaningful ways."

1

22. Spirituality

"My spirituality guides and supports my daily existence. | 2

23. A sense of purpose

"I am connected to my community by my contribution to it." | 1

24. A sense of connection to others

"My relationships define me and create meaning in my life." | 9

Subtotal Meaning and Community | 13

25. Challenging activities

"I have many interests and activities that fulfill me, help me grow, and give me pleasure. I'm never bored." | 2

26. Commitment to personal growth

"I devote a significant amount of time and energy to personal growth. I know that I am a wiser, more caring, and stronger person than I was 10 years ago." | 7

27. Commitment to professional development

"I devote a significant amount of time and energy to increasing my skills and knowledge. My services are worth substantially more today in the career marketplace than they were 10 years ago." | 5

Subtotal Personal and Career Development | 14

28. Joy in living

"I really enjoy my life. I have fun, and laugh a lot. This is a journey, not a race. I live and love in the now." | 4

29. Personal empowerment

"I'm in charge of my well-being, and I do a great job. I'm fulfilled, I'm content, I'm happy." | 2

Subtotal Personal Fulfillment

Note: in the following section, please define work in the broader sense, to include retirement, education, and/or unpaid work in the home and/or volunteer sector. | 6

30. Professional satisfaction

"I love my job. I feel I'm really good at it and yet I'm constantly challenged and growing. I know I'm making a contribution." | 1

31. A sense of direction

"My career path is mapped out. I know exactly where I want to be in five years, and I'm on my way. I'm confident I'll make it, too." | 1

32. Balance	
"My work leaves me with time and energy to enjoy my life and relationships."	2
33. Prosperity	
"My work provides me with a good living."	7
Subtotal Career	11

As if that wasn't challenging enough, you now have to define the "score" that is acceptable to you; what requires improvement, and to what degree. The importance we attach to each of these issues is as individual as we are. For instance, a person with a significant weight problem may feel that her quality of life is low even if her score is high in every other area of her life. In my own experience, however, I found that my constant struggle to maintain my ideal weight disappeared when I found the time to nourish myself and find outlets for my creativity. Likewise, I am much more effective in my career when I work out. My relationship with my spouse improved a hundred-fold when I started making time for fun on my own.

You may wish to write a vision statement for each of the aspects of well-being that you feel need improvement or growth. Motivation occurs naturally within the context of an overarching vision. For the moment, however, let's keep it as simple as possible. Wherever your score is lowest and most in need of improvement (in your own opinion), try and think of small, relatively painless changes you could make to bring you closer to your vision. Think tiny. I'll go first.

SMALL CHANGES

I'll have a big glass of water before my morning coffee.

I'll eat three pieces of fruit each day.

I'll commit to seeing my dear friends at least once a month, no matter what.

I'll go for a bike ride this weekend.

I'm going to sign up for that seminar to increase my _____ skills.

_____

_____

_____

Now we'll move back to the world of money and the task of measuring cash flow. For as Charles Dickens so wisely stated, "Nineteen pounds in, eighteen-nine out—contentment. Nineteen pounds in, nineteen-two out—misery."

In order to enjoy life fully, we must spend less money than we earn.

Interestingly, this principle holds true at almost any level of net worth. The family with millions of dollars is still less than content when their expenses are continually higher than their income. For those of us with less than millions, spending more than we earn is a sure recipe for distress.

Hopefully, you've been recording your expenditures for a while and you can bring exact figures to the task. If not, use the figures you do know (rent/mortgage, hydro, insurance) and estimate the ones you don't. Beware, however, the big mystery amount.

Many of my clients come to me with cash-flow statements that look like this:

Monthly net income from salary	$4000	
Monthly net income from investments	$ 120	
Living expenses		$2500
Debt repayment		$ 500
Total	$4120	$3000

"That's great," I say. "So, you must be saving about $1120 per month, then."

"Well, no," is the usual reply. "We each put a couple hundred dollars a month into an RSP, but the rest just seems to disappear."

"Miscellaneous spending" or, as I call it, "walking-around money" worth less than 5 percent of income is perhaps acceptable. Unaccounted spending worth 20 percent of income is not. When you prepare your cash-flow statement, aim to record at least 95 percent of income as recognizable expenditures or savings.

It can be as simple as the statement above, but I find it is far more useful to break the expense categories down. If you are recording your expenditures, you are already doing this, but a cash-flow statement will give you a clear synopsis of money in and money out. It is a good idea to prepare one at least once a year, or whenever your expense/income situation changes significantly.

Enter your monthly income and expenses below. Start with a list of annual expenditures, divide by 12, and enter the appropriate amount in the monthly columns.

Then do the same with any lump-sum annual income, e.g., bond or GIC interest.

CASH-FLOW STATEMENT

ANNUAL EXPENSE	APPROXIMATE AMOUNT	AMOUNT ÷12
Car insurance $		
Home insurance $		
Vacations $		
Car tune-ups $		
Furnace tune-up $		
Contact lenses $		
Lump-sum RSP contribution $		

ANNUAL INCOME	APPROXIMATE AMOUNT	AMOUNT ÷12

MONTHLY INCOME & EXPENSES

Description		Income	Expense
Income from salary	$		
Income from bonus or commissions	$		
Rental income	$		
Self-employment or professional income	$		
Income from investments	$		
Child support or maintenance	$		
Pensions	$		
Other	$		

Description		Income	Expense
RRSP contributions	$		
Savings or investment programs	$		
Loan or credit-card payments	$		
Mortgage/rent	$		
Home or contents insurance	$		
Property taxes	$		
Home repairs and maintenance	$		
Utilities—gas/electric/water	$		
Telephone	$		
Cable	$		
Domestic help	$		
Groceries	$		
Takeout and fast food	$		
Dining out	$		
Household maintenance items (cleansers, supplies, etc.)	$		
Car payments	$		
Car maintenance and repair	$		
Gas and oil	$		
Parking	$		
Public transportation	$		
Car insurance	$		
Pets—food, veterinary services, licensing, etc.	$		
Clothing	$		
Education and school fees	$		
Personal care (cosmetics, vitamins, fitness-centre fees, hairstyling)	$		
Baby-sitting	$		
Daycare	$		
Entertainment	$		
Crafts and hobbies	$		
Vacations	$		
Medical insurance	$		

Description		Income	Expense
Prescriptions	$		
Dental	$		
Disability insurance	$		
Life insurance	$		
Bank charges	$		
Professional fees (lawyers, accountants, etc.)	$		
Optical expenses	$		
Gifts	$		
Memberships	$		
Charitable donations	$		
Other	$		
Total Income	**$**		
Total Expenses	**$**		
Net Cash Flow	**$**		

Remember, we are just establishing where you are right now. There is no right place to be, no correct figure. It may be that you are pleasantly surprised at how much you theoretically have left over at the end of the month. More often, the opposite is true, and you begin to have an understanding of why you always feel so tightly stretched.

If this were the end of the story, it might indeed be a little depressing, but it is only the beginning.

Again, spend a few minutes meditating on your larger vision, that of the life you wish to create. With these images still fresh in your mind, make a quick list of things that you could do either to reduce your expenses or to increase your income. Remember to send the internal critic/judge to her room first—these ideas don't have to be practical, manageable, or even plausible—they are simply seeds of possibility.

_____

_____

_____

_____

_____

_____

_____

_____

Risk Management

As Scott Peck said in the opening line of *The Road Less Travelled*, "Life is difficult." And if we live it well, it is also glorious, challenging, and full to the brim with joy, laughter, and love.

We will face grief and loss. We won't get the job we had our heart set on, and lovers will betray us—sometimes on the same day. We will lose people we love. We may suffer illness, and at some point, we will die.

These are things we cannot change or control, but there is a lot we can do to shield ourselves and our families in difficult times. We can live fully, love deeply, and nurture strength of spirit. We can embrace reality and take prudent measures to ensure that whatever happens, we and our families will be OK.

Even the most brilliant financial plan can be derailed by an illness or accident that robs us of our greatest asset—our ability to earn an income. Statistics show that one in eight of us can expect to suffer an injury or accident severe enough to qualify us for long-term disability benefits between the ages of 20 and 65. We are far more likely to be disabled than we are to suffer untimely death.

We like to tell ourselves that the whole concept of insurance is too boring. In my humble opinion, our supposed boredom masks terror. In order to accept the need for risk management, we have to emotionally, as opposed to intellectually, accept the existence of risk.

Yes. It's true. We can get sick. We can get hurt. We plan on dying much later, but it could be sooner. We are like sailboats in the open water—we have control of our sails but not of the wind. All the worry or denial in the world will not change the course of events we may someday face.

What we do have control over is the course and quality of our days. Risk management is necessary not to affect destiny, but to provide peace of mind, and to ensure that we suffer whatever it is we must suffer in as much material comfort as possible.

Risk management has a face to me, that of the woman who lived in a basement suite a few houses away in my old neighbourhood. I used to see her out walking her Jack Russell terrier when I was walking my dog. One day she stopped and shyly asked me about the teenage girl who exercised Indy when I was at work. She wanted to know how much I paid, and if I would consider having her do it. She told me that she was recovering from a disabling car accident and really needed to earn some extra money. She had been forced into the tiny, dark basement suite because there was nothing else she could afford where she would be allowed to keep her dog.

I never knew her name. I never knew her story. It was obvious from the worn but expensive clothes she wore that she was used to a much more affluent lifestyle, and much easier times. It broke my heart every time I saw her gingerly walking her little dog.

As I write, I say a little prayer for her. I hope that her life is easier and smoother, now that she has healed, and is back at work and back in a home where there is sunlight and comfort. I say a little prayer for me. *Let me never be there, or anywhere like there, again.* I say a prayer for you, for all of us. *If we must suffer illness or injury, let us suffer it in the comfort of our own home with enough money coming in to pay the bills.*

Likewise, most of us can think of someone we know who was left bereft and impoverished by the untimely death of a beloved spouse. My friend and hair stylist, Teresa, insisted that her husband buy enough insurance to allow her to mourn in financial comfort for one full year. I personally want more than a year, but it is a very wise place to start. Recognizing the reality of our mortality is one of the most loving things we can do for our dependents.

Isn't insurance expensive? It certainly can be. However, insurance is as costly as it needs to be—there are very bright actuaries out there who use statistics to determine how likely we are to be injured, to be in a car accident, to be robbed, or to die, during any given period. Rates reflect the likelihood of having to pay benefits; therefore, it can be argued that insurance is exactly the right price.

I don't want to scare you. Although fear is an effective motivator, its side effects are devastating. So I wouldn't offer this story if I didn't also have an antidote—to both the fear and the challenge.

You need to know where you are, and you need to know where you want to be. Then we can develop an action plan to take you there. Insurance can be expensive—having a plan is not.

This is one area of financial planning where it is fundamentally important to consult a competent and trusted professional. I couldn't begin to do justice to this topic in one chapter. My intent is to prepare you for your role in partnership with that professional, to help you determine your wants and needs.

OK. Let's deal with issue number one: replacing your income or unpaid contribution to your family in the event you become disabled. Whether or not you have dependents, you must have enough income from employment, pensions or benefits, or investments to live on.

If you are in a committed life and financial partnership, it is a good idea to do these exercises together. Examine the alternatives if one or the other of you were to become disabled or die.

For the sake of simplicity, make two copies of this questionnaire and complete one each, recognizing both your individual expenses and your contributions to the family unit. If one partner is presently not earning an income but is contributing through unpaid services to the family, estimate the value. How much would it cost to hire care providers to replace these services?

Disability insurance only replaces employment income. Therefore, it is not available to unpaid caregivers. However, catastrophic illness and accident insurance is available and will provide a lump-sum payment that will make life far more tolerable should this type of event occur. It is also important to purchase life insurance for unpaid caregivers, particularly if there are young children involved. You cannot replace a mother, but you may be able to replace at least some of a mother's services to her family.

If you're on your own, of course, this exercise is equally important.

Take care to be honest. Guard against any tendency toward unrealistic optimism.

To answer the following questions, you may need information from your human resources department or from your benefit provider. This is sometimes ridiculously difficult to obtain, but don't give up.

RISK-MANAGEMENT NEEDS ANALYSIS

1. If I were unable to work, what is the least amount of income I would need to maintain my current lifestyle? (Calculate by referring to Cash-flow Statement, subtracting expenses related to employment, such as office attire, transportation to and from work, lunches out, income tax, CPP, and EI.)

   $_____ per month

2. If I were unable to work, how much would I receive in Employment Insurance benefits? (Remember, investment income, disability pension benefits, etc., may affect this. You can get information on EI payments as they apply to your situation by calling Human Resources Canada or visiting their Web site.)

   $_____ **per month for (   ) months**

3. If I were unable to work, how much would I receive in benefits from my disability insurance provider? Calculate this figure on a net basis—it is fundamental to determine whether your benefits are non-taxable (you have paid all of the premiums yourself) or taxable (your employer has paid for all or a portion of the premiums).

   $_____ **per month for (   ) months**

4. How many weeks would elapse between the onset of my illness or injury and receipt of benefits from EI and/or my disability provider?

   (   ) weeks

5. Based on my cash-flow expense calculation, how much money do I need in an emergency reserve fund to manage this period (between onset of unemployment and receipt of benefits)?

   $

6. How much do I currently have in an emergency reserve fund?

   $

7. If the reserve I now have is insufficient for my needs, do I have friends or relatives I could borrow from? Do I have a line of credit set up for this purpose? How much money could I access without changing my lifestyle or risking investment loss?

   $

8. Is there a difference between my long-term and short-term disability benefits? How much would I receive per month (net) if I were ill for more than a year?

   $

9. If I was severely injured or ill, and was unable to return to my career or job, would my long-term disability benefits continue until age 65? Or would they only continue if I was unable to do *any kind of work* (i.e., telephone soliciting, attaching mailing labels to envelopes, etc.)?

   ☐ **Benefits would continue as long as I was unable to return to *my* occupation.**

   ☐ **Benefits would continue as long as I was unable to return to *any kind of work*.**

Likewise, you can calculate your life-insurance needs and compare them to your current life-insurance programs. There are really two primary kinds of life insurance—purchased insurance, which allows you to share the risk of untimely death with a large pool of other individuals, or self-insurance.

Self-insurance is the accumulation of assets that will provide you with income whether or not you are able to work. The second is sweeter, but not always possible, particularly in the early years when your family needs your income most.

To determine your life-insurance needs, you need to ask yourself the following questions:

- What are my financial obligations?

- If my family were to lose my income or my services, how much would it cost to replace them? Again, it is important to look at your cash-flow statement and subtract those expenses related to employment.

- Would there be additional costs? For instance, would it be necessary to replace your current daycare arrangements with a live-in nanny? What about the approximately $8000 it would cost for funeral arrangements?

- What are my financial dreams for my family? Would I be content dying knowing that these goals wouldn't be met, or do I want to "insure" that they are reached with or without me?

The following table is an example of an articulated needs analysis:

NEEDS ANALYSIS

Cost of funeral and burial expenses	$ 8 000
Replacement of my net income for 10 years (during which time all dependent children will reach age 21)	$ 300 000
Cost of a live-in nanny for six years, minus the cost of 50% of daycare (spouse pays half now)	$ 72 000
University education and/or or small-business fund for daughter	$ 48 000
First home or business investment pool for son	$ 48 000
Debts that must be paid off by estate; taxes that will be triggered on my death	$ 3 000
Total funds required at my death:	$ 479 000
Subtract:	
Current group life insurance	($120 000)
Current assets and investments	($120 000)
CPP Death, Survivor, and Orphan Benefits*	($ 12 000)
Required life insurance	$ 227 000

*For a full synopsis of current CPP benefits, see the Glossary.

As most of the income-replacement requirements named in this example are short term, I would advise this individual to purchase a small permanent or term-to-100 insurance policy to cover burial expenses and estate taxes, and a larger policy of term insurance, the least expensive kind, to cover the balance. Permanent insurance, sometimes referred to as whole life, universal, or variable insurance, may be appropriate in those circumstances where you will need income or benefits no matter when you die.

Now that you have an articulated needs analysis, you can move to the action steps. Find an insurance professional who will guide you through the next phase, designing the best program for you. I think it's always wise to look for an adviser who is as objective as possible. If advisers are part of a captive sales force, that is, their job is to sell their company's products, it is natural that there will be some bias. Look for independent advisers, and ask them to help you compare the various insurance products available.

A word of caution. Traditionally, insurance advisers are paid a fraction of the commission on term-insurance products that they are paid on whole-life insurance products. If you find yourself being force-fed the full-meal deal, it may be appropriate to ask some tough questions. Yes, whole life insurance does provide a forced-savings/investment program, *but so does an automatic monthly investment program.* Yes, you can borrow your own money at a low rate of interest later on if you're strapped. *Wait. Borrow my own money at a low rate of interest? I think I'll just arrange a line of credit, thank you.* Yes, term insurance does get more expensive as you get older, and may not even be granted if you have health problems, *which is why it is best to get a "guaranteed renewal" option.*

There a number of differing opinions on the subject, but unless there are estate-planning or creditor-protection issues at play, I strongly advise keeping investment programs and insurance programs separate.

Current Reality Summary

Wow.

Let's stop for a few minutes to think about how far we've come. We've reviewed financial net worth. We've explored cash flow—where the money is coming from and where it goes. We've reviewed quality-of-life issues. We've articulated risk-management needs.

In the last chapter, you dreamed a life. Now that you have a clearer picture of current reality, it may be a good idea to go back and revisit that vision. Please don't reduce your expectations; at least, not unless you have come to understand that you simply don't want to pay the price. There is no question—I want to have a body like Karen Voight. I really do. But not enough to spend the three-plus hours that she spends working out every day. Therefore, I have reduced my expectations. My objective is now a toned, vital, strong, sleek Lori. And for that, I am willing to pay the price. In the investment world, the price that we pay for higher returns, for instance, is higher risk. The perfect investment for me is the one at the point on the continuum of risk/return where I am most comfortable. In reaching a clear vision and coming to terms with current reality, we begin to see the cost of moving from here to there.

I would like to live on a remote tropical island paradise, but not at the cost of leaving my friends, family, and the breathtaking seasons of British Columbia. It isn't a sacrifice; it is a decision. Of the two desires, I am choosing the sweeter.

That said, do not reduce your expectations because you think it would be impossible to get from here to the life that you dreamed. Anything is possible. Now that you have a crystal-clear, fully articulated, Technicolor vision of your future, you'll be amazed at how serendipity and creative power will unfold in your life.

7

Unleashing the
Creative Power of Vision

In the world to come I shall not be

asked, 'Why were you not Moses?'

I shall be asked,

'Why were you not Zusya?'

RABBI ZUSYA

I grew up near the Beaver River in Alberta. There was something so magical to me about the river's water, coming from great distances, flowing ever onward. Perhaps to the sea, they said; perhaps back to the sky to fall again as rain. That river was free.

In the heat of summer, my aunts and uncles swam there. As children, we weren't allowed to because of the currents, and I can still hear their laughter reverberating between its deep banks as we played, envious, in the sand of its shores.

Occasionally the Beaver would yield up something marvellous beyond imagining: a river oyster, with a tiny, rough freshwater pearl. A pearl. Even now, so many years later, it hurts a little bit to remember the disappointment of being told that these tiny, irregular grey seeds were not the precious pearls I read about in books—that they were not, in fact, considered precious at all.

Along the river's banks were sand dunes of a modest Alberta sort, and as I grew up, I would often make the two-kilometre-long journey there to sit alone and dream. As I was rather unpopular and desperate for the approval of my mates, my favourite fantasy was of the grand party I would someday host. I would decorate those very dunes with cardboard cut-out figures of elegantly drawn men and women. My entire class would be invited, and they would be so enchanted that they would come. The sun would shine brilliantly, and I would serve endless potato chips and all the Pop Shoppe soda that could be consumed. I would even play music, though in my wildest dreams, I couldn't imagine where I would get the radio from.

The party dream had endless variations. I would dance with Walter, the most handsome boy in class. No, I would sit quietly and chat of intimate things with Maureen, the best-dressed, most popular girl in the school, whose parents owned the town's only clothing store. No, I was dead and my class had gathered at my memorial service while my spirit hovered and listened to how much they missed me, how terribly they felt that they hadn't been kinder to me while they could, how much they had really admired me.

All in all, like the freshwater pearl, my childhood dreams were modest. When I wasn't dreaming of grand parties, I dreamt of having my own room, with a real bedspread, and a real dresser to keep my multitude of stylish blue jeans in.

If we can envision it, we can eventually create it. Unfortunately, our dreams tend to be limited by our experiences. Unless we have seen a model of the life we desire, how do we add colour and clarity—the details that will make it real for us? It is not enough to say we want a bigger house, or to be able to take a tropical vacation, or to have that mythical "financial security." Financial well-being is the product of discovering *our* dreams, *our* power.

If we watch TV, or listen to the radio, or even drive on city streets, we are inundated with images of things we cannot do without, unless we want to be excluded from the beautiful people; unless we want to be dull. Numerous advertisements even tell us not only what we should want but how we can pay for those things we need for the beautiful, exciting life we are destined to live. It's all as close as the right credit card.

What advertising doesn't tell us is how we will create the wealth we need to pay those credit-card bills. And it doesn't tell us how those fragmented bits and pieces of things are supposed to fit together to make a rewarding whole. It doesn't tell us who we are and what we want. It doesn't impart to us the perfect balance of things and time and sacrifice and pleasure that will give us, at the end of the day, a sense of a life exquisitely well lived.

Honouring our needs and affirming our desires is an art form. Some of us are born with talent. Some of us are blessed with life-well-lived mentors. As with any art form, most of us have to practise, painstakingly and at length.

When I began this journey, I knew that something was missing in my life, but like so many people, I wasn't sure exactly what it was. I knew that I wanted an orderly, light-filled, harmonious home, for instance, but I wasn't clear on what that looked like. I made buying decisions based on what was available and fashionable. I had few clues. I knew that I wanted an antique dressing table. I wanted a more comfortable wardrobe, and more art in my life. I loved books and the colour green. Other than that, I found that my personal style and tastes were a bit of a mystery, even to me. I sometimes said that I knew what I liked when I saw it, but it didn't quite ring true in light of the many things I had purchased and then came to hate after I'd had them for a while.

I felt lost in my own life, as if my larger "body," that of my clothes, my home, my leisure activities, and even my dreams, didn't fit me any more, if indeed it ever had. In order to become fully me, to live my life richly and deeply, I had to discover what it was that I loved and wanted in my life, and through those discoveries, who I was.

Blessings come in dark packages, and as most losses do, my husband's departure at this very vulnerable time brought unexpected gifts. For the first time in my life, I found myself decorating a home without considering any-one else's tastes or preferences. I can't even describe the weightless joy of having a bit of money and absolutely no one with whom to compromise.

My home became a metaphor for designing my life. I moved things around. Tried this, and that.

I studied. The wisdom and insights of other women inspired me to new explorations of my own. Through the pages of their books, I had the sense of sharing their lives, chatting at their kitchen tables. I found that though my path might be entirely unique, it didn't have to be solitary. After a lifetime of studying various religions, it was this sharing of experience, written and ver-bal, that taught me to hear the still, small voice within. The heart knows; my heart knows. What kind of home I needed, where I wanted to live. The secret was learning to listen. After years and years of being starved by a poverty mentality, my heart had to be wooed into disclosing its wisdom.

In the Recommended Reading section, you will find some of the many books that enhanced my life as I explored this new richness, and I hope that among them, you will find a few that speak to you. From these pages, and the wisdom of my friends and helpmates along the way, I gleaned a multitude of tools that allowed me to keep moving forward on the path when I might have otherwise given up. I am thrilled to share them with you, to encourage you to go out there and find your own. Like the things that make us happy, ulti-mately, the tools that work best for us are . . . the tools that work best for us.

A fundamental part of this process is learning to *worship* our uniqueness. Some of us flourish physically by devotedly going to the gym three hours a day; for others, a long, meditative walk every morning is the path to vitali-ty. Some of us want diamonds. Some of us want poetry. Embrace your idiosyncrasies. Love them. Devote yourself to them. How can you attract and create financial well-being if *you don't really know what you want?*

There is no one way to reveal your dreams and desires, yet you must seek until you find. There are clues. It may be images that set your imagination on fire, or a beautiful turn of phrase, or a warm waft of cinnamon apple pie from the oven. What is it that brings your dreams to the surface?

Whatever it is, seek it. Seek it with all your might.

Revealing the Definitive Dream

If dreaming my life was to prove miraculously powerful for me, it was my dream book that gave my creative endeavours direction and elegance. It provided the texture, the detail, the colour, the images that allowed me to see the road ahead so that my vision would be focused there. I hope that it will do the same for you.

What was it I wanted in my life anyway? What made me happy? What did I find beautiful? What replenished me? What was missing?

We spend so many hours of our lives focused on the small questions: how to make it to the grocery store before it closes, whether to send a cheque or use a credit card. To live our lives fully, we must turn our attention to the larger questions. Make a date with the *you* of the future, the happier, healthier, financially serene, wise woman who will one day look back over the years and say, "Oh, I was so much stronger, smarter, more capable, powerful than I knew. If only I would have known . . ."

Begin by setting aside a time that you can commit to. A time for you.

For me, it's that hour in the morning before the rest of the house awakes. Again, if you can't find a half-hour for yourself in the day, you must ask yourself why. Is everything in your life truly more important than your own fulfillment? Don't forget that this is also a gift you give to the people you love. My husband didn't leave me because I was a content, serene, happy, joy-filled person. The fact that I felt I had no time for myself *because* I devoted myself to my family didn't make him any happier in my miserable company. He became happy in my company when I learned how to be happy. Someone once said that the greatest gift a man can give his children is to love their mother. I would add that the greatest gift a mother can give her children, and the world in general, is to love herself. When I look back on my years in corporate management, my greatest regret is that I didn't care for myself better. Because I didn't, rather than contributing optimism, warmth, and all the things I value, too often I brought more anxiety, more fear, more conflict when healing was desperately needed.

My morning meditation hour has evolved over the three years. I read the inspirational works of others. At the moment, every day begins with an affirmation from Julia Cameron's *Heart Steps,* a daily meditation from a book by Emmet Fox, and a daily meditation from *Simple Abundance.* After reading, I enjoy a few minutes of contemplation. (My teachers used to call it daydreaming, but now I'm grown up and I'm allowed to call it "contemplation.") Then I take up my beautiful fountain pen, a gift from my husband that first appeared in my life as an entry in my dream book. My writing begins with my Gratitude Journal, recently made famous by Oprah. In my case, a beautiful, blank, hard-cover book in which I simply count my blessings—at least five every morning. Then I write in my journal—the place I leave both my epiphanies and my whining. It is on these pages where the noise in my mind comes to reside, leaving me free to focus on *life.* My journal has also become a record of that life. All of those greeting cards I had no idea what to do with now get pasted in its pages, along with holiday photos and ticket stubs and my daughter's seasonal artwork. My great-grandchildren may know entirely too much about me (yes, I whine about PMS and puppy training), but they will know me. More importantly, I will know me.

Then come some of my favourite moments of the day . . . my meander through my dream book.

Wonderful to wander through—wonderful to create. There are a million variations on this theme, and I've incorporated ideas from everybody from Julia Cameron to the minister of my church. Don't feel that that you have to follow a formula. The objective is simply to create an ever-evolving illustrated book of the life you want to live.

In my dream book appear images of gardens and islands and tableware and ocean views distilled into collages of the world I desired. At the front, in golden ink, I wrote the list of desires from my "Dreaming a Life" exercise: the people I wanted in my life, my job description, my home. I have a section for material accumulation—the art, books, and stuff I want: my fountain pen, an antique dressing table with a mirror and lots of drawers, a bicycle.

In a section I added after all the others, when I had the house, the soaker tub, and the view, and knew that something was still missing, I have written the essence of all of my longings: contentment, serenity, peace, order, fulfillment, quiet, solitude, accomplishment, harmony, loving relationships. There are no pictures in this section. Instead, I prefer to meditate daily on the images they bring to mind. These few minutes reveal so much about where I am and what I need in my life. When things are out of balance, it is here that I awake to what is needed.

Filling in the textures and colours of my dreams is one of my greatest pleasures. In some mystical way, it is the details that call them into being.

● EXERCISE 5 **The Serenity Dream Book**

You'll need a pair of scissors, a glue stick, and all those old magazines and catalogues you've been saving. I also have gold- and silver-ink pens—not necessary, but really, really great. If you aren't a saver of old magazines, it might be fun to make a trip to the nearest thrift store and buy a collection of other people's old magazines—you can often get a whole stack for a few dollars.

Begin by writing your dreams in the first pages. What is it you would like to change? Answer these questions for yourself.

- Would you like to be more physically fit? What does the "new, fit you" look like? What physical activity do you love? What foods do you love?

- Are your relationships as fulfilling and loving as you'd like them to be? Is your life full of people you admire and who admire you?

- Would you like to live somewhere else? Where? When? What does it look like? How is it different from where you are now? Is there anything you would take with you?

- Are you happy with your job? If not, exactly what would you like to be doing?

- Is there a trip you would like to take? Where? When? With whom?

- Are your finances in disorder? What does order look like to you? What does financial well-being look like to you?

- Do you feel that you are contributing enough to the world around you?

Jot down anything and everything you would like to have or accomplish. Remember, be specific. Not, "I'd like to travel one day," but "I'd like to spend six weeks in a rented villa on the water in the south of France in the year that my youngest child leaves home. I'd like to go alone and write and eat cheese and bread and drink wine. I want to sit on the terrace in the morning sun and sip espresso."

"I'd like to have a book of my poetry published in hard-cover."

"I'd like to learn to wind-surf before I'm 50."

"I want to have a pair of kick-ass, black-ostrich-skin cowboy boots with real silver toes."

"I want to spend a weekend in New York and shop at Bloomingdale's and have a $200 dinner by myself while I read a Harlequin romance."

These are not goals—although someday they might be. For now they are seeds, centres of gravity.

These "seeds" shape the future for me; they give it meaning and light and life. Just as importantly, they save me from striving for what I don't want. My dream book has saved me hundreds of dollars in purchases I almost bought but didn't because I knew I didn't really need them—they weren't in my book. Nothing is purchased without making it into the dream book first.

There are occasional deletions. About a year ago, for instance, I decided that it was time to start thinking about updating my Jeep Cherokee. Mine's an '88, so it's been well used. However, after pasting beautiful ads of new Cherokees in my book, it slowly dawned on me that I wasn't dreaming my own dreams. Some unconsciously absorbed advertising message was telling me that if I wanted to look prosperous, I needed a newer vehicle, even if I loved my old one and it served me well. I realized that looking more prosperous wasn't worth the extra $40 000 (I can't even imagine how many hours of work that represents) it was eventually going to cost me. I pasted over those pictures with scenes from the garden I will one day sit and read in.

If you do nothing else after reading this book (have I said this before?), make a dream book. Make a home for all those things you've been dreaming of, everything from learning to play the guitar, to a cruise around the Greek Islands, to learning to speak Spanish. Everything. The great set of white, ironstone, everyday dinnerware you'd like to have. A portrait of your dog. A dog. That perfect black dress. Create a place for the dreams you are going to have as your relationship between you and your financial well-being becomes ever more intimate and comfortable.

Even if you don't have a clear picture, write down the theme. Take the stuff from your list. For instance, I knew I wanted to own artwork: sculptures and paintings and prints. And books—I love books, not just to read, but to own—and bookshelves built into walls to put them on. So that is what it says in my dream book, and when I see a piece of artwork or a book that speaks to my heart, at a price that works for me, I add it to my dream collection.

I begin the process of creating my perfect body in my dream book, as well. Don't get me wrong—there isn't a picture of Barbie pasted there, or a Playmate centrefold. That isn't my idea of the perfect body (thank God!). Instead, I have a picture of a real, perfectly unique, beautiful woman with fabulous biceps; another with sturdy, muscled thighs above a pair of roller blades.

My career is mapped there. This book is the product of a dream mapped almost two years ago. There were many times it seemed I was going in the opposite direction, as if my goal was a long way off. Every time I meandered through my dream book, however, there it was, and it just kept calling me— the road ahead. Every time I realized I was moving in the wrong direction, I did a course adjustment. And here I am.

Play. Wander through those magazines and catalogues with the wonder of a child, a pair of scissors, and a glue stick. Don't feel obligated to finish it all at once. Much of the pleasure comes from finding a great photo in that pile of junk mail at your door on Saturday. As you probably have already discovered, it is not the great or important thing that you do today that will change your life. It is the little things you do every day—the things that are so much fun you *want* to do them.

At the back of your dream book, create a section for the dreams that have come true for you.

It is such a joy for me to review this section every morning. For years, my daughter and I wanted to go to Disneyland. When it was time for a holiday, however, either my husband and I desperately needed to get away alone together, or we did something the whole family (meaning my husband) wanted to do. We just never seemed to make it to Disneyland.

After Disneyland became a place in my dream book, it occurred to me that if I waited for Randy, we were never going. Within a few months, I'd found the money, booked the trip, and off we went. And my daughter and I have wonderful memories of a time that was incredibly sweet and magical for both of us.

Yes, my fountain pen is there, and the beautiful (affordable) artwork that has miraculously found its way to me. There is the bicycle I found in a second-hand store for $35—a Raleigh Sport, in perfect condition, an exact twin of the precious bicycle I had to leave behind when I left home at 14. My beautiful home with the view of the North Shore Mountains and the Burrard Inlet. My soaker tub!!! The beautiful, kindred souls who have found their way into my life, or back into my life, since I dreamt of them. The deepening, intimate, joyous relationships that have developed with old friends. My business. My business partner.

Miracles.

There are miracles untold just waiting for your invitation.

8

From Dreams to Action: Becoming the Architect of Your Financial Destiny

All is procession;

the universe is a procession

With measured and beautiful

motion.

WALT WHITMAN

As a financial adviser, I meet most of my clients for the first time when they decide to learn about investing. They come to learn about diversification, mutual funds, and compound returns, but my greatest joy is the first few hours we spend together, when we talk about what is real and meaningful in this business of personal financial planning. Who we are. What it is we want.

Money is only a tool, a unit of value that is convenient to exchange. A Stradivarius violin in the hands of a master may make the angels weep, but in the hands of a novice, it is only wood, string, and metal. The same principle is true of investment knowledge—and (dare I say it?) money.

Thus far on our journey, we have explored our beliefs about money, and the early lessons we learned that may no longer be valid. We've replaced invalid beliefs with empowering ones, through meditation, affirmation, and action. We've learned to channel our energies productively by creating and maintaining order in our lives. We've studied the importance of developing a crystal-clear vision of the future we desire, and learned ways of making that vision our directional True North. We've determined where we are now.

It is time to make a plan, to start carving out the action steps. Believe it or not, this is the easy part—as long as you can hang on to that vision. My

Disneyland trip, for instance, would never have happened if I hadn't finally figured out what it was I wanted. I didn't necessarily need a family vacation in Disneyland. I wanted to take my daughter there. Once I had that clear understanding, the action steps were obvious.

I informed my husband. That was interesting—he was, I have to admit, surprised. After all those years of hearing, "We should take the kids to Disneyland" and "I'd love to go to Disneyland," "Teryl and I are going to Disneyland at the end of May" was a bit of a shock. Then we went to the travel agent to compare prices, packages, and flights. As it so often does once the vision is clear, serendipity intervened. The travel agent loved Teryl and worked hard to get us the best package at absolutely the lowest price—it was far more affordable than I expected. I withdrew the money from an investment account in which I'd just had an unexpected windfall, and in a couple of days, we had plane tickets and Disney passes in hand.

It may seem that planning for retirement, buying that dream home, starting a home-based business, or other such weighty issues require a more strategic approach, but the steps are largely the same.

◆ Develop a crystal-clear vision of what you really want. Take your time. Use your dream book, or whatever tools work best for you. Do you want a new Jeep Cherokee, or do you want to look prosperous? Do you need an ocean view, or will a view of the pond in the park make you just as happy? Do you want a 270-square-metre house because you really do, or because you think that if you lived in a house that big, you'd have some peace and quiet? (Peace and quiet are cheaper.) Do you want a "comfortable retirement" at 65, or do you want the freedom to start your own business at 45?

◆ Get the best advice and help you can. There are wonderful, competent, caring individuals out there who are waiting to be of service to you and your dreams—you just have to find them. Whether it is a travel agent, a realtor, an accountant, or a financial adviser, creative, professional partnerships will make your life richer and more successful.

◆ Calculate how much it's going to cost to get from where you are now to where you need to be, and decide how you are going to pay for it. Did you just get an ugly feeling in the pit of your stomach? If there is no clear answer to this dilemma, please don't waste your energy worrying or wallowing in self-indulgent bouts of hopelessness. Please do not start telling yourself that you are being impractical, that you should let go of this fantasy. Just accept the fact that you don't know *right now* how you are going to pay. Trust that the answer will come to you. Keep your vision clear. Study your dream book religiously, affirm your divine right to a life beyond your wildest dreams, take the practical steps that are available to you, and wait. If you need $300 000 to start your own business, for instance, and only have $50 left at the end of the month after the necessities of life are paid for, save and invest that $50. Research other businesses like yours in the library and on the Internet. Join associations of business owners in similar fields.

◆ Begin.

With issues like these, it is so important to get the specifics. Almost all Canadians would list "a comfortable retirement" among their financial goals. Now, what does "comfortable" mean to you? What does "retirement" mean to you? When I do financial plans for clients who have no idea what their retirement should look like, I am forced to use the generally applied assumption that they will need about 75 percent of their current income to live on. In most cases, however, current income changes rather dramatically throughout life. In preparing a financial plan for a couple in their early thirties, we may be planning for a retirement income of 75 percent of $60 000. However, this same couple may be earning $120 000 a year by age 50, and have no intention of reducing their standard of living once they retire. One person's paradise can be another person's impoverishment, and vice versa. The happiest retired couple I ever met had $25 000 in savings and no assets except an old car. What makes you happy? What does it cost?

It is important to remember, too, that most of us spend a fair amount of money compensating ourselves for doing jobs we hate. What would happiness cost if we could sit on the verandah by the lake and play the guitar all day?

Do you really want to stop work entirely? Or do you want to stop doing this job? Or do you want to stop *having* to do this job? There are aspects of my work that I absolutely love, and would do for free if my family could afford that luxury. I don't plan to retire in the usual sense. I would like to be writing, counselling clients, and presenting workshops when I'm 90. But I don't want to have to do it for the money—not when I'm 90, and not when I'm 50, either. Planning for my retirement means planning my life. I'm not interested in spending all my time accumulating a pile of assets. Money truly isn't everything. On the other hand, freedom, to me, really is everything, and much of freedom is paid for with dollars and cents.

Therefore, I have a list of goals that I will accomplish within stated time frames. A goal without a time frame is a daydream. Not that daydreams are bad—they are the seeds of goals, and nothing grows without a seed, remember?

My goals:

◆ To live in an affordable home with a view, a soaker tub, order, peace, and harmony.

◆ To create an RSP for my son that he can use as a down payment on his first home at age 30+ (10 years from now).

◆ To create an education fund for my daughter to use for university or to start her own small business at age 21 (11 years from now).

◆ To save and invest 10 percent of my income in growth-oriented investments every year from now until I die, leaving a legacy for my family and for those social organizations I want to contribute to.

◆ To maximize my RSP contributions from now until age 55, so I don't have to worry about being comfortable in my golden years.

◆ To maintain an insurance program that will meet my goals for my children and provide for home and childcare should anything happen to me.

Pretty simple. As a financial planner, I know that if I stay with my investment plan, and I do not take undue risks, I will achieve my goals comfortably. Perhaps even more importantly, now that I have an articulated plan, I have both peace of mind and financial well-being. Today—this moment. The only moment that really counts. In my practice, I generally find that financial goals boil down to some or all of the following:

◆ Financial independence: having enough money in reserve to walk away from the job you hate or the relationship that's gone wrong.

◆ Having all your bases covered: knowing that your family will be OK if something happens to you, and that *you* will be OK if something happens to you.

◆ The "comfortable retirement": knowing you won't end up eating cat food out of old sour-cream containers or pushing your wardrobe in a shopping cart.

◆ Education funds—if you have children or grandchildren.

◆ A comfortable home, preferably owned by you, as opposed to joint ownership with the bank.

◆ The freedom to realize your grand dream: a year of travel, a recreation property, a trip "back home."

◆ The ability to leave a legacy to your children, grandchildren, or a favourite charity or institution.

Feel free to borrow the appropriate items off this list and add your own. Write them in the spaces provided below.

EXERCISE 6 **My Financial Future—The Vision**

_____

_____

_____

_____

_____

_____

_____

_____

_____

_____

When you've clarified your vision, I strongly suggest working through the next steps with a financial adviser to figure out how much it's going to cost, and how you are going to pay for it. At this point, you have to start thinking about things like "present and future value," rates of return, tax issues, and inflation. It can get very complex. Financial advisers have access to computer programs and other tools to assist in the various calculations you need to do.

If for some reason you are intent on doing it on your own, I would recommend that you buy Graydon Watters book, *Financial Pursuit*. Mr. Watters provides each of the forms, tables, and calculations you'll need to do all of this, but plan on devoting considerable time and energy. There are also a plethora of Internet sites and marketing materials from financial institutions that offer forms and calculations. Proceed with caution. As some wise pundit once said, "There are three kinds of lies—lies, damn lies, and statistics." Statistics, calculations, numbers—the same premise applies. Without professional advice to assist you through the process, it's possible to use the wrong calculations, or to overlook a fundamental piece of the puzzle. If you haven't yet found a financial adviser you're comfortable with, you may wish to check out some of the suggestions in Chapter 13. Most people find they feel more in control of their financial destiny with the benefit of professional advice than when they try to manage on their own. Peace of mind comes with knowing that everything has been taken into account and planned for, and it's far more likely that will be the case when you have expert assistance.

Whatever you do, do something. Please. Far too often, I meet with women in their sixties and seventies who have not planned for their futures. In most cases, they were simply too busy taking care of other people. Often, they thought "retirement plan" and "husband" were synonymous, and in a way, they were right—the retirement plan left in the same direction as the husband.

This isn't just about money. This is about quality of life. It is about the happiness and peace you will share with the people around you, with the world. God knows we need your contribution.

A Time for Everything Under the Heavens . . . and the Reality of Being Women

Birth, kindergarten, primary school, secondary school, first job, first marriage, first child, first house, first grey hair . . . significant events marching one after another unto death. Within, or perhaps above, this linear vision is another level of experience. A series of cycles within cycles. Imposed upon the railroad track of this linear perspective are the seasons of our lives.

This linear perspective creates much of the anxiety we feel around the issues of money. Remember when you planned to be a millionaire by age 30? Or, God forbid, marry a millionaire by age 30? The quality of our lives is determined not by the scoreboard, but by the grace of natural progression: seeding, emergence of the tender shoots, growth, the blossoming, fruit and harvest.

To come to peace with the issues of money, it is not enough to understand where you are, even to know where you are going. You must remember what you have achieved, how far you've come. The greatest accomplishments are too often buried in tragedy. Survival itself is worthy of celebration.

Most of the people who come to see me for planning advice, especially women, feel they are not doing very well. Perhaps they rent rather than own their homes. They don't contribute the maximum to their RSPs. They don't pay off their credit-card balances every month.

Interestingly, only 44 percent of eligible Canadians made contributions to their RSPs in 1996, and the average contribution was about $3000. Among those who contributed, the largest demographic group were in their fifties. Yes, in light of all we hear about the threatened state of government-funded retirement programs, this is a frightening statistic, but it tells us something else as well. Despite the media images to the contrary, the Joneses are not doing as well as we may think.

Those of us between 25 and 34 are invariably net borrowers. Between 34 and 45, we are net accumulators. Our income is increasing, but we spend it on paying down the mortgage we took out for our first home at approximately age 34, and on raising and educating our children. Forty-five to 60 are our highest earning years, and they are also the years in which we become net savers. We are often net savers until the age of 68, when we start living off the fruits of our labours.

There is some comfort in acknowledging that our financial struggles are not a reflection of personal ineptitude. Rather, they are almost inevitable by-products of our life cycles.

Complacency, however, is not our helpmate. Fear is a negative and crushing way to incite action, yet we must recognize the realities of being women. As women, we face numerous economic handicaps. It is fundamentally important that we come out of whatever trance we are operating under.

There are some painful realities we have to acknowledge before we can transcend them.

Perhaps you are not in a life partnership right now, or you don't feel these issues are of concern to you. Sharon, an extremely intelligent 20-something woman I worked with, described herself as "postfeminist." She's educated, capable, and she has never faced discrimination on any level. According to her, the issues that Gloria Steinem and Germaine Greer concerned themselves with simply don't apply any more, certainly not to her and her generation. It's over. I'd love to believe that's true, but based on my own experience in the world of business, my unspoken response was, "Not yet."

When I was Sharon's age, if I thought about the issue at all, I felt the same way. It was only after I began moving up the corporate ladder that gender became an issue. I felt I had to work harder for equal recognition and remuneration, and I had to do it with a huge handicap. I didn't have a wife who took care of 80 percent of the domestic and child-care responsibilities.

There is no question. We have come a long way. Opportunities in the workplace are creating new challenges for women. We are earning more money. We are being promoted. The education gap is closing, and there are more women than men graduating from many university programs. If we choose not to have children, or if we can find partners who agree to share domestic and child-care responsibilities equally, the gender bias we face will be inconvenient as opposed to disabling. The rest of us, those in the majority of families in North America, are left to cope with the reality of childbearing in a world that too often places more value on making money than it places on raising the next generation. Yes, we know it is one of the most important contributions we can make to the world we live in, and no, it isn't fair. As one Vancouver mother was quoted as saying, "We live in a world in which we look after our money in glass towers and our children in church basements." Business values business.

I think of it this way. As a capable, modern woman, I have completely equal opportunities: to work harder than anyone else in my office and then go home to my second shift of duty.

At a mutual-fund dinner I recently attended, I had the pleasure of sitting next to a very forthright brokerage-firm executive whom I shall refer to as Dwight in order to avoid potential litigation. During the course of the evening, I mentioned this book, and Dwight asked if I felt that the subject matter was still relevant. Was there really any difference between men and women when it came to financial planning?

I said that I felt that there were many differences, starting with the fact that women live longer, earn less money for equivalent work, and are often out of the work force and pension plans for extended periods of time.

Dwight disagreed. "There are more women graduating from medical and law programs now than there are men. There are affirmative-action programs that make it difficult to get a job unless you are a woman, handicapped, or aboriginal. If a woman gets a good education and applies herself whole-heartedly to her career, I believe she will do as well or better financially than an equally competent man will. If she decides to take time off to have a couple of kids, however, or leaves the office every night at four to pick them up at school, then of course she will suffer financially. That's a lifestyle choice. The last thing we need in this world is more people. If you decide to have children, you should be prepared to pay the price."

His obvious frustration and honest political incorrectness made me laugh out loud.

"Dwight," I replied, "I can't argue with your opinions. I do, however, have one question for you. Why should women have to make that choice when men do not?"

His answer floored me. "Because women want children more than men do."

Since then, I've been conducting an informal survey among my male acquaintances, and it appears that Dwight may indeed be speaking for a majority of men. However, this is far too complex an issue to explore in this forum. At its core, the debate is moot. The truth remains that raising children is an incredibly expensive endeavour, and women bear the greatest portion of the economic disadvantages of child rearing. We face prejudice in the workplace when we are in our child-bearing years because employers are nervous that we will begin a series of maternity leaves just about the time we become indispensable to the firm. Even job sharing and flexible hours can ultimately serve to ghettoize mothers—you can stay in the work force through job-share programs, but you won't get promoted to those jobs that demand more than 40 hours a week, as in almost all management and executive positions. We lose RSP contribution room, Canada Pension Plan benefits, and private pension benefits. We are more likely to start our own businesses or choose occupations that offer flexibility as opposed to long-term benefits, so it is far less likely that we will have access to a pension plan at all. If we divorce, our husband's economic well-being will invariably improve while ours is diminished.

As the mother of two amazing children, I wouldn't do it any differently for the world, but facing these realities has been wonderfully helpful to me. First, I was able to give myself credit for my accomplishments, and I was forced to decide what was most important to me. No, I don't have a PhD. I've never been to Europe, and I don't know how to golf, but I have raised two of the most beautiful people I know. Secondly, I was able to start negotiating a better deal for myself. If two people decide to have children together, it is imperative that they start with a financial plan that is fair to both. Thirdly, this information gave me a practical basis on which to begin taking advantage of the assets I do have. My financial picture is immeasurably better than my mother's or grandmother's, and I have opportunities that they couldn't even dream of.

Whether our income is increasing because of employment opportunity, or because divorce settlements are fairer, or because we live longer, we are seeing an undeniable trend. Women are controlling ever-larger portions of the nation's wealth. And our new opportunities are creating new challenges. What do we do with the money?

Before we begin, we have to commit to becoming the architects of our own financial destiny. This is not something that will happen *for* or *to* us. If we desire this quality of life, we must create it through our own efforts.

Most of the married women I see in my practice include their husbands in the financial decision-making process, which makes sense. How can a partnership not include participation in something so fundamental to happiness?

Unfortunately, this inclusion doesn't go both ways. I used to believe it was because men were excluding their wives, encouraging dependence. Then I began inviting women to planning workshops, and was absolutely blown away by the number of times I heard, "My husband takes care of all that stuff . . . you should talk to him." I realized that I was seeing the equivalent of "my wife is better at taking care of _____ (the cooking, the cleaning, the kids . . .)." Yes, until you connect the dots and realize that *money is the stuff of life,* this can be boring, mundane, intimidating work, and yes, I know how busy you are. If there were one thing that I could convincingly say to every Canadian woman, it would be this: take responsibility for your own financial well-being. A life partnership should be a partnership. Two equal partners with equal power, equal responsibility, and equal access to information that affects the partnership. It may feel unloving to insist on being equally involved in all financial-planning and money-management matters, but it *is* unloving to burden our significant other with a role that can only be effectively managed by both partners.

Too many women, myself included, have been socialized to believe that their husbands will be the primary source of financial security. Without thinking about it too deeply, this was my world view: "Yes, I will do the majority of the cooking and the cleaning and the child caring and the compromising. And you, having the higher income-earning potential ($1.00 for every $0.64 I can earn, comparing the earnings of married women to married men, as of 1996) will ensure that my sacrifices are rewarded and I have a comfortable future."

Then I started sitting across my desk from women and listening to their stories. I came to understand in my heart what I had known previously only in my head:

- ◆ Marriages fail. One out of three marriages will end in divorce. (The other two apparently end in death.) The men in our lives can leave us, and when they do, so does their earning power. Most of their pension. All of the financial strength and promise.

- ◆ People get sick, or have accidents, and lose their income-earning ability. And if you have been focusing on getting the laundry done and the kids to Little League, it can be a big shock when you realize that you are either going back to work or losing your home. Either way, the lifestyle you enjoyed is a thing of the past.

- ◆ People die. My next-door neighbour lost her husband last year to a heart attack. He was a healthy, vital, trim 41-year-old man. It was absolutely heartbreaking watching her leave for work in her IGA uniform, often with tears in her eyes, in the months after his death. Please God, let me (or my family) mourn with dignity—and a comfortable insurance settlement. It can be worse than having to go back to work after a two-week "compassionate leave." I've spoken with women who had no idea how in debt they were until they lost both their partners and their lifestyles.

◆ Even great income earners can lose their jobs. If the primary income earner in your partnership is in middle or upper management, or is an executive, you should know that the average time before someone in these positions is re-employed is one to two years.

◆ People cannot share identical hopes and dreams, or the same investment style, or the same tolerance for risk. As a matter of fact, when it comes to finances, opposites really do attract. Allowing someone else to take care of the finances can leave you with some really nasty surprises: "You invested all of our money in Latin America? Now why would you do that?"

If you are in a traditional marriage, or end up in one some day, you may find yourself in a little non-verbal dance that goes something like this:

Since you are the man, you must know more about money than I do because that is what society expects of you, and of me. So, even though I'm pretty good with money, perhaps even better than you are, and care more about it, we'll pretend that's not true and you can take care of it. Because if I act too competent or controlling, you may not feel as much of a man, and that would be worse than losing our money.

I don't mean to imply that all men are this way, or all women are that way. We all know exceptions—we may be exceptions. However, I know there are some things that I'm more likely to have in common with my women friends than I have with my husband. Those differences are important—precious. They include the way I see the world, the way I use language, the way I think, the way I make decisions. There was a time I denied these differences, because I had been socialized to believe that those traits that we view as feminine were less valuable. It was better to be stoic than sensitive, better to be left brain than right brain. Better to make decisions based on pure logic rather than logic *and* emotion. Nonsense! There is no "better." There is only balance. Imagine a world in which we both acknowledged our differences and revered them.

Every day, I see women who are unprepared for the future, who are living lives diminished by the sacrifices they've made. Why?

One of my friends told me recently that she has encouraged her daughter to marry a man with money. When you're 40-something, it is plain to see that "in love" is probably just another term for infatuation, and that it is easier to maintain a relationship after the bills are paid than when you are lying awake at night worrying about them. As a financial adviser, however, the advice I give my daughter is somewhat different. I couldn't say it better than Joanne Thomas Yaccato at one of her recent presentations: "I decided that as far as money was concerned, I wanted to *become* the man I wanted to marry!"

When I was in the process of awakening from my own trance, I had a heart-stopping epiphany. It occurred to me suddenly, after 20-some-odd years of struggling with the concept. The all too rare best-case scenario is this: my husband continues to earn a good income, and he is generous, never leaves me, never makes me need to leave him, outlives me, and invests well. Without taking responsibility for my own financial well-being, the most I can ever hope for is to be *dependent* on a financially independent man.

I realized that I had to learn to meet my own needs. I needed money of my own, money I didn't have to ask or account for. And this was the source of much distress in my home for some time—I had to learn to share domestic tasks more equally, so that I had the energy I needed to create the financial well-being I was seeking, and to replenish myself on the journey.

For many women, the first step on the road to financial freedom doesn't really have anything to do with money. It is that point at which we recognize that we are in charge of our own financial well-being—not our husband, our boyfriend, or our partner. By educating ourselves, by insisting on equal decision-making power when it comes to investments, and by planning for our own retirement needs, we liberate both ourselves and those we may have depended on.

9

The Stepping Stones of Investment Success

Money, which represents the prose of life, and which is hardly spoken of in parlours without an apology, is, in its effects and laws, as beautiful as roses.

RALPH WALDO EMERSON

Despite the fact that they had to raise us, the parents of my generation may have been the luckiest people in the history of the world. Not only did they seem to lead charmed lives in which acceptance into the university of their choice was a given and jobs came easily, but everything they bought tended to immediately increase in value and continue to do so until they sold it. When our parents say that "things were different when we were kids," they're right. From a financial perspective, it was easier.

Why? Largely because we homo sapiens love to do what comes naturally, and when the soldiers of North America returned home after the Second World War, they celebrated their survival and victory in the oldest way known to humankind. They procreated at an unprecedented rate. I know, the last thing we want to think about is procreation and our parents in the same context, but, believe it or not, it gets worse.

You'd have to be living in a cave to escape the fact that the baby boomers have shaped trends and created economic reality for the last 40 years. The huge mass of bouncing babies born between 1946 and 1964 (perhaps the world's longest postwar "celebration") continues to move through life with all the subtlety of glaciers moving over the continent during the Ice Age.

When the boomers wanted cars, Lee Iococca became a superstar.

When we all went to work, jobs became scarce. When it was time for us to settle down en masse and raise our families, real estate prices skyrocketed. Interest rates went higher and higher as millions of boomers lined up to apply for mortgages.

The New Investment Landscape

In the '80s, as our parents and then our oldest siblings, the early baby boomers, began preparing for retirement, real estate prices and interest rates were at an all-time high. Of course, the largest bulge in the baby-boom stream was 30-something, and they were lining up to buy a house. The '80s were also the last decade in which we also still believed, at least to some degree, in the concept of spending our career with one company and then retiring in the benevolent grace of the corporation's pension plan.

As recently as a decade ago, it was possible to live a financially comfortable life and prepare for retirement without ever entering the murky world of investment, and many did. We could get along just fine without ever knowing what "standard deviation" was. The stock market was for rich playboys with too much time and money on their hands, and a bond was something that Grandma gave us on our birthday when she was feeling flush.

Times have changed. Just as women can't rely on their husbands to be their retirement plan, and none of us can rely on corporations to provide security, we have had to let go of the idea of investment ignorance as bliss.

Today, we know that what we don't know *can* hurt us. Pension plans are too rare and getting rarer. Social retirement programs are threatened. And our homes will not always increase in value—certainly not enough to fund the 30-plus years we may live after retirement.

Will Rogers once said that "the best investment is real estate, because they aren't making any more of it." David Cork, co-author of *The Pig and the Python,* has a fabulous response to this. "Yes," he says, "but have you flown over Canada lately?" That's a *lot* of underdeveloped real estate.

The baby-boom generation is fully one-third larger than the generation behind it, due to the depressed birth rate of the Depression period, and is followed by a generation only three-fourths its size. When we went out to find houses, there simply weren't enough out there, and prices soared. What's going to happen when we are ready to sell?

Real estate prices will not automatically go up for the next 30 years, as they have for the last 30. If you doubt this statement, just ask yourself this question: If the next generation is 75 percent smaller than mine, who is going to buy my house when I want to sell it? Well-located, attractive properties will continue to attract buyers, but in all likelihood, we are looking at a buyer's market, probably for the next 20 years. In the simplest terms, we have three buyers for every four sellers.

It's a twofold insult to our pocketbooks. Firstly, we are in a time when treading with caution is in order when buying a home. We need to think down the road, to the buyers who may or may not be there when we're ready to sell. (More on this in Chapter 12.) Secondly, if we can't count on an increase in the value of our home to fund our retirement, we better get serious about doing that ourselves.

The bottom line is this: your nest is no longer your nest-egg. Not only has buying and selling home sweet home become a rather precarious adventure, but we can no longer saunter through life in sweet ignorance of stocks, bonds, and mutual funds.

What About GICs?

What the hay is going on with interest rates anyway? Whatever happened to the days when Canada Savings Bonds paid 15 percent? Yes, it's those darn baby boomers again. In our quest to borrow money to fund our expensive home purchases, we drove interest rates up astronomically in the 1980s. There were certainly other factors at play, and as egocentric as we tend to be, North America is not the only player on the world's economic stage. It is difficult to argue, however, with statistical charts that clearly illustrate interest rates rising at exactly the same time as the baby-boomer bulge moved into their first homes.

What's happening with baby boomers now? The largest group of us has been housed for some time, and our children, Generation X, are of university age or older. So, what are we thinking about? Retirement. Saving for retirement, to be exact. Therefore, there are comparatively more money lenders (which is, of course, what a GIC owner is) than there are money borrowers (which is what a mortgage holder is). The law of supply and demand is putting vast downward pressure on interest rates.

Do today's low interest rates mean that GICs are to be avoided?

No. The integrally important factor that most investors overlook is this: When Canada Savings Bonds reached the interest-rate peak of 15 percent in the '80s, inflation was 12 percent! If you held your Canada Savings Bonds outside of an RSP and were in the highest tax bracket, you paid 50 percent of that 15 percent in tax, leaving a return of 7.5 percent. Now, subtract 12 percent for inflation and you have a return of negative 5 percent on your investment. As I write, I'm earning about 4.25 percent on my one-year GIC, and the last report I read showed inflation to be running at less than 1.85 percent. As I hold my GICs in my RSP, as should we all, taxes aren't an issue. Therefore, after inflation is factored in, my "real return" is positive 2.4 percent. Even if I unwisely chose to hold my GICs outside my RSP, my real return would be positive .275 percent. I can't stress this point too strongly. Interest rates are *more* favourable now than they were when they were in the double digits.

This small blessing, however, it not going to fund our retirement by itself. Over the long run, it is equity investment—investment in business—that has historically provided the greatest returns.

To flourish in this new environment, we as investors need to be educated, aware, and active. At the risk of being redundant, it is so important to get professional advice. For now, though, let's just take a look at the basics.

I don't profess to be anything but a conservative, road-weary, once-burned-twice-shy veteran of the financial industry, both personally and professionally. I've seen investors prosper and lose fortunes, and my family and I have been in both camps. I can only offer you the truth as I know it, and the truth as I know it can be reduced to the following statements:

◆ As *Money Magazine* once stated, "There is no one right investment. However, we believe that the one that comes closest, for most people, is a mutual fund." I emphatically agree. However, as Duff Young, author of *FundMonitor*, so succinctly puts it, the key to successful mutual-fund investment is separating "the winners from the dogs." The mutual funds I own and recommend to my clients are managed by veterans with proven track records in both bull and bear markets. They outperform their peers. They do not take undue risks, and they do not deviate from their stated objectives to chase returns in changing times. They've been around, and they provide superior management. (More on this in the next chapter.)

◆ The rate of return you can expect will always be matched by the degree of risk you are exposed to. There are no exceptions. This is a universal principle that applies to both life and investment.

◆ Unless you're an adrenaline junkie, an investment that provides stable returns of 10 percent will add more to the quality of your life than the fund that provides a 30 percent return one year and drops 20 percent the next.

◆ Must we really invest in the equity markets? In a word, yes. Once consumer debt has been paid off, and risk-management and cash-reserve needs have been met, it is time to look to the future. Unless interest rates rise dramatically in relation to taxes and inflation, which is very unlikely, only business ownership will provide the returns we need to outpace inflation and see our net worth grow. For most of us, the most practical way to participate in business ownership is by purchasing shares (or stocks, or equities—the terms are interchangeable) through mutual-fund investment. However, there are as many ways to invest in the equity market as there are cars to buy. Don't let yourself end up in a Corvette if you're a Volvo kind of woman, or in the Formula 500 when your idea of a good time is a Sunday drive to the Farmer's Market.

Getting Started

A few weeks ago, a girlfriend and I were discussing her investments, and she mentioned that a particular financial adviser had done such a fabulous job for one of her colleagues that he was able to retire eight years ahead of schedule. Early retirement was such an appealing possibility that she was thinking about moving her accounts into the care of this master adviser.

"Wait a minute," I said, perhaps a bit jealous, "that isn't what financial advisers do. We help people make the right decisions and avoid the wrong ones. But we don't control the markets. I would bet anything that your colleague started with a relatively large portfolio 10 years ago, invested in Canadian and U.S. equities, and simply stayed invested through what turned out to be the greatest bull market in history. His adviser helped him make the right decisions: to invest in equities rather than lending his money to banks so that they could profit from it, and to avoid panic selling during the downturns. Did the adviser create the bull market? No. Did he predict the strength and duration of the bull market? Did he pick the highest-returning stocks or mutual funds? It's very, very unlikely, and if so, frankly, he was incredibly lucky."

Conversely, an acquaintance recently mentioned to me that his adviser had "lost him money last year." Advisers don't do that either.

This is the thing. The stock market goes up and the stock market goes down. Over time, however, it goes up because stocks represent businesses, and the economy of a society is driven by the growth of its businesses. It is possible, however, even likely, to buy the right investments for the wrong time frame, or for the wrong investor personality. It is nothing short of dangerous to invest without the clear vision of an articulated financial plan.

My driving instructor once told me that an accident is the result of three separate but connected errors, never just one. Similarly, investment success is the product of three connected, equally integral forces. There is only one, unfortunately, that we as investors have complete control of—our behaviour.

I. *Successful Investor Behaviour*

Successful investors are aware that there are certain things they have to take care of prior to worrying about where to invest, or with whom. As is said of charity, investment success also begins at home, with the following fundamentals:

1. Having money to invest. By paying yourself first and avoiding debt, you can send your money out to work for you early and often. It's so simple. No money, no investment. Expecting a financial adviser or a magical investment to make up for the saving you didn't do sets you up for failure by stimulating the two demons of money management: fear and greed. Fear and greed then make you vulnerable to bad decisions, unnecessary risks, and empty promises.

2. Working with a comprehensive financial plan that ensures you've got the basics covered. You don't seek to earn 12 percent in taxable income on your mutual funds while paying 16 percent in after-tax income on your credit-card balances. You have a cash reserve, and disability and life insurance where appropriate. Stock markets go up and down in value. If they didn't, there would be little real opportunity. Lows can benefit the savvy investor as much as the highs. However, if you have to cash in your investments when the market is down because you've lost your job or suffered a health crisis, it doesn't matter how fabulous your investments were, or how much they eventually earn for other people. Good investments will never compensate for poor planning.

3. The ability to have effective professional relationships. Just as in your personal life, success in professional relationships depends on both *finding* the right person and *being* the right person. You need effective communication skills, you need to know what you want, you need to be able to stick to a plan, you need to be able to trust when trust is appropriate and end the relationship when it is not. I could go on for pages about this, which I'll prove in Chapter 13, where I cover all of the fundamentals of financial professionals, what they do, and how to identify and find the advisers you need.

4. Understanding the principles of investment, and the nature and purpose of the investments you own.

II. The Benefits of Professional Advice

Financial advisers don't create investment returns, and we can't even predict them on anything but guaranteed investments. We aren't psychic, and if we say we know where the stock markets or interest rates are going, or what is going to happen in Asia, we're either lying or hopelessly deluded. However, a financial adviser can help you develop a plan, help you to stick with it, and help you sort through the absolutely overwhelming amount of information out there in order to determine what's relevant to you. With the help of tax and legal professionals, we can help you pay the least amount of tax you are legally obligated to pay, and to structure your affairs in a way that most benefits you and your family. We can talk you out of buying that Internet stock that's about to go to the moon that you heard about in the bathroom at the mall. We can monitor your investments and advise you if adjustments to your portfolio become necessary, so you don't have to worry about it.

III. The Investments We Choose

Let's take a look at investing from the inside of the industry. It's important to understand what these things called "shares" or stocks or equities, are, and what purpose they serve to the corporations that issue them. Believe it or not, this part is pretty simple. As a matter of fact, it is so simple, I'm going to let my 10-year-old daughter and 11-year-old niece demonstrate it for you.

Teryl and Shari were and are young entrepreneurs. At ages six and seven, they developed an intricate and laborious plan to open their own printing studio when they reach their teens. Shari, a talented artist, plans to do all of the artwork, and Teryl, a budding photographer, will take the photos. Their intent is to produce one-of-a-kind calendars, postcards, and greeting cards.

Teryl has an investment trust account that she plans to use to fund her share of the initial costs of the business—the darkroom, paper and photographic supplies. Shari hopes to arrange a loan from her mom. They have decided that they will share a bedroom, either Shari's or Teryl's, and make the other bedroom into their darkroom. My home office will also, apparently, be their office.

As they discussed their future plan on our way back from the beach one day, I asked how they were planning to market their products. Were they going to sell at craft fairs or through stores? After intense and heated discussion, they decided that the best way to sell their work would be through the Internet and mail order. They know they won't be likely to make a lot of money on any one product, so they sure don't want to share their small profit with a store owner, or pay for a craft booth.

"We can get Uncle Marty to set up a Web site for us," Shari said.

"That's a good idea," I said, "but how will people find your Web site? Do you think people will just do a search for Teryl and Shari's one-of-a-kind calendars and cards and find you? Maybe you should think about advertising."

They both agreed that advertising was a good idea, but it wasn't in the budget. They were going to have to raise some more money.

I explained that there are two ways a business can get more money or "capital" in order to grow. The first is to borrow it. When you have a small business, that usually means borrowing from friends and relatives. When you have a medium-size business, you borrow from the bank. And when you have a big business, or you are a government with almost unlimited powers to raise money through taxation, you issue a bond offering. A bond offering is an arrangement whereby a corporation or government offers investors the opportunity to lend it money in exchange for a certificate (bond) that states that the money (principal) will be paid back on a specific date, along with a stated rate of interest.

This is where the investors come in. When a company or government issues a bond offering, it has to be reasonably certain that investors will want to lend it money at the rate of interest it is offering. Obviously, the higher the risk of the company/government *not* being able to meet its obligations, the higher the rate of interest it will have to offer in order to attract buyers. That means, if the interest rate you are being offered is higher than the current market rates, you can be absolutely sure that the risk is higher as well. For our purposes, we will limit discussion to the highest grade, AAA bonds.

Over the last 30 years, high-grade corporate and government bonds have provided an average annual return of 7.7 percent, or 2.4 percent after inflation. Canadian equities, stocks representing ownership in Canadian businesses, provided average annual returns of about 11 percent before inflation, or 7.3 percent after, for the same time period. So why would an investor choose to buy bonds over equities?

The answer is in the time frame. What do you plan to do with the money, and when?

An Equitable Suggestion

The bottom line is this. If your time horizon is long enough, you will earn the greatest returns by investing in a well-diversified, high-quality, well-managed portfolio of equities, that is, by investing in business. However, a too-short time horizon makes you vulnerable to market cycles that may last a very long time. If you don't have at least a 10-year time horizon, you probably shouldn't be in equity investment. Yes, the market could go through the roof next year. If it does, fabulous. But it could also go through the floor, and if you need your money next year, what do you do? Well, perhaps you can take out some money on your line of credit and wait for things to turn around. But what if they don't turn around for three years? Or 10? If you invested in certain sectors of the U.S. equity market, for instance, at the height of what was known as the "go-go market" in 1968, the value of your holdings did not make it back to the amount of your original investment until 1982. That is a long time to wait to get back to zero. Is that likely to happen again? Probably not. However, it is a possibility, and one you have to be aware of when structuring your affairs.

The following graphs explain risk more clearly than I ever could.

The first graph shows us average annual returns over a 30-year period. As you can see, there are a number of years that were not very pretty. Seventeen, as a matter of fact. And what a lot of investors miss and too many advisers don't point out is that you don't start at zero and go up or down. When you invest, you invest at whatever price the investment is at the moment you hand over your cash. So if that investment does not go up but down in value, you go with it to the lowest price, and then you have to make

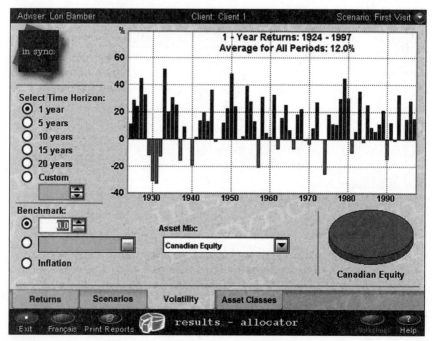

Source: Trimark Investments

your way back to the price at the time of your original investment. In that way, my 1998 RSP contribution into an equity fund that earned minus 2.1 percent last year actually went down almost 9 percent for me, because I invested at the very height of its value in 1998. Similarly, if someone had invested in 1979, 1980 would be an ugly year.

As you'll note, between 1924 and 1997, the average return on Canadian equity investment was 12 percent. Lovely. We like 12 percent, but that's the average over a 73-year time period. However, there were 17 one-year periods with negative returns. We don't like negative returns, but we can live with them—unless we have to sell during those periods.

The graph below shows why equities are not only suitable as a long-term investment but eminently desirable. This is for the same time period, beginning in 1924, but you are shown one-year returns averaged over ten-year periods. That is, during a ten-year period, returns may have been up 20 percent for the first five years and down 20 percent the latter five, which means the annual return would be zero for that ten-year period. Each line in the graph represents the ten-year period ending that year, so for 1933, for instance, you are seeing the average return, per year, for the years from 1924 to 1933.

As you can see, if one had the luxury of staying invested in Canadian equities for at least 10 years, there was only one period in which average returns over that 10-year period were negative: after the crash of 1929. Sounds

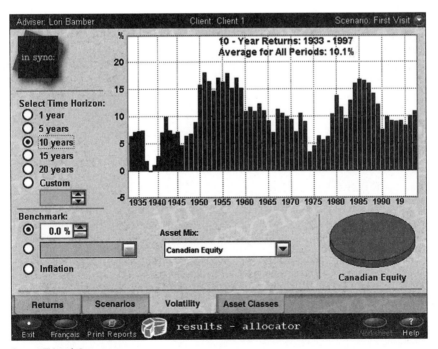

Source: Trimark Investments

simple, doesn't it? Does that mean that everyone that invested in Canadian equities and held them for 10 years made money? Absolutely not.

The figures shown are *averages.* They represent a basket of stocks, or equities, some of which did extremely well, and some did very poorly. If you owned the former, you might have made a lot of money. If you owned the latter, you might have lost some or all of the money you invested. So how do you know, in advance, which stocks to buy? My answer to that question is, "You don't." Trying to pick the stocks that are going to go up in value and avoid their poorer-performing siblings is called "stock picking," and in my opinion, it's to be avoided at all costs. If you indulge in stock picking, or allow someone to do it for you, you run the risk of investing in companies that fail. Perhaps they are poorly run, or produce only products that are no longer in demand. Perhaps they simply fall prey to overwhelming competition. Whatever, the bottom line for us as investors is a) we lose money and b) we don't make money, which is why we're investing in the first place.

In my humble opinion, there is only one way to make money over the long run in equities, and that is to invest in a **well-diversified portfolio of blue-chip companies.** For many of us, those with less than $100 000 we can put aside for at least 10 years and forget about, that leaves two options.

The first is to invest in companies like Disney, Coca-Cola, and GE, that are really not companies but conglomerates, with more power and economic stability than most countries. However, even these companies have on-again, off-again love affairs with stock buyers. You're still putting your eggs in one basket, even if it is a basket the size of Mount Everest.

The second is to invest in mutual funds, which merit their own chapter. Stay tuned, it's coming up.

Bonds and Diversification

As evidenced by the graphs above, there are times when equities in general simply fall out of favour with investors. There are an endless number of reasons for this, or more accurately, an endless number of theories as to why this occurs. At its core, however, a bear (or declining) market is the result of a loss of faith. Things have occurred that lead investors to believe that stocks will decline in value. They stop buying and start selling, thereby creating the reality they feared. At times like this, it is comforting to own something other than equities, which brings us back to bonds.

In addition to creating a vehicle with which corporations can borrow large sums of money, bonds serve three purposes in the investment market. Professional and sophisticated traders buy bonds in order to speculate on interest rates. If rates go up, the value of the bonds they hold, paying the old, lower rate of interest, go down. If rates go down, the value of the bonds they hold, paying the old, higher rate of interest, go up. If you think you're up to it, go for it. I know a lot of bond traders, but not a lot of rich bond traders.

The second and more common reason investors buy bonds is diversification. Implied in the old adage "don't put all your eggs in one basket" is the very real possibility of dropping that basket. As we know, stocks, or equities (the two terms are interchangeable), sometimes drop. When they do, it's nice to have another basket. Let's call it our "bond basket."

Stocks and bonds tend to move up and down together, because when interest rates are high, bond prices are down. High interest rates also depress business growth and profits leading to lower equity prices. However, stocks go up and down a lot, and bonds go up and down a little. If your equity portfolio is down 30 percent, as it may have been in September/October '98, it is nice to know that your bond portfolio is only down 5 percent or 6 percent. If the worst happened and you did have to sell something, better to have the option of selling an investment that is down 6 percent than one that is down 30 percent, right?

The third reason that investors buy bonds is that high-grade bonds, the kind issued by governments and large, stable corporations, are very secure. Bonds are almost always backed by the assets of a company or organization; that is, if the worst occurred, the assets of the company would be sold and the proceeds paid out to the bondholders. In the case of a government, the collateral is the government's almost unlimited ability to continue squeezing taxes out of the citizens it represents. Unless the company or government that issued the bond fails, both the yield (the interest or rent paid to you for the use of your money) and the principal (the money you lent) are secure. In this way, bonds are like the GICs issued by banks, but they often offer a slightly higher rate of interest. They are also an attractive alternative for high-net-worth investors who are concerned about the limited $60 000 CDIC (Canadian Depository Insurance Corporation) guarantee on their bank investments. (See the Glossary for further information on CDIC coverage.)

Now let's return to Shari and Teryl and their printing business. Their printing business will definitely be small, meaning they will have to put the squeeze on my sister and me for their advertising costs. For the sake of this discussion, however, let's pretend that they started their business when they first conceived the idea four years ago. Now it is a huge success. They sell more calendars and postcards than McDonald's sells hamburgers. However, they now need money to fund their latest huge expansion into the European calendar market.

On the advice of their agents, wheeler-dealer types from a major bro-kerage firm, Shari and Teryl decide to do a common-share offering. They like the idea of "going public," because it allows them to take some of their profits out of the company without having to sell it or lose control of its management. With common shares, the investor usually has voting rights in the management of the company but is not guaranteed either dividends or interest.

If the same corporation had issued bonds, preferred shares, and common shares, any income over operating expenses would be used first to pay inter-est to bondholders. Secondly, the preferred shareholders would receive any dividends—their share of the company's profits—due to them, hence the name preferred. Any remaining profits would be distributed as dividends to common shareholders. All common shareholders get to vote on manage-ment issues, but unless they control a majority of the shares, no individual controls the destiny of the company.

After making their decision, Teryl and Shari begin by having a team of professional business evaluators come in and evaluate the business, including everything from supplies and buildings to the value of the "goodwill" that Teryl and Shari have developed with their regular clientele.

Through their advisers, Shari and Teryl apply to a stock market, the Toronto Stock Exchange, or TSE, to list their stock, creating a public mar-ket in which to buy and sell shares. Their initial share offering is called an Initial Public Offering, or an IPO, and investors are very excited about being able to participate in this hot new business. The moment that Teryl & Shari Inc. starts to trade, the markets go wild. Analysts and savvy professional investors have been watching this company, and they know about the European expansion. They believe that the company's profits are going to skyrocket, taking their stock price with them. They can't buy TSI fast enough, and because they all want the same stock, the price keeps going up, just like it would at any other market.

Uh-oh. After a few weeks of prices that go up like a hot-air balloon, the market sniffs bad news. Some bureaucrat in Europe is stonewalling TSI's expan-sion. Share prices plummet. The bureaucrat then meets with Shari and Teryl and is charmed. The press reports it and share prices skyrocket. And so on.

Eventually, however, whether the investment world welcomes them with open arms and wallets or with disdain that results in falling prices, these "new issues," as they're called, generally settle into pretty stable trading patterns. If the stock market in general goes up 5 percent in a day, TSI goes up 5.2 per-cent. If the stock market goes down 3 percent, TSI may go down 4 percent.

Why the variances? Who knows? The experts will offer dozens of theories, all of which sound equally plausible, but next time, there will be dozens of new theories that are equally plausible and equally unlikely to be proven. The key to protecting yourself from the unknown is diversification. If you own the stocks of fifty companies and five of them diminish in value, your portfolio will still do well. If equities all go down in value and you also hold bonds, which don't, you're in much better shape than if you owned only equities.

Diversification

This may be the most important concept in investment and financial planning. There are many levels of diversification, all of which are intrinsically linked. However, it is important to understand each level individually:

1. Diversification of asset type: stocks, bonds, GICs, real estate, and "hard" assets such as oil, gas, and gold, which tend to go up in value in times of high inflation. If you're wondering why I haven't mentioned mutual funds, it is because each of these investment types can be held within mutual funds. Mutual funds are pools of investments, not investments themselves.

2. Diversification of industry: stocks and/or bonds issued by corporations in banking, technology, utilities, health care, communications, etc.

3. Diversification of geographical location: Canada, the U.S., global, Europe, or more speculative investment in defined developing markets such as Asia or Latin America. Many investors think of global investment as being rather risky, but in fact, Canada represents only 3 percent of the world's equity markets. We all know, or have at least heard about, investors who lost their shirts in Latin America or Asia. Indeed, this kind of concentration on a specific geographic region where volatile growth is anticipated is risky. Investing in global mutual funds that seek opportunities in diverse locations is not.

4. Diversification of time horizon—the very essence of financial planning. Short-term (less than five years) cash-flow needs must be met through income-producing investments in which there is virtual certainty that capital will not be diminished. Therefore, GICs and short-term bonds are most suitable but produce a low return and unfavourable taxation. Medium-term cash-flow requirements (five to ten years) are most appropriately met through a balanced combination of "secure" investments (five-year bonds, for instance) and "blue-chip" or "value" style mutual

funds with low volatility. Long-term investment requirements may be met with a diversified portfolio of equity investments, with a foundation of globally diversified blue-chip equity investments. It is in the long-term investment program (more than 10 years) that you can take advantage of diversified growth-style investment opportunities, trusting that history will repeat itself and provide occasions to sell at a substantial profit.

5. Diversification of maturity dates. In the '80s, this was usually as complicated as investment planning ever got. High-interest yields on guaranteed products allowed investors to avoid the higher risk/volatility of the equity markets altogether. Sound financial planning was regarded as the process of staggering maturity dates to ensure that cash was available when needed, or that rising interest rates could be accessed through investment of maturing funds. Further protection was offered against falling interest rates, as only a portion of an investor's portfolio would require reinvestment at a given time. In today's vastly different financial universe, this is still an important concept.

There you have it. The basics of investment planning. There are innumerable variables out there: options, futures, strip coupons, debentures, convertibles, commodities, REITs, LPs, etc., etc. If you need more information about these terms, please refer to the Glossary. However, unless you plan on taking up investment planning as a vocation, it doesn't have to be that complicated.

At this point, we move on to mutual funds, the great investment vehicle that has made broad diversification available to investors with as little as $50 in their pockets.

10

Mutual Funds: Pooled Prosperity

. . . if two be together, then they have heat: but how can one be warm alone? And if one prevail against him, two shall withstand him, and a three-fold cord is not quickly broken.

JOHN STEINBECK, *THE GRAPES OF WRATH*

A group of people come to the simultaneous realization that they don't have the time, experience, or knowledge to figure out which stocks are going to do well and when. They've also realized that as individuals, they don't have enough money to buy a well-diversified portfolio, but that if they pool their money together, they do.

An investment analyst who has been analyzing and studying the behaviour of stocks and companies for some time, hears about the group and proposes a joint venture. They put up the money; the analyst and her organization supply the expertise and buy a portfolio of investments she believes will provide strong returns. For a fee. Included in that fee is the cost of administration, marketing, tax reporting, and record keeping. The investors review the investment analyst's record of success, decide they like what they see, pool their money together, and, *voilà*, an equity mutual fund is born.

Now, of course, it doesn't happen exactly this way. Instead, mutual-fund organizations market their funds to potential investors. Really, they market the expertise of their fund managers. Either they hire a staff to tell their story to potential clients, as in the case of bank or no-load funds, or they tell their story to financial advisers. If the financial advisers believe the story is a good one, they tell it to their clients, and if their clients are convinced, they invest their money in the mutual fund. The end result is the same. We have a group of people with money to invest. We have an organization that can provide record keeping, tax reporting, and administration services. We have an investment analyst guru, or a team of them. We have a mutual fund.

Mutual funds are sold in "units," which are valued at the close of each business day by dividing the total value of the underlying holdings by the number of outstanding units. New investors buy in at the current market value, called the Net Asset Value, or NAV. Their money is added to the investment pool, which increases by the new amount and is then divided by that day's unit value. If the units are valued at $10.00, and the investor puts in $1000.00, she receives 100 units. If the price rises to $10.50 the next day, her investment has increased in value by $50.00, or half a percent. Conversely, if it drops to $9.50, her investment has decreased in value by $50.00. Since 1924, as we saw in Chapter 9, Canadian equities have returned an average of 12 percent. In any given month, year, or certainly day, the value will fluctuate. If historical averages hold true, however, and your profits are reinvested in the fund, a service the fund manager will provide at your request, you can expect your $1000.00 to grow to $29 959.92 over 30 years. Dreamy!

With more than 2000 mutual funds to choose from, it can be somewhat challenging to identify those that best meet your needs. This is where professional advice comes in, but it doesn't have to be wearing a suit—a jacket will do. There are a number of excellent mutual-fund books published every season, and they all do a relatively good job of explaining the basics of mutual funds, mutual-fund performance, and comparative analysis. Check out the Recommended Reading section for some of my favourites. If you're on the Internet, the Web is now rife with mutual-fund analysis tools—it will blow your mind. And if you find yourself becoming confused or overwhelmed, you can always call your financial adviser.

A mutual fund's returns and risks are determined by its underlying holdings. To understand risk, we first have to define it. "Risk" in the investment world is the likelihood that a particular investment will not do what we expect it to. To analyze risk, we often rely on a measure we call "standard deviation," which tells us how often the investment deviates from its expected return. The deviation can be positive or negative. If we expect an equity fund to return 12 percent, for example, a deviation will occur when it dips to 6 percent and when it rises to 18 percent. When I'm recommending investments, I always look at how often the returns for a particular fund were negative. The zero benchmark has real emotional value to most investors. It is far easier to sleep when an investment is up 1 percent rather than down 1 percent, even if the difference is only 2 percent, simply because we never want to see our investment drop below its latest, greatest value.

Stocks or Mutual Funds?

This is a question that financial advisers still hear quite often. I find that even clients who have invested successfully in mutual funds for years come in for their portfolio review and ask if they should be buying Microsoft or some hot new Internet stock. There is a certain cachet to buying and selling individual stocks. It seems more sophisticated somehow . . . more fashionable. Mutual funds have become so pedestrian.

Stock picking is certainly more challenging to profit from. I'm racking my brain trying to think of one stockbroker, among the dozens I know, who became rich by investing his or her own money in the stock market as opposed to earning a bundle on commission income by selling stocks to clients. Mmmm, no. Can't think of one. They are out there, I'm sure; they're just very rare. What does that tell us about stock picking, then? If the professionals aren't getting rich doing it, what are the chances for the rest of us?

Personally, I quite happily pay management fees in order to employ the expertise of managers like those at Templeton Growth, AIC Diversified Canada, and Ivy Canadian. "Past performance," that is, the record of a fund's returns over a period of history, does not tell us anything about what that fund will return in the future. It does, however, provide a glimpse into the ability of the fund managers to outperform similar funds and the market under various conditions.

Why try to outguess seasoned professionals with proven ability? As Ann Eynon, a seasoned, well-respected financial planner with the Rogers Group in Vancouver, once said to me, "The longer I'm in business, the more conservative I find myself becoming. When clients asks if I think they should be investing in Asia, for instance, my response is now usually something like, 'Well, maybe. I don't really know. But if Asia is the place to be, I do know that the managers of Templeton Growth will be there long before we hear about it.'"

Experienced planners like Ann know something we should all remember: success in any venture is a product of knowing what we are good at and delegating the rest to the experts in that area. There are good funds and bad funds, and a financial adviser can help you determine which is which. Once you've determined which are the best funds, there is simply no point in chasing short-term returns. If everyone is talking about a particular investment, it's pretty likely that the party is already winding down.

Fund managers make mistakes and have bad years. Templeton Growth, with an average annual return of *15.6 percent since 1954,* a stunning performance record, had a comparatively bad year last year. It zigged, the market zagged. I ask you, if it can happen to Templeton, what are the chances for the average investor? Or for a broker, the one who is still earning a living from commissions? Is this evidence that mutual funds are a bad idea, or that we should seek out the greatest expertise and experience available to us? I really believe it's the latter.

Mutual funds do have their dark side—management expenses. Management expenses are the costs you pay to participate in a fund. These are annual fees collected by the fund managers directly from the investment pool to pay their salaries, the cost of administration and reporting, and the cost of distribution. If you are blessed with a large portfolio, the Management Expense Ratios, or MERs, as they are known, can be hefty. It is therefore important to compare MERs along with performance and volatility when shopping for funds. Speaking only for myself, I'm absolutely thrilled with the value I receive for my fee dollars. Remember, a fund's returns are reported net of MERs. If your mutual fund reports a return of 14 percent in 1998, and has an MER of 2.3 percent, the fund's returns were actually 16.3 percent. You can get information on MERs, and almost everything else you need to know about a fund, from its prospectus. As I tell my clients, you don't have to read these from cover to cover if you'd rather not—they can be both intimidating and dull. However, you *absolutely must* read the sections on fees, charges, and risks. If you can't be bothered to read the section on risk, girlfriend, it is probably best to stay with GICs and Canada Savings Bonds.

The Three Basic Asset Types

OK. Let's take a closer look at the various types of mutual funds. Reduced to its very essence, asset allocation comes down to diversification among the three fundamental asset types:

1. **Cash.** In this category, we have savings accounts, GICs, Treasury Bills (or T-Bills) and bonds that will mature in the near future, usually within 90 days. In the mutual-fund world, we have Money Market funds, sometimes known as T-Bill funds or Cash Funds. We keep our emergency reserve in cash, and we park money here that doesn't yet have a home, for example, when it is March 1 and we don't know where to invest our RSP contribution. Cash adds a stable base to our portfolio. It won't fund our retirement, but it will never dip below our original investment. Money Market funds often come in both Canadian- and U.S.-dollar varieties.

2. **Fixed-income investments (sometimes called debt securities).**
This category includes bonds, mortgages, and other investments that pay
a "fixed" rate of income. Obviously, these are divine for people who rely
on their investments to provide income, but they also work well for
those of us who prefer golf carts to roller coasters. However, there is
something that you should definitely know, and most people don't,
about bond funds. That is, they are not the same and do not serve the
same purpose as bonds. The worthiest purpose for bonds, in my estimate, is to hold until maturity, guaranteeing a fixed rate of return over
a stated period of time along with return of original principal. With a
bond fund, you don't control the maturity dates, and the fund manager
doesn't control the redemption period. If bonds take a beating because
of a significant rise in interest rates, fund holders will start redeeming.
When fund holders redeem, the manager must sell some of the bond
holdings to meet the cash requirements—at a discount. Bond-fund
returns are not guaranteed, nor are they "fixed." They will fluctuate, generally not as dramatically as equities, but their value can rise and fall.
Bond funds are not a risk-free investment, and they are definitely not
the same as holding a high-quality bond. However, they will add a
degree of stability and diversification to your portfolio.

Something you should be even more careful about with bond funds
is the MER. It is harder for a fund manager to provide added value (i.e.,
higher returns) to offset management-expense charges in bond funds
when interest rates are low and fixed, and the bonds are all high-grade
corporate or government issue. Yes, large investment pools do have opportunities to purchase bond offerings that the average investor does not.
Bond funds can and often do increase in value in addition to providing
interest income when interest rates go down. A bond manager can create capital gains for the fund investors by selling at a profit in these times,
an opportunity that a bond owner may miss. However, shopping for the
lowest MER is always worthwhile.

The fixed-income category includes **mortgage funds**, which invest
in, yes, mortgages. **Dividend funds,** which generally invest in preferred
shares that pay comparatively high and "preferred" dividend income, are
also sometimes referred to as "fixed income." They are also sometimes
referred to as equity funds, which is most accurate. Whatever we call them,
as the companies that offer these returns are often the largest, strongest,
and most profitable, these funds tend to offer lower volatility as well as
tax-advantaged income. High-quality preferred shares have become
rather rare in Canada, so buyer beware—some dividend funds have a

heavy weighting in common shares, which are more volatile and whose dividends are obviously not "preferred."

3. **Equities.** Canadian equities, global equities, U.S. equities, small-cap equities, sector equities, special equities. A long list of equities. Actually, I think these deserve their own section.

I know I said there were three asset classes, but you might read or come across a fourth, known as hard assets or inflation hedges. Hard assets include precious metals, oil and gas, and real estate. The reason for holding hard assets is that they will always rise in value with rising inflation, and tend to do well when both stocks and bonds are floundering. There are many that would disagree, I'm sure, but I believe that if you own your own home, you own enough "hard assets."

Equity Funds: Our Opportunity to Own the World's Greatest Businesses

A few short centuries ago, with rare exception, the only way to own a business was to be born into wealth. Then came the North American dream, the wild frontier in which anyone with perseverance and determination could win both fame and fortune. However, the risks that these individuals faced were considerable—they stood to win everything, or to lose everything. Why? Because in most cases, they couldn't afford diversification. By necessity, they had to invest all of their time, energy, and money into one business. If that business succeeded, the individual flourished. If it didn't, they failed.

Then along came the stock market. At the stock market, which began as a large room with a table in the middle where wealthy men came to play, investors were given the opportunity to spread the risk of business around. With participation in a number of businesses, the failure of one business became less devastating. Unfortunately, at certain points in history, this group of wealthy men forgot that they were buying businesses and began playing with the paper "stocks" themselves, bidding them up far beyond the value of the underlying business, or in fickle, often unconscious collusion, selling them at deep discounts. At its best, however, the stock market became a wonderful, inclusive opportunity, allowing people who were formerly excluded from owning businesses to participate for the first time. There is a dark side to every story, and we now know that too often, these "newbies" became victims of naturally self-interested insiders and unscrupulous brokers. Someone had to buy the stock that was overvalued—someone had to buy the paper that was suddenly revealed to have no real worth. The stock market became known as a scary place.

Then came mutual funds. They've been around for a while, but it wasn't until low interest rates forced us to take another look at the stock market that they began their amazing ascent in popularity. Mutual funds, in one sense, serve the same purpose that labour unions did in the 18th and 19th centuries, but they go a step further. For the first time, equity mutual funds put insiders, corporations, brokers, and new investors *on the same team*. If one did well, we all did well. By pooling our efforts, we created co-operatives with everything we needed to flourish: insider expertise and power, huge pools of capital, efficient record keeping and tax reporting, and teams of skilled analysts to stay on top of the myriad corporate and economic changes that affect our investments.

Mutual funds have created a deeper level of market efficiency. It used to be that a corporation with shares to sell had to go out and market its story to individuals investors. As you can imagine, the costs of doing so were enormous. Today, these corporations market to a handful of fund managers, vastly reducing the costs that have always been passed on to the investor through reduced profitability.

Equity Fund Types

One thing we have enough of in the Canadian mutual-fund market is variety. Before you test the waters, it's important to know what's what.

1. **Canadian Equity.** Funds that invest in large, small, or medium-size Canadian corporations. In the absence of another label, like "growth" or "sector" or "biotech," a Canadian equity fund is usually one that invests in larger, blue-chip Canadian companies. A Canadian equity fund can invest up to 20 percent of its holdings outside Canada and still qualify as pure Canadian content for RRSP investment, and many of them do.

2. **U.S. Equity.** A cab driver on my Disneyland vacation described Canadians as "unarmed Americans." As our artists, writers, and film producers are all too aware, Canada is a teeny, tiny market in relation to our southern neighbour. Keeping all of our investment dollars in Canada is a little like hooking our rowboat to a cruise ship. It is likely we will move in the same direction, but negotiating the wake could get tricky.

3. **Sector and Special Equity.** The premise behind sector management is that certain industries do better than others at certain times, and during these times, fund managers with sector (industry) expertise will fare better than your run-of-the-mill equity manager. Maybe. Some of the performance records certainly bear this theory out. However, my problem with sector funds and geographically specific funds is this: If we invest in a biomedical fund, and the fund manager realizes that biomedical corporations are losing favour in light of rising interest in homeopathic health care, he or she can't call us up and say, "Whoops, we're in the wrong sector. I think we should move to plan *B*." This year, we've seen a raft of consolidations as Asian and Japanese funds became "international" funds, but the Asia crisis happened an eon ago. I want my fund manager to have the freedom to go where he or she believes the profits are, unrestricted by a too-narrow mandate.

Sector, special equity, and geographically specific funds tend to be an answer to a marketing need as opposed to an investor need. They give the financial adviser something a little bit sexier to recommend to their clients, and a product to take off the shelf for the client who calls up and says, "Do you think I should put some money in technology stocks? What about Latin America?" My advice? If you need something sexy, go to a lingerie shop. Your investment portfolio should be as dull and reliable as possible.

4. **International Equity.** Canada represents only 3 percent of the world's equity markets. You need diversification. However, unless you like to play with your money, I advise avoiding geographically specific funds that invest in countries where our rules don't apply. There is an ethical question here, as well. I need to know that I'm not investing in companies that employ children, or pay their adult employees the price of one day's food for one day's labour.

5. **Small Cap (sometimes referred to as "growth").** Higher potential returns, higher volatility. These funds tend to invest in smaller, new corporations that the fund managers believe are about to make it big. Depending on the economy, there can be great profits here, but for the last few years, small caps have fallen out of favour as investors brought their investment ships into safer harbours.

6. **Balanced Funds and Asset Allocations Funds.** These funds strive to provide a balanced portfolio of equities, bonds, and cash within one package. Some are great, some aren't.

7. **Index funds.** Until last summer, the stock markets seemed to go nowhere but up for a decade, and as a result, index funds have really gained in popularity. Essentially, for a very low management fee, usually half a percent or less, you can participate in the returns of those companies that make up a particular index (the "basket" of blue-chip stocks whose prices are tracked to measure the performance of a particular stock exchange). I prefer active management, largely because the market isn't always on its way up. However, index funds are an excellent option for anyone who must buy stock on their own but can't afford real diversification.

Management Styles

When you start comparing equity funds to equity funds, you'll hear about something referred to as "management style." Essentially, management style is just the label that is applied to the criteria that a manager uses when deciding what to buy and what to sell. I love the way Veronica Hirsch, former Fund Manager of the Year and manager of the Hirsch Resource Fund, responds to questions about her management style: "The only style label you can attach to me is opportunistic."

As she so often does, Veronica gets right down to the bottom line. Management styles are too often a label that promotions departments attach to their managers in order to make them more saleable. The reality is that, as an investor, I don't care much about the label. However, when practising **strategic asset allocation,** which is a process of diversifying portfolios across asset types and geographic regions, management style is the third criteria. When I began studying mutual-fund performance graphs, I was amused and surprised to see how similar their up-and-down movements in value were. As investors, we too often think we own a diversified portfolio when in reality we own five Canadian large-cap value-style equity funds that hold essentially the same companies. *Different management styles should result in different underlying portfolios, and therefore provide true diversification.*

1. **Bottom-up.** Where do they come up with these names? A bottom-up investment style involves looking first at the company, not at the stock prices or the markets. How sound and capable is the management of the corporation? How long and impressive is its history? How are its products or services likely to fare over the long run? Is it profitable? Is its debt load reasonable? Is it broadly diversified in terms of products and/or potential markets, or is it likely to suffer under certain market

conditions? Is it vulnerable to the fickle tastes of consumers? To competition? To inflation? Bottom-up managers study a corporation's earnings, cash flow, fundamentals, possible merger activity, management, and the image it enjoys (or suffers) in the public eye.

2. **Top-down.** I can't remember the last time I heard a fund manager say they practised a top-down style—it is rather out of favour. Top-down is obviously the opposite of bottom-up. These managers study the markets and economic trends looking for opportunity.

3. **Value.** A variation on the bottom-up style that is very much in favour. Value managers seek only the strongest companies and buy them when the market, for whatever reason, discounts their stock.

4. **Growth.** Growth managers look for value, but their first priority is finding companies that are likely to experience significant growth in profitability. Growth funds are generally more volatile than value funds because it is usually smaller and medium-size companies that will experience the greatest increase in profitability over the short term. On the other hand, they may not. Hence the volatility.

5. **Momentum.** If a corporation's earnings increase rapidly in relation to previous earnings or earnings of similar companies, momentum managers make the assumption that the trend will continue for some time, creating upward pressure on a stock's price. If everything else is in order, they buy. When earnings drop, they make the assumption that this will cause downward pressure on the stock's price and they sell.

6. **Small-cap or small capital.** Small-cap managers look for the new kids on the block. They may embrace a value, growth, or momentum style, but they seek small companies with big potential for growth in their stock value. As smaller companies are often newly listed companies without much of a historical track record, small-cap investment is at the high-risk end of the equity investment continuum.

Buying and Selling Basics

You buy mutual funds when it's time to invest. Simple as that. You do not try to time the markets because the markets resist timing, even by the virtuosos out there who attempt to do it for a living. You don't buy anything but money-market funds with the money you've put aside for potential car repairs, or for the condo you want to purchase next year. To put mutual-fund investment back into perspective, let's review your financial plan to this point:

1. You have a crystal-clear vision of the life you want to create.

2. You've created order in your affairs, and you have a detailed picture of your living expenses and cash flow. You've cut out any non-pleasure-inducing expenses, and have all your bills debited from your chequing account on payday. You've made monthly contributions to your emergency reserve fund, and will do so until it reaches the amount of three months' net salary.

3. You've reviewed your disability and life-insurance needs with an insurance adviser, and you're comfortable that you have both an adequate disability program and a suitable life-insurance plan. You have the other insurance stuff covered, too, as in car insurance, home insurance, or contents insurance if you are a renter.

4. Either you pay your credit-card balances off monthly, or you have stopped using your cards and have a monthly repayment program in place.

5. You are making monthly contributions to your RSP.

Step five leads us right into mutual-fund investment because one of the smartest ways to invest in equity mutual funds is through monthly pre-authorized purchases into your RSP. You get the benefits of dollar-cost averaging, which means that whether prices are up or down, you invest the same amount every month. When prices are down, you buy more units, thereby lowering your average costs over time. You benefit from disciplined investing, paying-yourself-first peace of mind, and long-term wealth benefits. When everyone else is panicking about what to buy and where to get the money in RSP season, you're laughing all the way to the mailbox with your completed tax returns.

If your employer is willing to make the monthly contribution directly to the RSP trustee as opposed to paying you and having you make the contribution, you can actually have the tax your employer withholds reduced. This is a good news/bad news story. The good news is that if you're in a 40 percent tax bracket, a $400 monthly contribution will only bite $240 off your net pay. The bad news is that you still pay the same amount of tax in the end, so if you would otherwise get a tax refund, don't hold your breath.

In the Years to Come

Now, what to buy. Think diversification. A rule of thumb that some professionals apply to asset allocation is equities minus your age. So, if you are 33, subtract 33 from 100 for a target of 67 percent equity investment within your portfolio. Frankly, though I occasionally employ this rule of thumb, I don't think it applies at all to younger investors—those under 50—and certainly not to those who have their financial houses in order.

This is my advice. It is only my advice, and you should discuss your individual situation with a trusted financial-planning professional who can both educate you about the consequences of your decisions and ensure that nothing has been overlooked. Also, *this advice assumes that you have your financial plan in order to the degree we just went over.*

Sit down and map out your cash-flow needs for the next year. Any money you will need within the year should be in a money-market or savings account, T-Bills (with larger amounts), cashable Canada Savings Bonds (not the new Premium Bonds), or a short-term GIC. Do not put money you'll need over the short term into equities or bonds with maturity dates that extend beyond the time you'll need the money. In the next year, for instance, you may know that the roof is going to need repair, and that you are going to need a tropical vacation. This is not investment money. It is savings.

Now, plan for the next five years. Do you want to upgrade your condo? Buy your first home? It makes me crazy when clients who have earmarked money for their retirement come in and say, "Well, yeah, but we want to take advantage of the Homebuyer's Plan and use it as a down payment." Fine! I mean, that's fine. But your financial adviser should know about that prior to advising you to put your *retirement* money into equities that are now down 7 percent from your original investment *last year.* OK. I'm over it. But you get the picture. For this time frame, it might be alright to put your money into conservative fixed-income funds, but it shouldn't be in equities.

Look further into the future, five to ten years from now. Your needs might include things like returning to university for your master's, having a baby, or taking an extended sabbatical to write a book or see the world. This is why it is so integrally important to have a vision of your future, and why many investment plans go off the rails. If you don't know what you are going to use the money for, you might have the wrong investment plan. Once you have a vision of your family or your sabbatical, you can be clear on the timeline. If it's close to ten years, you may choose a balanced or conservative equity fund. If it's closer to five years, you might invest a small portion in equities and the rest in fixed income.

Now, you have your retirement fund, your freedom 45 money. How do you invest it? That depends on who you are. I'd like to believe that once you've read this book, you are at least a moderately prepared investor who will not panic when the stock market dips 30 percent, but will smile as your monthly purchase buys 30 percent more units. However, I strongly believe that exceeding your comfort level is a universal recipe for disaster. Before you decide to invest, think about how you will feel if this happens. Actually envision it—close your eyes and imagine looking at the numbers on your statement. They are 30 percent lower than they were just last month. The people at your office are talking about Y2K, global recession, and another Great Depression. How do you feel?

If you are in touch with your inner world, you can truly imagine this scenario, and if your response is a shrug of the shoulders and an "oh, well, it will go up again," you may want to think about a broadly diversified equity portfolio. Period. Now, remember, we are talking about money that will be invested for 10 years plus. Historical averages prove beyond a shadow of a doubt that equities provide the highest returns over the long run.

If your response is a sick feeling in the pit of your stomach and a worried call to your financial adviser, you need a significant income component to calm those potential butterflies. In this case, you may want to apply the equities-minus-your-age formula, but you should probably do a risk-tolerance exercise with the help of your financial adviser.

If you can't imagine anything other than selling everything as quickly as possible, don't buy equities at all. Put your money in guaranteed investments. Buy a few more books, read them, do some meditation. Don't tread where you aren't comfortable.

There is nothing wrong with having a low tolerance for risk. There is a prevalent myth that women are more risk averse than men, and that this is the result of a lack of knowledge or sophistication in combination with either a lack of courage or an inability to act with logic rather than emotion. Bull pucky. First of all, it is very smart to avoid what you do not know. When faced with unfamiliar data, it may be manly to pretend you understand completely, but it is not wise. Secondly, I'm finding that many very astute women are simply too busy to stay on top of this stuff. Between holding down full-time jobs, advancing their careers, doing the majority of the domestic and child-care duties, they are just too busy to keep up with the latest jargon and trends. They are not averse to risk. They are averse to complexity. Thirdly, many women still have less money than many men. Often, we work harder for it. Twenty-two percent harder for every dollar, remember? Therefore, we can't afford to take unnecessary risks. In spite of what the language of many investment books would imply, this isn't a game. It is about our families, our well-being, and our quality of life.

Now, you've decided how you will allocate your investment between the asset classes. As Canada represents only 2 percent to 3 percent of the world's equity markets at any given time, it is imperative to aim first for geographical diversification. Then, look at management styles—you don't want to end up buying into two funds with the same underlying holdings. You know, of course, whether or not you are buying funds within or outside an RSP, and if you are shopping for domestic or global funds.

Separating the Best from the Rest

Now you know exactly what kind of fund you want to buy—how do you decide which fund company to buy it from?

Financial advisers have an undeniable advantage in that they are inundated with information on mutual funds every day. Information begins to make much more sense when it's filtered through years of experience. Experience and, hopefully, a certain degree of cynicism, are two of the benefits of professional advice. It is really important to remember that most information provided to prospective buyers is *marketing material,* professionally designed and written by people who are paid big money to minimize any weakness and highlight any strengths.

With more than 2000 funds available, it isn't possible to analyze each one when making a recommendation. Every financial adviser has his or her own strategy. My partner, Rob Potuzak, and I begin by sorting out the funds that don't rate—we don't spend any time analyzing funds that have underperformed for the last three years. Then we sift through the following positive benchmarks:

1. In the asset category in which you're interested, which funds have the best five-year, three-year, and one-year performance records? Which funds appear in the top ten of all three categories?

2. If the top performers haven't been around for five years, did the fund managers previously manage other mutual funds? What was their track record there?

3. Of the top five funds in each period (one-year, three-year, five-year, and ten-year), which are the least volatile? Are there funds that should be taken out of consideration because of high volatility?

4. Should you have any concerns about the fund managers? That is, have they moved from fund family to fund family, or are they new to the industry? Have they proven that their style works equally well in both bull and bear markets?

5. Should you have concerns about the fund family? Is it losing an inordinate number of strong fund managers to other companies? Although it may have one or two strong funds, are there too many disasters in its roster?

6. Which funds tend to do best under the current market and economic conditions? We don't know where the market is going tomorrow, but we do know where it is today.

7. Do you have any concerns about the major holdings of the strongest funds? Are there economic factors looming that threaten this fund's ability to perform?

8. What are the tax advantages or disadvantages of this fund's management style? If the fund is to be held outside of your RSP, what are the tax advantages or disadvantages of this fund's management style?

9. How does the fund's management expense ratio compare to similar funds?

Knowing When to Let Go

It is a mistake to get emotionally attached to your investments. They might perform for you, but they will never love you back. On the other hand, our emotional and psychological design means that not only is it unnatural for us to make good selling decisions, it is likely we will make bad ones. Believe me, investors do far more poorly, in most cases, than their investments. Why? Because we buy high and sell low. Like clockwork.

Every single time we've had a market correction over the 11 years I've been in the industry, there have been clients who call and insist on selling their equity holdings. Their financial adviser's advice is fine when they're buying, but somehow loses its validity when the market dips. They assume that this time is different. This time things aren't going to get better. I'm getting to the point where I won't process equity trades for clients unless they agree to have the Dow Jones Index graph laminated to their coffee tables.

In all honesty, I don't know. It might be different this time. They might be right. But I do know that so far, they have always, eventually, been wrong.

The market goes up and down, but over time, it has always gone up. I also know that if you sell when the market is down 30 percent, you're too damn late.

Unfortunately, our money is close to our hearts, and our stomachs. When prices start dropping, we feel sick. We react as we do to all threats to our well-being, with an adrenaline rush. Fight or flight. Since the market is usually a long way away and we wouldn't know what to do there, that leaves flight. We want to get out, get out now before it's too late, before it drops to zero.

Now, if I owned a portfolio of penny stocks, I'd be worried about it dropping to zero. But let me take another look at the companies in my mutual funds. The Royal Bank. GE. Bombardier. Coca-Cola. Berkshire-Hathaway. You know what? I don't think they are going to zero. And if they do, it won't matter, because our economy will be so shockingly bad that I'll be melting my credit cards to get the minerals from the magnetic strips.

So When Do We Sell?

Find a competent financial adviser you trust and take that person's advice. When your adviser recommends that you sell, sell. When a fund's performance has lagged behind that of its peer funds for three years, sell. If the market fundamentals have changed, get professional advice. For instance, we've seen a lot of turbulence this year and expect more with Y2K on the horizon. While things are still good, we've been moving many of our clients with shorter time horizons into more defensive portfolios. We're not alone. Balanced and income funds have attracted a huge percentage of new money flowing out of equity funds.

The best reason to sell, however, is the same best reason to buy: it's the right time for *you*. Buy when it is time to invest, sell when you're going to need the money. When your situation changes, and your money requirements demand that your ten-year-money is needed within five years, let your financial adviser know and start looking for an opportunity to move out of equities.

Fees and Commissions

Some day I'd like to make a living from book royalties and workshop and seminar fees. My dream is to provide financial planning as a community service because, unfortunately, the people who need it the most are the least likely able to pay. For the time being, however, I live on commission. The truth is that sometimes I earn more from my work with a particular client than I have contributed, and sometimes I earn less. I can put in days of work creating a financial plan and earn $20 in the first two years, or I can have someone come in off the street and place a trade that generates hundreds of dollars in commission. It's a wacky way to earn a living.

I look forward to the day when financial-planning services are provided the way accounting services, legal services, and consulting services are provided: for a stated, agreed-upon-in-advance fee. However, my position has softened over the years because I find that my clients prefer commissions, particularly deferred sales-charge commissions, which don't come out of clients' pockets unless they decide to leave the fund prior to the redemption period. In addition, studies have shown that deferred sales charges can actually increase investor returns by discouraging us from redeeming during scary market periods.

There are arguments to be made on all sides of the equation. For now, let me just explain the way things currently work:

Front-end, Initial Sales, or "Low Sales" Charges

The term refers to a sales commission paid at the time of a mutual-fund purchase and is sometimes called an acquisition fee. This fee is charged on a percentage basis ranging from 0 percent to 9 percent, with an average of 3 percent to 5 percent. There is heavy competition at the lower end, however, with many institutions selling at 1 percent to 2 percent, and even lower on purchases of a minimum dollar amount.

Shop around, and negotiate—but make sure the service package that you buy will meet your needs. The sales charge compensates a financial adviser or planner for services rendered. A lower sales charge can mean warehouse-style service, or an adviser who promises and intends to deliver excellent personalized service but is too busy to return your calls.

There are two alternatives to front-end load: no-load (no fee) and deferred sales charge, or back-end load.

No-load, Zero Commission, "No Objective Help" Funds

There are a number of excellent no-load funds in Canada. However, the nature of the sales environment demands that these funds be sold with economical, "retail" service levels. Salaried staff sell the funds, which may make it more difficult to get an objective opinion. No-load funds generally work best for extremely sophisticated investors who feel comfortable with their knowledge of the market and global economics. For less sophisticated investors, purchasing no-load funds can result in poor investment returns because of "buying high and selling low." It is natural to be drawn to invest when a fund is performing well, and natural to be anxious and sell when a fund is not performing well. Following these natural instincts guarantees poor returns.

A sound partnership with a professional adviser adds another level of protection from panic-driven decisions when self-doubt reaches destructive levels.

Deferred Sales Charges (or DSC)

These funds have taken the market by storm since they became available in the 1980s. With a deferred sales charge, the fund company pays the sales commission on your behalf, but you must leave your investment with that family of funds for a stated period of time, usually six to seven years. If you withdraw earlier, you will be charged a fee on a declining scale. This information is available in the fund prospectus. This is a good option if you plan to leave the funds invested at least long enough to reduce the sales charge to 1 percent to 3 percent because it leaves your principal intact to work for you from day one. Be aware, though, that the DSC is sometimes charged on the full redemption amount rather than the amount of the individual purchase (again, review the fund prospectus).

"Free Units"

Most funds that are sold on a DSC basis allow you to redeem up to 10 percent of your investment per year without charge. It may be a good idea to do this, even if you just move the redemption proceeds to the same fund's front-end equivalent because your free amount does not accumulate, but expires at year end—you only have 10 percent free at any given time, rather than 10 percent the first year, 20 percent the second year, etc. This also provides an opportunity to "crystallize capital gains." That is, in the eyes of Revenue Canada, although your assets may have gone up or down in value, no capital gain or loss has occurred until you create a "deemed disposition" (see Deemed Disposition in the Glossary). Therefore, if you have capital losses you wish to use, or if your income is lower than usual in a given year and it makes sense to declare some capital gains, you can apply this strategy. The same can be true of capital losses if you have capital gains that would otherwise be taxed.

What You Need to Know About Segregated Funds

One of my friends called me the other day with excellent news. She had found the perfect, high-return, risk-free equity investment. Not only was her principal guaranteed if she left it in for 10 years, but she could reset the guarantee amount, up to twice a year, to include any increase in value. She would avoid probate and executor fees, and her funds were creditor-proof.

It does sound pretty dreamy, but this is the catch. In a segregated fund, your principal is guaranteed because you've paid insurance premiums in order to guarantee it. If the value of your fund goes up, the insurance company pockets your premiums with nary a thank you. If your funds drop in value, the insurance company steps up to the plate and pays the difference between the value of the fund 10 years ago (the purchase or reset date) and the value of the fund on the day you cash it in. Premiums can range from 0.35 percent (for fixed- income-type funds) to 1.75 percent (for more volatile equity funds), and they aren't generally guaranteed for the life of the fund, meaning that they can be increased at the manager's discretion. Seg funds are hybrids—mutual funds married to insurance products.

Again, there is no perfect investment, just the right investment for you. In my friend's case, many of the benefits of segregated funds didn't apply. For instance:

- Because they are also insurance products, segregated funds can be creditor-proofed, meaning that if you name certain beneficiaries, usually your spouse or dependent children, the assests may be protected from creditors in the event of personal litigation or bankruptcy. If this is a concern, seg funds offer a definite benefit. If you are university professor with an impeccable financial plan in place, like my friend, this isn't much of a concern.

- Unlike non-segregated investment funds, you can name a beneficiary, meaning that, on your death, the proceeds will be paid out directly without being exposed to probate process and fees. If your assets are in an RSP or RIF, however, you already have this benefit.

- The principal is guaranteed and you can "reset" the principal amount, along with any increase in value, usually up to two times a year. However, this is only true if you hold the fund for 10 years after the guarantee reset date, or die. CIBC just introduced guaranteed funds with a five-year guarantee period, so we may see more of these.

If you refer back to the graph (on page 139) on annual returns averaged over 10 years, you'll remember that there has only been one 10-year period since 1924 when average annual returns were negative. Therefore, the insurance companies are getting very good odds on their guarantee. On the other hand, there is a minute possibility we may see a situation like the one in Japan, where the bottom fell out of the equity market and stayed down for what seemed like forever. In that case, my question would be this: Do the insurance companies have enough money to make good on all those guarantees? The guarantees are only as good as the insurance company that makes them, so be sure you know how solid the company is.

I don't mean to scare you. However, the reason seg funds have become so popular is that they allow participation in the equity markets with the security of knowing you won't lose your original investment. However, the insurance premiums paid for this benefit significantly reduce the benefits of equity-market participation. All else being equal, if you really believe that there is a significant chance of losing part of your principal, you may be better off in a GIC or bond, particularly if the funds are registered.

I'll tell you why. As I write, there are five-year GICs available paying 5.35 percent per annum. In an RSP or RIF, tax isn't a consideration, inflation is currently less than 1 percent, and the principal is guaranteed to $60 000.00 per investor. Over five years, compounded, a $10 000.00 investment at 4.3 percent will be worth $12 373.25. Assuming that real return of 4.3 percent is possible on a guaranteed investment, a guarantee of principal actually represents a loss of $2373.25 in income over five years. If you extend this over a 10-year period, the impact is even more profound. So, if you believe your principal may be at risk, you may want to consider high-grade bonds or GICs. And if you don't believe your principal is at risk, why would you pay a hefty insurance premium?

That said, segregated funds are worthy of consideration under the following conditions:

◆ You believe equities will increase in value over the long term, but for whatever reason (and don't apologize for that reason) you can't sleep comfortably at night knowing that they may go down in the short term. You want to own equities, but are willing to pay an insurance premium in order to also have complete peace of mind.

◆ You work in a litigious field, own your own business, or are just very concerned that someone may sue you or you might one day be forced to declare bankruptcy. Remember, if you are planning to declare bankruptcy or expect to be sued, it is a total waste of time to dump your assets into seg funds. If the courts feel that you have taken any action simply for the sake of protecting assets, they have the right to claim the funds.

◆ You have substantial non-registered assets that you wish to shelter from probate. In this case, ensure that you know exactly how much probate fees will cost. Don't spend $1 in premiums to avoid 50¢ in fees.

The Bottom Line

For those of us in the earlier wealth accumulation stages, or with little extra time to devote to analyzing companies and following the markets, mutual funds offer unparalleled value and opportunity.

They are not a magical path to automatic riches, and should be approached with the same caution, care, and professional advice with which you would make any other significant purchase.

If you follow these steps, you will avoid any major mistakes:

1. Know what you want the money for, and when you'll need it. Don't gamble that things will go your way—always work within the law of averages and appropriate time horizons.

2. You don't need to own 20 different funds to achieve diversification. As a matter of fact, until you have at least $15 000 invested, try to stay within one fund family. Choose one that offers superior performance in each of the asset classes, locales, and management styles you seek. Try to keep a minimum of $5000 in each fund you buy, and try not to exceed a dozen funds, whatever the size of your portfolio. Why invite complexity?

   The exception to this is in your RSP, where you have a 20 percent maximum foreign-content limit. Always ensure you have close to the 20 percent maximum invested globally, even if your 20 percent is just a few hundred dollars.

3. Seek unbiased, professional advice. If you are receiving free advice from the staff of no-load mutual-fund companies, or your bank, for instance, be very clear on the fact that their job descriptions includes selling you *their* funds—not necessarily the *best* funds. If for some reason you'd rather do it without a professional financial adviser, at least read a couple of books on the subject before you start shopping.

4. Don't be unduly influenced by the performance numbers. Whatever the performance of a particular fund, ask to see a comparison of its performance to similar funds from other fund families.

5. Never buy on the basis of short-term performance. We absolutely do not care what a fund has returned over the past three months, six months, or one year, unless its longer-term performance numbers are equally impressive. There is no reason to believe that short-term performance will be repeated. *Look for superior long-term performance in comparison to similar funds.*

6. Ask what the greatest loss within the fund was in a single month and in a one-year period. If you owned it at that point, could you live with it?

7. Never buy anything, not one thing, until you understand why it best meets your needs, what the charges and fees are, and what the risks are.

8. Buy segregated funds for their estate-planning and/or creditor-proofing benefits, not for the sake of the guarantee.

Empowerment, Taxation, and RSPs

Out of your vulnerabilities
will come your strength.

SIGMUND FREUD

The process of weaving financial planning into the fabric of our lives some-times takes us to places we'd rather not go.

Here, for instance. Taxes. Yuck. I think most of us would rather not think too deeply about the sense of powerlessness we feel as money disappears from our paycheques to pay for things we can't see. It's a big complex world of rules and regulations that we could never hope to keep up with. So rather than keep up, we give up. Sigh, curse occasionally, shrug our shoulders. Vote governments "out" rather than "in," hoping that the next party will some-how relieve our sense of hopelessness.

The most important change we can make doesn't have anything to do with government. If we wait for someone or something to give us power, it can always be taken away again. We needn't all quit our jobs and run for office, unless that is what calls us, but it is important to reclaim the power that rightfully belongs to us as voters, taxpayers, and citizens.

Let's just begin by exploring how we feel about these matters beyond our control. Frustration? Rage? Hopelessness? Cynicism? Distrust? And what's underneath that?

We might be surprised to find that we don't hate taxes as much as we think we do. We may hate the amount of tax we pay, or the fact that we seem to have no voice when it comes to how those dollars are collected and spent. Still, most Canadians share my opinion that Canada is the greatest country in the world to live in. We are, for the most part, both proud and grateful to have incomes that allow us to contribute. We're glad to drive on decent roads maintained by capable crews, and we're content with the quality of education our children receive from the public school system. We're happy to share our well-being with those unfortunate people who, for whatever reason, cannot support themselves, and most of us seem to think that our medical system is fine.

Finding Our Voice

We are, however, up against inefficiency, waste, and bureaucracy. Why do our politicians have to fly around the world in jets to lavish summits and trade conferences? Haven't they heard of the Internet? Teleconferencing? Is it necessary for salaried politicians to live like kings and queens? My latest source of frustration is the multimillion-dollar advertising campaigns, paid for with our tax dollars, that are supposed to convince us how wonderfully our current government is doing.

It is time we stopped being so polite about the inexcusable ways in which our tax dollars are squandered. Yet, like most people, I think, I feel helpless. Whom do I call or write? Whom do I even vote for? But I can speak. I can write. I can e-mail. And when I do, my tax dollars begin to mean something to me again. A source of power rather than a source of disempowering frustration.

In addition to voicing our concerns, there are two very practical and immediate ways to empower ourselves in the face of taxation.

The Luxury of Giving

A powerful way of re-empowering ourselves is to contribute *actively,* by giving as much money as we desire and can afford to the charities of our choice. There is nothing quite so satisfying as knowing that we have made a positive difference in someone else's life, and yet, in Canada, we have, for the most part, given both the responsibility and the joy of giving to a government that may or may not share our values. We already pay so much in taxes that we choose not to give, denying ourselves.

It doesn't have to be this way. At the moment, we receive a tax credit of 17 percent of the first $200 that we donate to registered charitable organizations, and 29 percent on amounts over $200. For this reason, and because you're allowed to, always declare all your family's charitable donations on one spouse's tax return. As well, if you are considering a substantial charitable gift, consult a tax professional. There are significant tax benefits to contributing securities rather than cash.

The second thing we can all do to protest the inefficient way in which our tax dollars are spent is to pay as little tax as possible. All Canadians have the right to reduce their taxes to the amount required by law, but because of inadequate planning, most of us are paying more than we have to. Just as an example, only 13 percent of allowable RSP contribution room is actually used. It's tragic.

The Great RSP Misunderstanding

Please begin this section by flipping to the jacket of the book and looking at my picture. Now imagine me hopping up and down and pulling my hair.

"An RSP is not an investment! An RSP is not an investment! An RSP is not an investment!"

OK, then. Now that we are clear on what an RSP is not, what is it?

An RSP is a tax-shelter vehicle devised by our government to encourage us to look after our future selves. RRSP stands for Registered Retirement Savings Plan. The key word is "registered." We can purchase two identical investments, but if one of them is an RRSP, the financial institution will advise Revenue Canada of our purchase and we'll get whatever tax slips we need to attach to our return. I tend to use the diminutive "RSP," which stands for Registered Savings Plan, because it's a reminder that there is far more to life than retirement.

When you contribute money to your RSP—within prescribed limits designed to keep supposedly wealthy people from becoming unduly wealthier at the expense of tax coffers—Revenue Canada says something like, "Catch ya later." Tax on income you earned during the year is *deferred*, allowing your savings to grow within the RSP, unscathed by further taxation on the investment earnings until you withdraw it from the registered plan. When you withdraw it, you will pay tax on it at whatever rate you are required to pay in that year.

Why do you need to know this? For a couple of reasons. The first is my friend Ann, who retired 15 years ago on an income that forces her to baby-sit for her neighbours in order to have money to go to the movies once a week (which wouldn't be so much of a problem if she liked kids). I asked her once why she never put any money aside in RSPs when she was working.

"Oh, those RSPs! What a scam that was! I did buy one once. I put $4000 into an RSP at my bank, and when I took it out, they took $400 from me, and then the government took even more money when I filed my income-tax return! Ridiculous! I never did figure out why they were so popular."

"Well, yes," I replied, "but you would have received a tax refund when you made the contribution. The $400 that the bank withheld was just an install-ment on the tax that you owed to Revenue Canada after making the withdrawal, so that you wouldn't have to struggle to find the money at tax time. You get a deduction when you put it in; you pay tax when you take it out."

"No, I never got a tax deduction," Ann insisted.

As it turned out, Ann had bought a registered GIC at her bank, not real-izing that it was a tax-deferral device. Because it was RSP season, the rate was a quarter percent higher than regular GICs because the bank was trying to attract RSP business. She received a tax receipt, but just filed it in her record-keeping folder where she was able to find it 15 years later to show me. No one at Revenue Canada caught the fact that she had RSP income even though she had never deducted an RSP contribution. This poor old lady, baby-sitting for $4 an hour, paid hundreds of dollars in unnecessary tax because she didn't know what an RSP was.

The second reason is that too many people stress themselves out trying to decide which RSP investment to make. It is important to separate the two things in your mind. When you find yourself in the unfortunate position of having to make a contribution in February, it is probably best to park the money in a registered mutual-fund money-market account or savings account, and meet with your financial adviser in March to figure out where to put it. Likewise, you can't "buy an RSP" every year and assume you've taken care of your investment needs.

Qualified RSP Investments and Types of Plans

Once you have taken care of the RSP contribution part of the equation, you can buy almost any investment or savings product with your RSP dollars, so let's start with what you can't do. You can't hold your art collection, your antiques, your collector coins, or foreign currency. You can't hold real estate, except within a real estate investment fund (REIF) or real estate investment trust (REIT). You can't hold some of the more esoteric investment devices that you shouldn't be buying anyway unless you are an investment profes-sional or a professional gambler. At the moment, although there is strong pressure on our government to change these restrictions, you can't invest more than 20 percent of your "book" value outside Canada.

You can hold your own mortgage, under certain conditions, but the fees are high both initially and over the long term, so get professional advice before moving ahead. Be sure to understand both the costs and the benefits. It sounds appealing to pay yourself interest for a change, but it must also make sense from a dollars perspective.

There are essentially three kinds of RSPs:

1. **Managed RSPs.** in which someone else decides where and how your contributions will be invested, paying you a prescribed rate of return. The most common managed RSPs are registered GICs and savings accounts offered by banks, credit unions, and trust companies. Managers are paid the difference between what they are able to earn with your money and what they pay you. Your principal is generally guaranteed to prescribed limits.

2. **Mutual-fund RSPs.** Somewhat like managed RSPs, but generally with more risk and more potential for returns. Rather than receiving a stated return, you participate in the success (or failure) of the investment pool. No guarantees.

3. **Self-directed RSPs.** A whole different animal. In this case, a "trustee" administers your qualified investments and registers the plan with Revenue Canada. Unlike managed and mutual-fund RSPs, in which the managers make money by investing your money and keeping some of the profits, self-directed RSP trustees rely on fee income. The benefits to the plan-holder are flexibility and consolidation. You can move your RSP money from one investment to another without having to fill out transfer request forms and wait for the cheques to be moved around. You receive one consolidated statement showing all of your RSP holdings. In addition, because foreign content is limited to 20 percent of the book value of any particular plan, not all of your RSPs, a self-directed plan allows you to maximize your foreign content. If you have more than three different RSP accounts, or more than $25 000 in RSP assets, it may be time to think about a self-directed plan. Remember, with a self-directed no one will make decisions for you, so you must either be a knowledgeable investor with time on your hands or have a financial adviser to assist you.

Self-directed plans are only as good as the investments they hold, and it is the investment choices that determine the level of security as well. When I acted as a self-directed RSP administrator, many plans held only staggered maturity GICs. For high-net-worth individuals, it was a way to consolidate accounts and ease administrative headaches while still keeping investments with any particular institution below the maximum CDIC guarantee. On the other hand, we had many self-directed RSPs that held only VSE penny stocks—one day they were worth $50 000, the next $5000. Or vice versa. It's up to you and your financial adviser.

The kind of investment you choose will largely determine the kind of plan that's best.

I can't say this emphatically enough. Every Canadian citizen with earned income should have an RSP. Without one, *you pay more tax than you have to.* Even in the lowest tax bracket, a $1000 contribution costs $740—that is, Revenue Canada kicks in $260 that would otherwise be lost to you. Yes, you will have to pay that tax some day, but in the meantime, you get to invest it. You get to participate in the magic of tax-sheltered compound returns. For example, if I contributed $200 a month to an RSP from age 39 to age 69, earned 10 percent per year on my investments, and had an effective tax rate of 40 percent, I would have a nest egg of $452 100 when I retire. If I do the same thing outside an RSP, I will have just $200 900, because I pay tax every year on the income. Even if I cashed in my entire RSP at age 69 and paid taxes at the highest rate, I would still be astonishingly ahead. But I don't have to do that. I can roll the whole thing into a RRIF (Registered Retirement Income Fund) and continue to defer taxes until I'm 99!

Do not let anyone, anything, or any opinion discourage you from making RSP contributions as early and as often as you can. You may want to defer *claiming* an RSP contribution in a year when income is down, or if you expect to be in a higher tax bracket the following year, but at least start sheltering the returns. If you are one of those very lucky people who has more than $300 000 in your RSP prior to age 55, ensure you get professional advice because at that point, it may be advisable to focus on non-registered investment strategies as well. Before you begin worrying about it, remember that we should all have your problems. The chart on the following page shows us an example of the benefits of investing inside an RSP as opposed to outside one.

The least effective way to contribute is to wait until the end of RSP season. If you happen to have the money lying around, contribute January 2 of every new year, which allows you to shelter an additional 14 months of growth. I know . . . "Ha!" However, if you hold non-registered investments such as Canada Savings Bonds through your payroll savings plan or from Grandma, or inside non-registered mutual funds, you can make an "in kind" contribution in January and shelter the income on those investments for the whole year. (In kind means that you contribute the value of the asset itself as opposed to an equivalent amount in cash.) If you are in a 50 percent tax

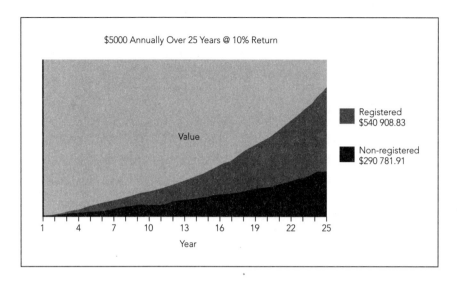

$5000 Annually Over 25 Years @ 10% Return

Value

Registered
$540 908.83

Non-registered
$290 781.91

Year

bracket, for instance, and make a contribution of a $10 000 bond earning 5 percent in interest income, you will save yourself a tax bill of $250 in just one year.

Two-hundred-and-fifty dollars is a respectable sum, but let's take a look at how this adds up over the long term. If you contribute $1000 a year for 30 years at 10 percent, you will earn an additional $6730 just for contributing at the beginning of the year instead of at the end of RSP season. I don't know about you, but I can think of a million ways to spend an extra $6730.

Beware. There is a weird Revenue Canada rule lurking around here. If you make an in-kind contribution, it will be treated as a "deemed disposition" of the asset, as if it had been sold, and you will have to pay tax on any gain. However, if there has been a loss, it disappears in Revenue Canada's eyes. Poof. Therefore, plan carefully. Don't contribute securities that have incurred a capital loss, which you could otherwise use against capital-gains income.

If you aren't lucky enough to have money or investment assets lying around, get on a monthly contribution plan. The long-term effects are slightly less staggering, but still very impressive. And again, if you can talk your employer into contributing directly on your behalf, you can contribute before-tax dollars, meaning your contribution will not cut as deeply into your take-home pay. A picture is worth a thousand words, they say, so in the chart on the following page let's compare the effects of contributing $5000 a year at the beginning of the year, at the end of the year, and monthly, over a 25-year period.

Ideally, the only time you should be contributing in RSP season is when

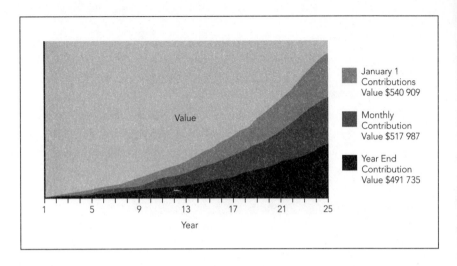

you discover you've got the money and room to top up your monthly contributions, or when you have to borrow to make your contribution.

Borrowing to Contribute

If you don't have the money to contribute to an RSP but have contribution room, taxable income, and adequate cash flow to make the payments, borrow. Shop around for the lowest rate, and don't be overly optimistic about how much you can afford to pay. Too many people sit down and add up their rent, groceries, phone, and car payments, and assume that the $600 left over can be applied to a loan payment. Do you have $600 left at the end of the month? If not, you can assume that you are spending the money somewhere, and that you're going to miss it when it's gone. If you can spend less, great. However, if you are going to start racking up your credit cards, you are driving in reverse without a rearview mirror. Before you arrange a loan, always do a realistic cash-flow/life-expenditure statement.

One of the most common financial-planning oversights I see in my practice has to do with tax refunds. In my financially dysfunctional days, I used to end up in a worse financial position after I received my refund than before. Every year, I would get the cheque, celebrate my good fortune, and spend the next two weeks bleeding money, catching up on all my delayed bill paying and shopping. Invariably, I overestimated how far one lump sum would stretch and ended up spending part of the grocery money. Feast followed by famine—I'll probably always associate tax refunds with Kraft dinner.

These days, there is a new twist to tax-refund madness. With RSP loans, you are often offered the option of deferring your first loan payment for 90 days with the assumption that you will pay down the loan with your tax refund. Deferring payment is almost never a good idea, but in this case, it also encourages you to apply your refund to an RSP loan that is usually offered at a very low rate of interest, while you continue to carry your credit-card balances at ridiculously high rates of interest.

If you aren't paying off your credit cards monthly, pay them off first and put them away. If you can't put them away, you might as well continue paying interest at 16 percent and pay down your RSP loan, or you may have them maxed out again in six months and still have your RSP loan.

Spousal RSPs and Income Splitting

I love processing spousal RSP contributions. What an act of love and faith— contributing to a retirement plan on behalf of a beloved other in the belief that you will retire together to enjoy your golden years. I used to get misty-eyed when I saw couples kissing. Now I'm moved when the higher-income earner writes a cheque. Oh, how our definition of love changes with experience.

With the defeat of the senior's benefit program, income splitting continues to be a sound practice. Income splitting simply means planning the financial affairs of spouses (legal or common-law) to ensure that you both pay as little tax as possible by equalizing your retirement income.

There are a number of ways to do this.

1. If you have a family-owned business and one partner stays at home, it makes sense to hire someone to do some of the domestic work and have the spouse do paid work within the business instead. Unfortunately, our government doesn't recognize domestic work as work, but if you hire a housekeeper to clean your house, your spouse can receive an income (which may be taxed at a lower rate) to clean your business offices. Your business can then deduct the cost as an expense. Stupid but true. Likewise, you can't pay your spouse to care for your children, but you can, theoretically, pay your spouse to run a company daycare that then provides free daycare to employees of the company.

2. Plan your investment buying wisely. The higher income earner should always pay living expenses, allowing the lower income earner to invest his or her income. That way, the investment earnings will be taxed at the lower tax rate.

3. Then there are spousal RSP contributions. This simply means that either spouse can contribute to an RSP owned by the other spouse. Your contribution room does not increase—that is, your total contributions,

regular and spousal, cannot exceed your allowable maximum contribution room. Once it's in, it's in. The money doesn't belong to the contributor any more, but to the annuitant, the spouse whose name the RSP is in. You can't transfer it back and forth. If you withdraw the money, it will be taxed in the hands of the contributor for three calendar years following the date of the contribution. After the third calendar year, withdrawals are taxed in the hands of the annuitant.

If one partner is giving up income in order to provide more of the child care or domestic support, a spousal RSP contribution can be an extremely fair and pragmatic way of saying thank you.

RRSP Contribution Room, Overcontributions, Carry-forwards, PAs, and PARs

This used to be pretty complicated stuff. Now it's simple. I'm going to give you a table with the maximum RSP contribution limits, etc., because I don't want you to think I overlooked it. However, rather than studying it, go dig up your Statement of Assessment, that thing Revenue Canada sent you after you filed your income-tax return. Flip to the page on RSP contribution room. There you go. End of study. That's your maximum contribution room, including any Pension Adjustment (PA) reduction (the amount that your contribution room is reduced by if you participate in a pension plan), carry-forward (unused contribution room), Home Buyers Plan repayments that are due, overcontribution amounts, and Pension Adjustment Reversal (PAR). If you can't find your Statement of Assessment, call Revenue Canada. (And go back and redo Chapter 4.)

At the moment, if you don't use your RSP contribution room, you can carry it forward indefinitely. Try not to. Money almost never gets easier to come by unless you make it easier.

Your pension adjustment, if any, reflects the benefits of any company pension plan you belong to. If you leave that company, losing your pension benefits, you will get a Pension Adjustment Reversal statement, or PAR, that gives you back some of the contribution room you lost.

If you are over 18, have money or investments lying around, and plan to leave those funds within your RSP for at least 10 years, consider overcontributing. You are allowed to overcontribute up to $2000 without penalty; after that, it gets ugly, and you are charged a penalty tax of 1 percent per month on any excess.

Here's the promised table for you not to study:

MAXIMUM RSP CONTRIBUTIONS	
Year	18% of Earned Income from Prior Year to a Maximum of
1999-2003	$13 500
2004	$14 500
2005	$15 500
2006	Indexed to inflation ($15 500 plus the rate of inflation)

Here is a list of income that is defined as "earned" for the sake of calculating earned income:

- My favorite—royalties
- Employment income
- Self-employment income after expenses and losses
- Rental income after expenses and losses
- Alimony

Conversely, the following are *not* considered earned income:

- Investment income
- Pension income
- RSP or RRIF income

Taking Full Advantage of Revenue Canada's Graciousness

Self-employment

I'm an Aries. The oldest daughter of five children. As I say in response to each job offer I receive, I have a pathological inability to take direction. I'm willing to make a lot of sacrifices to be in charge of my own destiny. Still, the bottom line is that money makes us free.

Whether we call them Boss, Mr. Client, Partner, or Dear, our lives are shaped by the people who provide our income. Freedom is measured according to our ability to say No. "No, I will not go there." "This is when I am available."

Oddly enough, a pathological inability to take direction is one of the things that Revenue Canada rewards us for with cool tax breaks. The tax collector calls it entrepreneurialism, which isn't for everyone, obviously, but if you have a job providing administrative, technical, or professional services, you may want to at least consider the possibility of eventual self-employment.

You don't even have to quit your job initially. As a matter of fact, that may be one of the last things you do. Even if your employer is willing to consider becoming one of your contracts, think about the loss of any benefits and security (ha!) before you make the leap. And don't make the mistake of believing that it's as easy as quitting and calling yourself a business. If your employer tells you what to do, how to do it, when to do it, and provides the tools and space for you to do it, you're an employee. Probably an employee without benefits, but still an employee, and your expense deductions will be disallowed. Although there is no concrete test, you are more likely to be considered self-employed if—

◆ your contract is negotiated based on a clearly stated objective and time frame, and remuneration is based on measurable progress toward the stated objective

◆ you are actively seeking other contracts and are likely to have at least three within any one-year period

◆ you decide your hours and location of service

◆ you are not a member of the employee benefit program

◆ your services could be replaced by another contractor without unduly disrupting the business of the company

However, you can be a full-time employee and still operate a home-based business. Set up a home office, begin developing your business, and you can also start writing off business costs relating to that potential income. It doesn't have to be either/or—you can grow into independence.

Your new endeavour may or may not be in the field in which you work. One woman I know works as an accountant for a large corporation during the day and operates her own import/export business in the evening and on weekends.

Obviously, you can deduct expenses relating directly to the completion of work or the development of new business. Advertising, printing, software, dedicated telephone lines, long-distance charges, cell-phone charges, answering services, stationery and office supplies, vehicular expenses relating directly to your business—the list is long. For instance, as a writer, I'm forever buying books as research materials, either for their content or to study the writing style. Therefore, I can deduct these costs. Save every single receipt.

The real benefits come from deductions for things you would pay for anyway. A home-based business is an efficient use of space. Don't be greedy—

you can only deduct the space that is used solely for business. For instance, I use the third floor of my house as an office where I also present workshops. I have a bathroom off that space that is dedicated to client use and for me when I'm working, so I have measured the square footage of office and bathroom, and calculated it as a percentage of the entire house. I deduct that percentage from my rent, hydro, and contents insurance. It would be greedy of me to deduct the stairs to the third floor, a percentage of the entrance, and the kitchen space where I prepare tea and coffee for my clients. Greedy and likely to attract an audit.

I also rent a small, inexpensive office downtown for meetings with my partner and any clients who don't want to come to the suburbs. If Revenue Canada was able to prove that this was my primary office, it would disallow the deductions for my home office. Therefore, I keep very careful records of appointments in each location.

The same is true of vehicle use and parking. Driving to your office is not considered a deductible expense, but if you stop to see a client or potential client on the way there and on the way home, it is. I try to schedule all my house-call meetings for early morning and evening.

In order to deduct expenses, you must be able to prove to Revenue Canada that it is reasonable to expect a profit at some point in the near future. There is no time limit, but if you've declared losses for more than three years, start expecting an audit. If you don't ever make a profit, and decide to give up, you don't have to pay back the tax benefits of your deductions.

If you are thinking about making the leap to self-employment, I highly recommend Joanne Thomas Yaccato's new book, written with Paula Jubinville, *Raising Your Business.* There are also some great books out there on the tax aspects of self-employment. I find myself referring to Tim Cestnick's latest, *Winning the Tax Game.* I'm not a big fan of baseball, or sports metaphors, but the information is well laid out and a pleasure to read.

Still, there is no substitute for professional help, particularly when it comes to starting your own business. Ask around until you find a keen accountant who specializes in home-based or start-up businesses, and have this person walk you through a tax-planning strategy before you get started. Even if you insist on doing your own tax returns, have your accountant prepare your return the first year and then review your work at least every three years after.

Investment and Taxation

1. If you own them anyway, try to keep most of your interest-bearing investments inside your RSP and most of your dividend and capital-gains-bearing investments outside your RSP. If you own any of the hybrid diversified, derivative-based, or RRSP index participation mutual funds, it's important to own them in your RSP. (*Seek professional advice. Seek professional advice.*)

2. If you're investing outside of an RSP, plan your investments with tax efficiency in mind. The least tax-efficient investments are those that pay interest, such as money-market funds, bonds, CSBs, GICs, mortgage funds, bond funds, and international funds that are structured to be 100 percent RSP eligible. In the middle are balanced funds, which have an interest-earning component, and dividend funds. Although dividends are taxed at a lower rate than capital gains, they are less tax efficient because tax is paid in the year the dividend is paid. Capital gains are sheltered until the asset is actually sold.

Of greatest efficiency are equity funds that provide capital gains, particularly those funds that practise a buy-and-hold strategy. Every time a stock is sold within an equity fund, there is a capital gain or loss that must be distributed out to unit-holders. The longer the stock is held, the longer its value can increase without triggering taxation. However, you will pay now, or you will pay later. Tax deferral should not be the primary criterion for choosing an equity fund.

When buying mutual funds, you will want to consider the fund's "turn-over" rate, which is a measure of the fund's sales or purchases divided by the average value of securities held during the course of the year. There is no "right" turnover rate; it is simply a measure of comparison.

The chart on the following page, from the AIC Group of Funds, illustrates the tax advantage of a buy-and-hold strategy as opposed to a trading (high-turnover) strategy.

Beware, too, of those situations in which deferring capital gains is not an advantage. In a child's trust account, for instance, up to $6700 can be earned in capital gains without any tax being paid. In this situation, a buy-and-hold management style may be a disadvantage, creating an unduly large tax burden when the investment is finally sold.

Always be aware of the tax implications when selling an asset. What seems like an uneventful shift in your portfolio from one fund to another, for example, can evoke a hefty tax bill. You may want to make the change over a two-calendar-year period, or crystallize a capital loss at the same time.

As an example of the different rates of taxation on investment income, let's look at the amount that Gloria, who lives in Ontario and is in the highest tax bracket, would keep on each dollar of income earned in 1998:

AFTER-TAX AMOUNT

Interest and rental income	$0.497
Dividend income	$0.66
Capital gains	$0.623

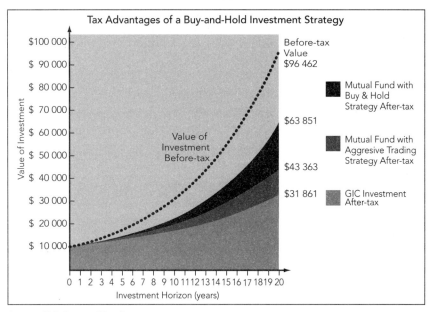

With the exception of those beloved RSPs, and RESPs (to be covered in a later section) avoid tax shelters unless—

◆ your RSPs are maxed out

◆ you're a very knowledgeable investor with a high tolerance for risk

◆ you're in the highest tax bracket

◆ you have no consumer debt

◆ you have trusted professional advice, preferably from more than one source (e.g., both your financial planner and your accountant or tax adviser)

Even then, be afraid. Be very afraid. There is no point in losing $1 to save 50¢. Judge every investment on its potential for returns and its vulnerability to failure. Remember that very few tax shelters offer liquidity, which in itself increases risk dramatically. Once in, you are in to stay.

One exception worthy of consideration may be the Labour-Sponsored Venture Capital funds available. Although their very purpose makes them high-risk and speculative in nature, the substantial tax credits do mitigate risk to some degree, and there are some that have been very successful. Don't dismiss them out of hand, but do seek professional advice prior to concluding that they are automatically more profitable than non-tax-advantaged investments simply because of the tax credits.

Other Deductible Bits and Pieces

1. Don't assume that everyone who charges to do tax returns is an expert. If you've got the time, energy, skill, and desire to do your own return, invest in a tax-help program like QuickTax that will walk you through all the possible deductions and common omissions. If you can't because you don't have a computer, for instance, have your tax return professionally prepared at least once, and then use it as a benchmark for future returns. Be sure to tell your accountant about any investments you have, all property you own, all income you have on T4s or otherwise. Their work is only as complete as the information you provide. Sort and add up your receipts before you go in. If it takes you two days to sort that mess, how long do you think it would take someone who has no idea whom you took to dinner on February 17 and why?

2. As mentioned previously, if you are in a marital partnership, deduct all charitable donations together on the highest income earner's return. Changes in the 1997 budget did away with the benefit of having the spouse with the lowest income claim all medical expenses. Medical expenses must now exceed 3 percent (or a minimum $1614, whichever is less) of family income. However, you still have the option of claiming expenses for any 12-month period ending in the year for which you are filing that haven't already been claimed. That is, if you had significant expenses in the last quarter of 1997 that didn't exceed the minimum, but had additional expenses in early 1998, you can choose to claim September 1, 1997, to August 31, 1998.

3. If you move at least 40 kilometres closer to your place of employment, you may be able to deduct many of the costs of moving, including some major expenses such as the real estate commission on the sale of your house. There are restrictions—check with your accountant.

If you receive bonus income, and you have the contribution room, ask your employer to make the bonus payable to your RSP trustee. That way, unless it's more than $10 000, your employer is not obligated to withhold tax (make sure your employer knows that).

12

Family: Certainties and Dreams

Love does not consist of gazing into each other's eyes, but in gazing together in the same direction.

ANTOINE ST. EXUPERY

No matter how fast or slow we go, no matter how exquisitely or superficially we live, none of us is getting out of this alive. Until we have assets or people who depend on us, we can deny this truth, but once we have family and stuff, it is time to acknowledge the reality of our mortality. No one likes to dwell on this at great length, so I'll just move quickly through the basics.

1. If you have no dependents and no assets, you don't need a will. If you have basic-use assets, such as your car and clothing, you can prepare a holograph will, which is a will in your own handwriting that says something like this:

I, Lori M. Bamber, being of sound mind and body, leave my 1988 Chevy Malibu to my mother, Marie Simpson, and my diamond earrings to my father, Derek Bamber.

Sign it, date it, and keep it with your underwear. It doesn't need to be witnessed. Everything I read about holograph wills says something like "may leave family with legal complications or financial institutions may be reluctant to honour your wishes." If you don't have any financial assets, I'd say that the worst outcome would be that your mom might get the diamond earrings while your dad gets the Chevy. As soon as you have financial assets, get a real will.

2. If you have dependent children, you need a will to establish your wishes for guardianship. Don't let your last thought be, Oh, God, I wish I'd taken care of that. When making your decision, ask yourself the following questions:

- Whom would your children choose to live with? Are your children mature enough to be consulted?
- Does the person(s) you are considering as a potential guardian have the health and energy required to take care of your kids? How old is this person? Will he or she have the health and energy required to care for your children when they become teenagers?
- Does this person share your child-rearing values?
- Does this person have children? Would your children be welcomed by all family members?
- Have you provided sufficient insurance or assets to allow the guardian to raise your child? If not, can the guardian afford to raise your child or children without your financial support? Would he or she be willing to take on that responsibility?
- Do you wish the guardian to also act as trustee of whatever financial estate you leave? If so, have you made arrangements for this both in your will and with your financial advisers?

Once you've made a decision, have a heart-to-heart talk with the person or persons you've chosen. Make sure they understand the responsibility, and be forthright about the way you'd like to see your kids raised. In a situation like this, a "no" response can be as loving as a "yes."

3. You need to designate an executor. Most people name their spouses or one of their adult children. There is no perfect solution. Remember, this is not an honour as much as it is a weighty responsibility. Before you choose an executor, ask yourself these questions:

- Does this person have the time necessary to carry out all of your wishes? Is his or her work flexible enough to allow for the inevitable office-hour meetings with financial advisers, etc.?
- What about location? Will this person have to travel or conduct extensive business by telephone?
- How is this decision going to affect family dynamics? In my family, for instance, my mom has named my brother as executor, which bothered me a bit at first—as I'm a financial adviser and he's a forensic anthropologist! However, I am one of four sisters, and I eventually concluded that she'd done the right thing. If she would have named any of us, it may have created tension.

Will this person be capable of wading through whatever emotional issues arise between family members in the course of the estate settlement? It may be that you need two executors—perhaps a respected and trusted family member and a financial professional to take care of the administrative requirements. It is a lot easier once you've been through the process a few times, believe me. An executor has a long list of duties, including preparing a statement of asset and liabilities; making a year-of-death RSP contribution if your will provides that instruction (and it should); settling all of the liabilities of your estate, including funeral costs, and money owed to creditors; submitting the will for probate, if necessary; arranging the funeral, if requested; completing and submitting all insurance claims on behalf of beneficiaries or the estate; distributing all assets in accordance with the will; managing all ongoing trusts, including investment and distribution; filing the final tax return, submitting taxes owing, and arranging for releases on the estate from Revenue Canada.

4. Once you've decided on a guardian and an executor, and they have accepted the designation, make your wishes known in a will. Tomorrow would be a good day to begin. Or even better, today. Prior to meeting with a lawyer, call and ask if a will-preparation package is available. Many firms can provide you with a lengthy questionnaire that will guide you through each of the decisions you need to make. By the time you actually meet, you will be relatively clear on your objectives. You can therefore minimize your legal bill by relying on your lawyer only to point out any pitfalls or oversights, and to prepare the document itself.

5. Go through the insurance-planning section in Chapter 6, and do whatever is necessary to ensure that your family will be OK if something happens to you. Term insurance is really very reasonably priced, particularly if you're a non-smoker, and it will provide immeasurable peace of mind.

6. If you're in a marital relationship, name your spouse as beneficiary of your RSP and insurance plans. Name an alternate beneficiary, perhaps your children, in case you and your spouse die together. Wherever possible, register non-RSP assets jointly, with right of survivorship, so that ownership will pass directly to the surviving spouse without probate costs or administrative wrangling.

7. Remember that all investment assets will be treated as if they were sold in the year of your death, so if you'd like them to go to family members, see a financial adviser about arranging insurance to pay the tax that

will be required. If you're thinking of your stock portfolio, it may not be a problem, but if you have a beloved recreation property that's been in the family for generations, you may not want it sold to strangers to cover the inevitable capital gain.

8. If you are leaving a legacy to charity, arrange to leave investments rather than cash.

9. Death can take a long time. While you're having your will prepared, you may wish to arrange for a Power of Attorney that will allow a significant other to care for your affairs if you are incapacitated. Remember, you are putting your life in this person's hands. Don't designate your new boyfriend no matter how sweet he seems.

10. Perhaps because of our excellent medical system, long-term care insurance hasn't become wildly popular in Canada. However, if you are in your late forties or beyond, it is something to consider. Although public medical insurance pays for basic health care, ongoing home care can put a tremendous burden on family members. It is a very loving act to prepare for the possibility of declining health by making arrangements for your own care. Your insurance professional can furnish the details on the plans available. The younger and healthier you are, of course, the less expensive it is to purchase.

11. I'm hoping that you've already taken care of all this, but just in case you skipped a chapter or two, when you go, leave decent records. By now, you should have complete cash-flow and net-worth statements. Be sure that the rest of your family is familiar with these.

12. Make your wishes and plans known to your family. Talk about it. Do you want a burial or cremation? Have you completed your organ-donor card and informed your family of your wishes? Where do you keep your will? Insurance documents? Investment certificates?

13. You may also want a Living Will that decisively states your wishes about medical treatment in the event of serious illness.

14. Review everything annually. Are the guardians you've named still healthy and willing to take on the responsibility? Are they still married to each other? As life changes, and assets are hopefully gathered, you may wish to make changes.

15. At the very least, review your will following any significant change in your affairs: if you change your insurance program, if you marry or divorce, if you receive an inheritance, or win a lottery.

EXERCISE 7 **Estate-planning Checklist**

1. Designate a guardian and executor(s); choose financial, legal, and tax advisers.

2. Keep complete records of all financial matters and advise your family of their location.

3. Review your life-insurance needs and make any necessary changes.

4. Arrange a Power of Attorney.

5. Arrange a Living Will.

6. Arrange for Long-Term Care Insurance if desired.

7. Avoid unnecessary taxes and probate fees by naming beneficiaries and holding assets jointly where possible.

8. Set up any trusts, RESPs, etc., that are required to fulfill your wishes for your inheritors.

9. Review annually and/or after any significant changes in legislation or your personal situation.

10. Discuss your wishes and arrangements with your family.

That's enough of that. Now we can forget about dying and get back to the business of living. Deep living. Rich living. Sweet living.

Money As Seen Through the Eyes of Our Children

I am appalled when I think about how little I knew about money when I had my own children. Like most parents, I think, I tried to shelter them from the realities of our struggles, but my son grew up hearing about what he couldn't have, sometimes even wondering whether dinner would eventually appear.

I have to admit to some regrets. When I was first married, money was something that my husband and in-laws took care of. I was a teenager—old enough to have my son but not old enough to know, apparently, what we had in the bank. When we bought our first home, my husband chose it, arranged the mortgage, and then excitedly showed me where we would be living. When we divorced, my ex-husband and his parents continued to take care of the money and our home—and I left with a lamp and my clothes.

I would fight harder today, not for myself, but for my kids. I would ask for help faster, and I would be more aggressive about taking advantage of the social programs that do exist for single parents. When I was struggling to buy groceries and charging diapers to my Bay card, for instance, there were day-care subsidies that would have given us an extra $400 a month. There were subsidized housing units, and communal-kitchen programs that provided access to bulk-food prices. I didn't know. Pride and a kind of mute acceptance kept me from asking. If I could go back, I would do things differently.

Thankfully, my daughter has been raised in a different world. She made me laugh last week when she rather aggressively asked how much money I had in my RSP. I have been rather clumsy of late, due largely to the distractions of finishing this book and my more-than-full-time financial-planning business. Teryl, however, has drawn the conclusion that it is my advanced age that is creating my accident-proneness, and has therefore started thinking about retirement on my behalf.

With my 40th birthday still before me, I don't really like being thought of as decrepit, but I was thrilled to find she was thinking about my future—and about RSPs. I'm lucky enough to have the opportunity to model by example, which is really the way children learn.

If you wish to teach your children about financial planning, and you should, because it isn't being taught in school, you must remember how you learned: modelling and experience. It isn't enough to handle money effectively, you must also share the experience. There are two ways to do this: by allowing your children to participate in the family's finances, and by establishing the much-revered allowance.

It is never too early to involve your kids in family expenses and vacation planning. If your children leave home knowing how to comparison-shop, for instance, they are already blessed. But if they've also been taught to calculate the number of hours of work required to make a purchase, they're likely to be wiser, wealthier, and more content.

Allowances

There isn't a right or a wrong way to handle the allowance equation. Some professionals suggest a dollar a week per year of age, so that a 13-year-old receives $13. However, it really depends on how much you expect your child to pay for. If your 13-year-old only pays for treats, even $13 may be too much. If your child pays for clothing and school supplies, it may not be enough.

In this case, the objective is everything. Sit down with your children individually and discuss allowance. What do they expect? What do you expect? Be ready to modify your plan as you move forward. Go over the following questions together:

◆ As an allowance represents children's first experience with money management, it is integrally important that they learn to spend some, save some, and give some away. Is the child mature enough to handle these basics, or is it advisable to have Mom or Dad take care of the saving and giving-away duties prior to handing over the cash?

◆ Is the savings portion for something far, far down the road, like university, or can it be accessed for the purchase of things like a bike or a Nintendo? Do you need to set up two savings accounts? What are the purchase-decision guidelines? How much input do Mom and Dad have on spending decisions?

◆ What are the guidelines on weekly spending, if any? There is a tremendous opportunity here to help children learn the importance of recording purchases. You may want to require a spending record—it will be helpful for both of you. One of my friend's parents did this: Debbie received $5 a week, which was a lot of money back then, but paid for all of her own clothes and personal items. Before she received the next week's allowance, she was required to account for all spending within 50¢.

◆ At our house, when Teryl needs new jeans, shoes, etc., I decide on a maximum spending limit. If she wants the designer brand, she then has the option of using her allowance to pay the difference. If you are going to pay for clothes and personal items, you may want to work out the same kind of arrangement.

◆ Believe me, I *know* how hard it is to resist, and I have failed miserably many times, but one of the worst things you can do for your children is to give them advances on their allowance. Talk about setting them up for credit problems. So what do you do when the movie absolutely must be attended or the birthday gift must be bought? One thing that works relatively well in our house is a job list. I have a list of things that I normally do and am willing to pay to have done. Unpleasant things, like cleaning the bathrooms and the dog-run area. Washing my car. Vacuuming the baseboards. When our kids are desperate for money, we let them decide just how desperate they are. A word of warning—never pay in advance, set a time frame, and be crystal clear about your expectations for performance.

◆ Where will the savings account be held? Involving your child in a discussion on services and service charges will benefit them for a lifetime.

◆ Is the allowance tied to household chores? Most professionals advise against this. It is important that children grow up seeing themselves as integral members of the family team, and not as paid employees. However, money is the single greatest motivator, and it's hard to resist the old threaten-to-pull-the-allowance trick in the face of unperformed chores. We've implemented a bonus program. Our kids receive an allowance that isn't tied to the performance of chores; however, if they do their chores on schedule and to an acceptable level of completion, they get an allowance bonus. There's no nagging, no reminding, no conflict, and if the chores don't get done, there's no money.

Until they get their first job, a sound allowance and spending program will provide the experience part of the learning equation. Now let's look at the modelling part. Depending on their maturity level, children of eight and up are normally ready to be involved in the financial-planning process. Once you've prepared your living expenses and net-worth statements, sit down with your family and go over it all together. Discuss how much you earn, and how many hours you must work in order to do so. (You may want to explain that this is private—most kids have no idea. Every single teacher my daughter ever had knew that she has a trust account with _____ dollars in it until one happened to mention it to me at parent/teacher interviews.) If you think they are ready, discuss what would happen financially if you lost your job, or were injured, or if you died. Today's children are inundated with information, and they worry. It can be very comforting to know that you have a plan. Go over the costs of running a household. On the other hand, you may wish to skip that step—your kids may never leave home. Discuss what's left at the end of the month, and how you decide where to spend it. Most children grow up with a sense that Mom and Dad get everything they want. It is never too early to learn that simply isn't true.

Whatever *you* do, your kids are likely to do, too. If you want them to pay themselves first and make monthly RSP contributions, show them your own good example. Talk to them about mutual funds and GICs, and the difference between them. Take them along when you meet with your financial planner.

Education Planning, Trusts, RESPs, and the CESG

Today's parents are facing double jeopardy. Youth unemployment is epidemic, and the educational requirements necessary for employment opportunities are rising—at about the same pace, it seems, as the cost of tuition. Although student loans are available, too many of today's graduates are starting their first real jobs with tens of thousands of dollars in high-interest debt. One of my son's friends, for example, will graduate in June 1999 with a bachelor degree in business and communication and a student loan of more than $20 000, on which the bank will charge a ridiculously high rate of interest.

Needless to say, a debt of this magnitude is a heavy burden for a young person to carry into today's uneasy job market. It isn't a situation that anyone wants to see their children in. On the other hand, how many of us have extra money to put aside for our younger children's future needs when their present needs are so compelling, not to mention, expensive?

With a little planning, and some very welcome assistance from the federal government, there is new hope. The 1997 federal budget delivered the welcome announcement of the Canadian Education Savings Grant (CESG), a program that is changing the face of education planning.

RESPs (Registered Education Savings Plans) have been around for some time, but their inflexibility made them less than attractive. With the changes in legislation and the assistance provided by the CESG, however, we are seeing a tremendous surge in the popularity of these plans. Unfortunately, like many government programs, it's a little confusing. These are the questions you'll need answers to:

◆ **How much can I contribute to an RESP?** Up to $4 000 per child per year, with a lifetime limit of $42 000 per child.

◆ **Can I contribute on my grandchild's behalf?** Absolutely. As a matter of fact, anyone can contribute to a single beneficiary plan. You can contribute on behalf of grandchildren, nieces, nephews, a beloved godchild—this is one way to make a profound difference in the life of a child. In a family plan, in which there is more than one beneficiary, the contributor must be related either by blood or adoption to each.

◆ **I heard that my contributions aren't tax deductible. What's the point, then?** A couple of things. The first is that the RESP is essentially a savings plan, and we've consistently found that saving doesn't occur without a plan. Those who wait "until we have the money" never have the money. Monthly investment is the key to reaching your objectives, whether those objectives are a snappy new car or something as important as your children's education.

Secondly, RESPs offer tax-sheltered growth. If you were to deposit $4000 in a non-RESP term deposit or Canada Savings Bonds for your child, you (yes, that's you, the contributor) would have to declare the interest income every year and pay tax on it at your tax rate, significantly diminishing real returns. If the investments are held in an RESP, the interest compounds free of taxation until the child withdraws the funds for secondary education. Returns are then taxed in the hands of the student, who presumably will be in the lowest tax bracket and will pay little or no tax.

Capital gains are always taxed in the hands of the child, whether or not they occur in an RESP. Therefore, if you have already taken advantage of the CESG and/or have made the maximum RESP contribution for a given year, you may want to investigate the possibility of opening an "in-trust" account holding a growth-oriented equity mutual fund. Before opening any trust account, it's a good idea to seek professional advice.

◆ **How does the CESG work?** The Canada Education Savings Grant is a program that matches 20% of contributions made to a child's RESP to a yearly maximum of $400 and a lifetime maximum of $7200. If you contribute $2000 a year from birth, your total contribution over 18 years will amount to $36 000. With the government's contribution of $7200 and an average annual return of 8 percent, your child will be going off to college with more than $90 000. That sounds like a lot of money—but if economists are correct, that is approximately how much a very ordinary secondary education is going to cost in 18 years.

To get the grant, you simply have to provide your RESP trustee with your child's social insurance number, which you can get by applying at your nearest Human Resources Canada branch with a copy of your child's birth certificate. Your trustee will apply for the grant on your behalf once you've provided the SIN and date of birth.

Unfortunately, children aged sixteen and seventeen are only eligible for the grant if contributions of at least $100 per year have been made in any four years before the age of sixteen, or, alternatively, if a minimum contribution of at least $2000 has been made prior to age sixteen.

◆ **Is there a deadline for contributing?** Yes and no. The deadline for RESP contributions in a given year is December 31, and you can't carry contribution room forward as you can with an RSP. At the moment, however, the CESG can be carried forward. If you contribute nothing this year, for instance, but contribute $4000 next year, the CESG will be $800 (20 percent of $2000 x 2). However, the maximum grant for any given year is $800, and if you contribute more than is eligible, you won't get the CESG on it next year. That is, if you contribute nothing one year, and $5000 the next, you'll receive a grant of $800. The $1000 cannot be used to apply for an additional grant the following year, so it's better to wait.

◆ **What kind of investments can be held within an RESP?** Qualified investments include mutual funds; segregated funds; GICs; shares listed on a prescribed stock exchange; and bonds and other debt obligations issued by governments, Crown corporations, or corporations listed on prescribed stock exchanges. Any RESP investments made prior to October 28, 1998, are considered qualified. New restrictions in regard to foreign investments are scheduled for the year 2001. If you are investing for younger children, it's important to bear in mind the long investment time frame and potential effects of inflation.

◆ **The last time we asked our financial adviser about education savings, we were advised to set up an in-trust account rather than an RESP. What's changed?** Quite a number of things, actually. The CESG is certainly a major and very attractive change, but there are others that are almost as important. The old restrictions were very onerous, and essentially, if Junior didn't go on to university almost immediately after high school, you received your principal investment back and the rest went to the Department of National Revenue. The new legislation provides much greater flexibility, and allows a longer time frame, 25 years from inception. If you open an RESP for your 13-year-old, for instance, it doesn't have to be collapsed until he or she is 38 years old.

Also, a full-time university program is no longer required. Funds can now be applied to tuition and living expenses required by any post-secondary program, as long as the course is more than 10 hours per week for three weeks.

And if Junior decides to eschew secondary education of any kind, you can transfer up to $50 000 to your RSP, assuming you have contribution room, transfer the RESP plan to another child, or apply the funds to upgrading your own education!

Contributions are returned without penalty or taxation, because they were made in after-tax dollars. Any Canada Education Savings Grant amounts will, of course, be returned to the government.

◆ **How do we get started?** There is never a better time than the present to start a monthly investment plan. In addition to being less painful than coming up with a lump sum, monthly investment allows you to take advantage of dollar-cost averaging, long-term growth, and the amazing benefits of early contribution on compound returns. You can purchase RESP plans through most financial institutions.

◆ **When is an in-trust account better?** Once you've received the maximum CESG grant, and assuming you have a long enough time frame to mitigate the risk, it makes sense to invest in a capital-gains-oriented mutual fund in-trust account. A minor child can receive up to approximately $6700 in capital gains without paying any tax, and there are no restrictions on withdrawals. An in-trust account can also provide funding for non-educational purposes—the down payment on a first home, or a start-up fund for a new business.

Home Sweet Home

There is perhaps nothing more emotionally satisfying that buying a home of your own. For years, this worked out well because residential real estate was also one of the most attractive investments available to the average Canadian citizen—not least of all because profits on your primary residence are non-taxable.

Over the last decade, the face of residential real estate in Canada has changed dramatically as high-ratio mortgages, those in which the down payment is less than 25 percent of the value of the home, have become increasingly common. The Canadian Mortgage Insurance Corporation (CMHC) is a Crown corporation whose function is making home ownership possible for more Canadians by insuring these high-ratio mortgages. However, CMHC premiums range from 0.5 percent to 3.0 percent of the entire mortgage, a significant expense for first-time home-buyers.

I'm amazed at the number of young people I see who have drained their RSPs through the Home Buyers Plan to fund the required 5 percent down on a home that then drops 15 percent in value over the first year, completely wiping out their assets. Not a pretty picture.

I guess what I'm trying to say is this. As we discussed in Chapter 9, real estate is no longer the risk-free, foolproof investment it was in our parent's time, largely because of demographics. If you're a late baby boomer, like me, born between 1951 and 1964, there is a generation following you that is 25 percent smaller than your own. Very simply, that means that there may be three buyers for every seller when you decide you need a bigger or smaller nest.

Home ownership is no longer an investment decision. When deciding whether to buy your own home, whether as a single woman or as part of a family, the deciding factor should be the cost. Compare the cost of renting a home to

◆ the cost of *interest* on your mortgage; plus

◆ the *opportunity cost* on your down payment; plus

◆ *maintenance* costs that you wouldn't have to pay on a rental property; plus

◆ *property tax;* plus

◆ *any condo fees;* plus

◆ *realty fees* amortized over the period you plan to be in the home; and

◆ *CMHC insurance premiums,* if any, amortized over the period you plan to be in the home.

For instance, if you put down $50 000 and could get a guaranteed rate of return of 4 percent per annum, your opportunity cost is $2 000 per year. If your mortgage is $150 000 at 8 percent, your interest cost is $12 000 per year. Add property tax, let's say $1200, maintenance costs of $500, and a real estate commission of $8500 amortized over 5 years, or $1700 per year. Your shelter cost is then $17 400 per year. If you can rent the same house for $1450 or less, you are better off renting. All other things being equal, if renting will cost you more, consider buying.

The fundamental deciding factor should be this: Do you expect the property to increase or decrease in value? No one rushes out to buy an investment that will lose money. Be cautious.

If your heart's desire is to own your own home, get the best professional advice you can. Shop for a realtor who is intent on finding the right home for you, not just on making a quick sale. Ask for her help in shopping for the best mortgage rates and terms. Consider a pre-approved mortgage, but ask for the best rate available between the pre-approval date and the actual signing date. A half-point deviation in interest rates can make a significant difference.

When you do buy, consider a shortened amortization period (10 to 15 years as opposed to 25) and weekly or bi-weekly payments. Your mortgage officer will show you the specific calculations, but you can plan on saving thousands of dollars.

The flip side of the home-ownership decision is your investment-planning program. Traditionally, mortgage repayment was the forced-savings investment plan of choice for average Canadians. If you choose to rent rather than buy because it is more economically prudent, *don't forget the other fundamentally important issue—paying yourself first through monthly investment.*

There is no higher purpose for money than making it into love. Managing your affairs well is perhaps the most effective way to express your commitment to your family, to society, and to your own well-being.

13

The Business of Relationships

The meeting of two personalities is like the contact of two chemical substances: if there is any reaction, both are transformed.

CARL JUNG

When we have a health problem, we generally go to a doctor. We don't call the nearest medical school and ask for an application. And if we're wise, we don't pretend that we don't have a problem and hope it goes away—at least not for long. We get help. When we need financial advice, on the other hand, it's amazing how often we choose to do without. There are any number of reasons for this inaction. The first, I think, is that financial advisers are often commissioned salespeople, and we've learned to distrust anyone who makes a living by selling us something. We are afraid we'll be pressured into buying something we don't want or need. There is sometimes a kind of inferiority complex at work. We are afraid we won't measure up financially. No one has less money and more debt than we do. No one is more ignorant about investments than we are. We might look stupid. We might waste their time.

When I was a teenager, I went to the same doctor my mother-in-law went to. Oh, was he mean! Nasty. He disdainfully dismissed my questions. When I asked him about an unusual bump, his response was, "It's nothing. Don't touch it." When I asked for an alternative treatment when a prescription didn't seem to be having the desired effect, he told me I was using it incorrectly. When I said I was using it according to his directions, he said, "You can't be." When I said something was painful, he said, "No, it's not. That's impossible." Looking back, I cannot believe that I saw him for four years. Why would I put up with being treated so disrespectfully? Maybe I assumed that was normal behaviour for doctors, and that he obviously knew best. As a matter of fact, his gruffness was almost reassuring. Surely he must be very knowledgeable if his patients put up with his manner. I was 30-something when it finally dawned on me that I wanted a female doctor—someone who had actually experienced a woman's body from the inside. I wanted someone who would take the time to explain things to me, who wouldn't disregard my opinions, wouldn't make me wait for half an hour in the waiting room, and who would view my symptoms or ailments within the context of my general health and life. Once I figured out what I wanted, it was amazingly easy. I mentioned my search to my friends, and it was only a matter of weeks before someone referred me to the doctor I still see today.

As I mentioned in Chapter 1, financial advisers often need financial advisers because *knowing* the right thing and *doing* the right thing don't always go hand in hand. A financial adviser should be more than an expert—he or she should be a coach, a source of information, and a service provider. For those of us who aren't financial professionals, it's even more important to work with professional partners. The benefits of a strong professional relationship are myriad and unique to the individuals involved, but these are just some of the advantages that you may expect:

◆ A trusted financial adviser can work with you to create a comprehensive financial plan, walking you through the early drudgery of things like disability, life insurance, and tax planning. If you don't get these basics covered, investment planning won't serve you in the way it should.

◆ A financial adviser can help you put together a team of financial professionals as your needs change. Most financial advisers and planners aren't also estate, legal, and tax specialists, but when you require that kind of help, they can refer you to someone who can provide it. They can also coordinate everything—communicating, for instance, with your accountant and your tax lawyer to make sure they have the information they need about your investments.

◆ I've been in the financial-services industry for almost 12 years now, and I still occasionally wake up in the middle of the night with a terrible knot in my stomach when the markets are off. The next morning, if my emotional-doubt-demons are still lurking, I go into my partner's office and give him the what-if speech. What if this time it is different? What if Y2K does trigger a recession? What if the markets are terribly overvalued? Rob pulls out his charts, graphs, and historical averages, and we go over it all one more time. Now, believe me, I know this stuff, but when the market is wonky and everyone I talk to is a messenger of pessimism and doom, my stomach hurts just like everyone else's. What I need, in order to alleviate my worry, is a refresher from an objective, trusted professional who knows his stuff. We all need that sometimes.

Now, let's say I'd never worked in financial services, and I own bank, no-load funds, or fund families whose representatives only sell *their* funds. I'm worried, and I call an in-house financial adviser. The adviser almost invariably tells me the same things: "Successful investing really isn't rocket science. It's about choosing the right investments and staying invested." The question is, will I believe in-house advisers whose job is to ensure I stay invested with their company?

Maybe. Maybe not. It probably depends on how worried I really am. But the bottom line is that without trusted, objective advice, I am more likely to make a fear-based decision rather than a wise one.

◆ As a financial adviser, I spend an average of two hours every business day reading materials relating to financial planning, investments, mutual funds, the markets, the global and Canadian economies, and Canadian tax issues. That's part of my job. The interesting thing is that never once have I felt on top of it all. If that is true for me, what are the chances for the rest of the population? Doctors? Lawyers? Working mothers? It is fundamentally important to educate ourselves on matters that impact our lives. However, a financial adviser should be an efficient resource, steering you in the right direction, pointing out the pitfalls, acting as devil's advocate, and helping you filter through the overwhelming amount of financial information out there.

If you have a financial adviser you trust and are comfortable with, fabulous. If you don't, I strongly recommend that you sit down now and write a list of the objectives you'd like to achieve within that relationship and the attributes you're looking for. It's a little bit like dating—you are far more likely to find the partner of your dreams if you first articulate your wish list. What's important to you? What isn't?

I recently had the misfortune of sitting next to a very brilliant and verbose investment adviser at an industry dinner. I'm sure he was a very nice fellow, but I actually left in the middle of dessert because I couldn't listen to one more word of his lengthy dissertation on the benefits of income trusts. If I were any more bored, I would have been comatose. If you're interested in two-hour lectures on comparative investments, however, he is definitely your guy. As my grandma used to say, "There's a lid for every pot."

Your lists might include some of the following entries. Check off the ones that apply or add your own:

OBJECTIVES

☐ I'd like to have a comprehensive financial plan prepared and implemented.

☐ I'd like to begin an RESP program.

☐ I'd like some advice on investing my RSP contributions.

☐ I want to learn more about investing and investments.

☐ I'd like to have someone explain my statements to me.

☐ I want to earn higher returns on my investments.

☐ I'd like to be sure that my investments are effectively diversified.

☐ I want to have someone take care of my investments so I don't have to worry about missing something.

☐ I want to be able to see the returns on my whole portfolio without doing a lot of calculating.

☐ I'd like to review my portfolio with a professional at least twice a year.

☐ I'm confused by the number of mutual funds available—I'd like someone to explain which funds are best for me and why.

☐ I'd like a financial adviser who can also give me basic tax advice and who will work with my accountant to ensure I'm minimizing taxes.

☐ I need someone to keep me on track. It's too easy to put things off. I'd like to work with someone who will call me when it's time to do something.

ATTRIBUTES

☐ I want a knowledgeable adviser, but someone who doesn't make me feel patronized.

☐ I want an adviser who is prepared to meet with me at least every six months.

☐ I don't have time to plow through a ton of information; I'd like someone who presents information concisely and gives me only the details I need to know.

☐ I want to be part of the decision-making process.

☐ I don't want to be part of the decision-making process; I just want to be told what's best.

☐ I'd like an adviser who is willing to teach me.

☐ I just want someone who will take care of it and report back with the bottom line.

☐ I want someone who speaks my language.

☐ I want to work with someone who sees the big picture.

☐ I prefer someone who is detail oriented.

☐ I want a casual, more intimate relationship.

☐ I want to deal with someone who's strictly business.

Now, think about the questions you need to ask. Ultimately, like everything else we've covered, there is no right financial adviser—just the right financial adviser for you. Even that might change over the course of your life.

For now, though, think about what's important to you. Ask around. If your friends rave about someone in particular, you may, too. But think of the process like any other relationship—it can be a real mistake to commit to a long-term relationship with the first person you date. You tend to know when it feels right. Don't discount those feelings. On the other hand, if you feel pressured, intimidated, rushed, patronized, or just uncomfortable, don't discount those feelings either.

Think of your first appointment with a financial adviser as a mutual interview. It isn't enough to work with someone who wants your business (as in commission dollars). Next to your health, there is nothing more intimate than money. Your financial adviser should be someone you're comfortable talking to—about your income, your spending, your fears, and your dreams. You should *like* each other. If you don't, you just aren't going to communicate as effectively as you need to.

It's always good to approach an interview with prepared questions. If you've written them down in advance, you won't forget, and the adviser you're interviewing should feel more comfortable, too. Explain in advance that you are looking for a long-term financial adviser with whom you feel comfortable, and that you aren't interested in investing immediately. If a potential candidate can't take the time to see you on that basis, great; that person is just one less candidate to interview.

Here are some questions you might want to ask:

QUESTIONS FOR A POTENTIAL FINANCIAL ADVISER

- How long have you been in the industry?
- Do you have any special designations, and if so, what do they mean? What did you have to do to achieve those designations?
- What type of client do you most prefer to work with?
- What do you feel is the most important aspect of financial planning?
- About what size is your average client portfolio?
- What is your educational background?
- Would you describe yourself as conservative, balanced, or somewhat aggressive in terms of investment planning?
- How many clients do you currently have?
- How often are you in touch with your clients?
- Do you send out consolidated statements? If so, how often?
- Do you provide newsletters? If so, may I see copies of the last few issues?
- Do you have any other marketing material you feel would be helpful?
- If we work together, will you prepare a financial plan? If so, is there an additional fee?

(continues)

(continued)

- How often will you review my account, and when you do so, will we meet in person, speak on the phone, or communicate by mail?
- Are there times when you would prefer that I call you?
- How do you get paid? If you're on commission, how does that normally work? How much would I end up paying on a transaction of $10 000?
- How long do your client meetings normally last?
- Will you come to my home if I prefer that? Are you ever available weekends and evenings?
- Do you tend to recommend a certain type of investment, and if so, what is it?
- How do you keep up with all the information out there?
- Would you describe yourself mainly as a financial planner, or mainly as an investment adviser?
- Do you tend to recommend stocks, bonds, mutual funds, or all of the above?
- Where would you recommend I invest my emergency reserve fund?
- Do you have a minimum account size that you generally work with?

These questions are all really just starting points for discussion. There are no right answers. As you move through the interview process, pay very close attention to the way you feel. Do you feel that your questions are being answered completely and respectfully? Is the communication process itself smooth and effective, or is it difficult to be understood?

Find someone you feel shares your values.

There are also a few things you should look out for, warning signs that should be investigated further. Watch out for—

◆ Anyone who tries to sell you something on the first date. How does this person know what's right for you until he or she knows who you are? What else you own? What your objectives are?

◆ Anyone who seems focused on selling you a specific product as opposed to designing a strategy and then finding the right products within it.

◆ Anyone who attempts to sell you more risk than you are comfortable with, or more complexity than you are comfortable with.

◆ Anyone who disregards your questions or concerns, or treats them lightly.

◆ Anyone who can't take no for an answer. If you aren't comfortable, you aren't comfortable, and that should be good enough.

◆ Anyone who makes you feel that your concerns are the result of inexperience or a lack of sophistication. That may be true, but then the adviser's job is to educate you, respectfully and patiently.

Lastly, if you weren't referred by someone you know, ask for references. Unless they are new to the industry, beware of advisers who give you the names of people they've been dealing with for a year or less. Everyone's wonderful in the courtship phase—I want to know how they behave when the honeymoon's over.

That brings us to the second part of the equation. You. A relationship is only as strong as its weakest link. I laughed last week when I heard a colleague's response to a client who was berating him for not calling her often enough. "Doesn't your phone have a dial pad?" he joked. If you need or want something, call.

Keep looking until you find an adviser you trust and feel comfortable with. Stay in touch. If you have concerns, speak. If you have questions, ask. Don't sabotage your overall financial plan by taking the advice of your third cousin, Bill, the plumber, over that of your financial adviser.

Trust your heart. Speak your mind. Get the help you deserve.

Conclusion:
The End of the Beginning

This we know. All things are
connected, like the blood which
unites one family . . . .
Whatever befalls the earth,
befalls the children of earth. We did
not weave the web of life, we are
merely a strand of it. Whatever we do
to the web, we do to ourselves.

CHIEF SEATTLE

Well, my friend. Our time together, at least on this leg of the journey, is almost at an end.

At the back of the book, you will find the Glossary—"The Language of Investment," a consolidated primer on terms you'll need and want to know. It was designed both to be read and to be used later as a reference. Do take the time to at least skim through it—you never know what you might find to talk about at the office tomorrow.

If I have succeeded in my role on this path we've shared, you now have the tools you need to create the life you want. You know that it is only fear that dares stand between you and a future rich with fulfillment—and that fear is powerless in the light of a clear vision. I do hope that this is one of those books you'll return to again and again, finding, in each cycle of your life, new ways of revealing and applying your inner wisdom. For now, if there is only one thing that you take away with you, let it be this: money, investments, and financial planning all exist for your benefit. They are useful only as tools in the creation of your dreams, and can be successful only if they are intimately linked to the unique desires of your heart.

At the end of the day, financial serenity is achieved by remembering and applying these six simple principles:

✄ Revere the wisdom of your heart.

✄ Choose your beliefs wisely and well—they will shape your future.

✄ Nurture a powerful vision.

✄ Save and invest 10 percent of your income.

✄ Give 10 percent of your income away.

✄ Get the help you deserve.

That's it. You now have everything you need.
You have the power to create a miraculously rich, abundant life.
Happy trails.

RECOMMENDED READING

If you'd like to continue down this path in the privacy of your own home, I heartily recommend reading any or all of the following books. All are available either in stock or by special order through any large bookstore, or you can find them in your local library. If you have any problem finding a copy, contact the publisher directly to order.

Inspirational

A GIFT FROM THE SEA, Anne Morrow Lindbergh. There are dozens of editions of this book—check with your local bookstore. One of those rare and precious reading experiences that make you wonder how someone so far away could know your inner heart better than you yourself; a book that offers the wisdom of our deepest understanding. I borrowed it from the library, and then ordered three copies from the bookstore the next day. Takes only hours to read, which is good—because you will want to read it again and again.

HEART STEPS, Julia Cameron, Jeremy P. Tarcher/Putnam Books. Simply life changing.

SIMPLE ABUNDANCE: A DAYBOOK OF COMFORT & JOY, Sarah Ban Breathnach, Warner Books. This book has been part of my morning meditations for more than 18 months now. My first copy was a gift—I have since bought more to give to loved ones. At about $20, this is a lovely gift to give yourself.

THE ARTIST'S WAY, Julia Cameron with Mark Bryan, Jeremy P. Tarcher/Putnam Books. I crossed paths with this book a dozen times before reading it—after all, I thought, I'm a writer, not an artist. By the end of the book, I understood that we're all artists, and that only that understanding stands between us and pure joy.

Investments

2000 BUYER'S GUIDE TO RRSPS, Gordon Pape, Prentice Hall Canada. The very best of the many RSP books around—a conservative look at all of the investment and other issues surrounding RSPs.

FUND MONITOR 2000, Duff Young, Prentice Hall Canada. A well-written and brilliantly analyzed review of Canada's top mutual funds, and a scathing review of "the dogs"—those funds to avoid.

RISK IS A FOUR LETTER WORD (THE ASSET ALLOCATION APPROACH TO INVESTING), George Hartman, Stoddart Publishing Co. Not an easy read, but a worthwhile one for anyone interested in mutual fund or equity investment.

Personal Finance

BALANCING ACT, Joanne Thomas Yaccato, Prentice Hall Canada. With a scintillating sense of humour and engaging personal anecdotes, Joanne takes a deeper look at the world of finance through a woman's clear eyes.

FINANCIAL FREEDOM WITHOUT SACRIFICE, Talbot Stevens, Financial Success Strategies. Can't find money to invest? This book has 150 strategies on ways to do so, and a good basic look at investment principles.

THE PIG AND THE PYTHON, David Cork with Susan Lightstone, Stoddard Publishing Co. Ltd. Cork & Lightstone do a masterful job of making demographic financial planning readable.

TAX PLANNING (FOR YOU & YOUR FAMILY) 1999, KPMG, Carswell Publishing. A reference book rather than a good read, this offers a comprehensive and detailed look at the taxation issues that touch you.

THE STRATEGY (A HOMEOWNER'S GUIDE TO WEALTH CREATION), Garth Turner, Key Porter Books Ltd. This well-known real estate expert takes a look at two very hot topics—today's real estate market and leverage investment programs. A must-read for anyone who owns a home or plans to do so.

THE WEALTHY BARBER, David Chilton, Stoddart Publishing Co. The very best place to start. An engaging, entertaining, easy-to-read overview of personal finance.

WINNING THE TAX GAME 2000, Tim Cestnick, Prentice Hall Canada. I hate sports analogies, but I have to admit that no one has ever made taxes more fun to read about than Tim has with this book.

YOU CAN'T TAKE IT WITH YOU: THE COMMON SENSE GUIDE TO ESTATE PLANNING FOR CANADIANS, Sandra E. Foster, John Wiley & Sons. When it's time to get down to serious estate planning, you'll want this book.

Other

THE PATH OF LEAST RESISTANCE, Robert Fritz , Random House. An intense and challenging read offering some remarkable wisdom and lots of verbiage—a great book for people like myself who are infatuated with the written word, and when choosing between two books, select the one with the most pages.

GLOSSARY
The Language of Investment

In order to navigate the world of finance and investment, you must learn to speak the language. Following is a list of common financial terms, in alphabetical order for convenience.

Accrued Interest Interest that has been earned but not yet paid out to the investor. This interest must be declared each year as income for tax purposes even if it has not been received.

Acquisition Fee Another term for sales charge or commission—the cost of acquiring or buying an investment. See also **Front-end Load.**

Actuary Professional analyst who calculates mortality rates and life expectancy for insurance purposes.

After-tax Cost The cost to an investor after calculating the effect of income tax. We hear this term in regard to tax-advantaged investments, like labour-sponsored funds, where the cost to the investor is offset by tax credits. If a tax credit of 30 percent is available, for instance, a $1000 investment would cost $700 after the tax credit was considered. The after-tax cost would be $700.

Amortization The process of gradually paying off debt or obligation—e.g., a mortgage—or of "writing off" value for tax or reporting purposes over an extended period of time.

Annual Report A report issued by a company to its shareholders containing records of the company's operations and its financial statements for the period reported.

Annuity A contract under which assets are turned over to an institution (usually an insurance corporation) on the condition that a stream of income will be provided for a specified period. **Life annuities** pay out over the lifetime of the "annuitant" (the person receiving the payments) and **fixed-term annuities** for a "fixed" period of time, generally until the annuitant reaches age 90. **Annuities** can also be **"deferred"** (payments are scheduled to begin at some point in the future) or **"immediate."**

Asset Allocation The planned distribution of investment assets (by percentage) into various categories, e.g., equities (stocks or equity mutual funds), bonds (or fixed-income funds), and liquid investments (T-Bills, term deposits, money-market funds).
    There are two primary types of asset allocation—strategic and tactical.
    Strategic Asset Allocation measures an investor's risk tolerance, objectives, and needs in order to design an appropriate portfolio. Examples include the Mackenzie Star Program and the Keystone Program.
    Tactical Asset Allocation is a kind of institutionalized market timing. Although there are all kinds of proponents of tactical-asset allocation and market timing, statistics prove that over the long run, it just doesn't work.

Averages and Indices (or Stock-market Index) The DOW Jones Industrial Average (commonly known as the DOW) is one, the TSE 300 Composite

Index is another. These are tools of statistical measurement, in which a basket of representative companies is used to determine the overall gain or loss of a market. In the TSE 300, for instance, the Toronto Stock Exchange performance is measured by recording the price changes of the 300 stocks that make up the index.

Averaging Down The process of buying more of a security for which the market value has declined in order to lower the average per-share or per-unit cost of the holding.

Back-end Load An arrangement in which mutual fund investors are not charged commission on purchasing a mutual fund, but may be charged a redemption penalty or "back-end load" if they redeem their holdings prior to an agreed length of time, usually six years. See also **Front-end Load.**

Balloon Payment A large, lump-sum payment due at the end of a stated term. Usually used in reference to mortgages, bonds, and debentures.

Bank Rate This is the rate at which the Bank of Canada makes short-term loans to Canada's chartered banks, i.e., the Royal Bank, CIBC, Toronto-Dominion, Bank of Montreal, and the National Bank.

Basis Point (also referred to as BPs or "Beeps") You will probably hear this in reference to bond and T-Bill purchases. It simply means 1/100th of 1 percent.

Bear Market A term used to describe a declining market. A "bearish" analyst is one who believes the market will decline.

Beneficial Owner The individual or institution that really owns the asset. If I own a self-directed RSP with ABC Trust, for instance, in which I own mutual funds, the mutual-fund account will be registered to ABC Trust In Trust For Lori Bamber a/c #123456-7. I am the beneficial owner, and ABC Trust (the trustee) would be the **registered owner.**

Bid The price a buyer offers to pay for a trading security or asset.

Blue-chip Stocks Stocks with good investment qualities. They are usually common shares of well-established, dividend-paying companies with established earnings histories. These companies are also invariably **"large-cap"** or large capital, meaning they have a market "capitalization" (shares outstanding) of $100 000 000 or more.

Board Lot The minimum number of shares that may be purchased without incurring additional commission. A purchase of shares that is less than a board lot is an **odd lot.** Unless you're planning to become a stock broker, you will probably never need to know this.

Bond A debt instrument issued by a government or corporation in order to raise working capital. A bond is a promise (or **covenant**) by the issuing government or corporation to repay the principal amount (amount purchased) on the maturity date plus interest payments on a stated schedule.

  Buying a bond with the intent to hold it to maturity is a secure way of managing cash-flow needs. Investing in bonds or bond funds to diversify a portfolio is a way of reducing the volatility of the overall portfolio. Investing in bonds with the intent to sell at a profit (a capital gain) when interest rates drop is a form of speculation.

Buyer beware—a 9 percent bond will not necessary yield 9 percent to the investor. In low interest rate environments, an owner of a 9 percent bond would not sell it without receiving a premium to compensate for the loss in income. That is, a $1000, 9 percent bond might be sold and purchased for $1070 (a $70 premium). Therefore, the yield to maturity (let's assume the bond matures in one year) would be $1000 x 9% = $1090 – the $70 premium for a real yield of $20, or 2 percent.

See also **Debenture, Diversification,** and **Discount.**

Book Value This term is usually used to describe the purchase price, plus reinvested dividends, of investments within an RSP. Book value can also be the market value at the time an asset is transferred or contributed to an RSP.

Book value is used to calculate maximum **foreign content** holdings. At present, foreign content is generally limited to 20 percent of book value, that is, 20 percent of the purchase amount of your assets plus any reinvested dividends.

In the stock market, or when analyzing companies, the term **book value** is used in reference to the worth of a company, the net assets belonging to the owners of the business as reported on the **balance sheet.**

Broker An agent who sells and buys securities on behalf of a third party. Usually used in reference to an agent who buys and sells stocks, an agent who sells a range of insurance products, or an agent who sells real estate.

Bull Market The opposite of a bear market—a market in which prices are increasing.

Callable This is a feature of some bonds or preferred stocks that allow the issuer to redeem ("call") the bond or stock prior to the stated maturity date at a prestated price.

Canadian Bond Rating Service (CBRS) An independent evaluator of the underlying credit worthiness (corporate credit rating). Ratings range from P1 (highest) to P5 (lowest). There are other bond-rating evaluators such as **Standard and Poor's** and **Moody's.**

Canadian Depository Insurance Corporation (CIDC) A Crown corporation formed for the protection of investors in Canada's banks and trust companies. Under CDIC, to which all banks and trust companies pay premiums, an investor is covered to a maximum of $60 000 (on principal deposits only—interest is not included) should a member firm become bankrupt.

Canadian Investor Protection Fund (CIPF) A fund created by the stock exchanges and the **Investment Dealers Association (IDA)** to protect investors from losses resulting from the bankruptcy of a member firm. All stock-brokerage firms in Canada must be members; however, securities and mutual-fund dealers are not members of the IDA and their clients are not covered by this fund.

A stock-brokerage firm is a member of an exchange, and although it may sell mutual funds, GICs, etc., its primary business is the trading of stocks and bonds.

Securities Dealers are licensed through their provincial securities commission (e.g., the BC Securities Commission) to sell mutual funds and certain securities not traded on an exchange. They may offer these products through a liaison with a member firm.

Mutual-fund Dealers are licensed through their provincial securities commission to sell mutual funds only. Again, they may offer other products through institutional liaisons.

Canada Pension Plan (CPP)   (For information specific to your situation, call the CPP hotline.)

We hear a lot about CPP in the news these days—it's going broke and we better prepare for retirement without it. In reality, CPP is not a pension fund per se—it only maintains a cash reserve of about two years. That is, if we all stopped contributing right now, CPP could continue to pay benefits for two years and then it really would be broke. CPP is a program that is fully funded by the current contributors—money in equals money out. Today, there are five employed contributors for each person receiving CPP benefits. By the year 2030, there will only be three employed contributors for each person receiving benefits. See the problem?

Due to demographic changes, there will be significant changes to CPP over the next 30 years. In any case, it isn't much of an income and certainly won't fund the life of your dreams. This is how it works: Throughout your working lifetime, you contribute a defined amount to CPP, and your employer matches your contributions. You can earn up to $3500 without being required to contribute, and you don't have to contribute a percentage of any earnings over the "maximum pensionable earnings" ($35 400 in 1996). In 1992, the contribution amount, as a percentage of earnings, was set at 4.8 percent. In 1998 it was set at 6.1 percent, and by the year 2016, it will be 10.1 percent. If CPP is to be sustained in its current form, contributors will have to pay about 14.2 percent of earnings by the year 2030. It's possible, but the ultimate question is "Is it fair?"

The Benefits

Full **retirement** benefits are provided to contributors when they reach age 65. The amount of the benefit is determined by calculating the number of years of contributory employment, and the amount contributed to the plan. Early retirement benefits are available from age 60 at a reduced rate; if individuals choose to continue contributing to age 70, their pensions at 70 will be 30 percent higher than normal benefits. The maximum benefit (at age 65) was $727.08 a month in 1996—not much. Worse news, women providing unpaid care services are not eligible to contribute. If their husbands die, they are eligible to receive 60 percent of this meagre amount.

Limited **disability** benefits are available if a contributor (who has contributed for at least five of the previous ten calendar years, or two of the last three calendar years) is unable to work at *any job or occupation*. This is a pretty limited view of disability, but CPP still paid out approximately $329 million in

1996. Maximum disability benefits are paid according to a flat-rate schedule and an earnings-related calculation. The maximum disability benefit in 1996 was $870.92 per month, with an additional benefit of up to $164.17 per month for each dependent child of the disabled individual.

Survivor benefits are paid to the spouse, estate and/or dependent children of a deceased contributor. There are three different forms of survivor benefits:

A "death benefit," which is a onetime payment, calculated as the lesser of one half of the benefits payable in the year of death or 10 percent of maximum pensionable earnings. The maximum dollar amount was $3540 in 1996.

A surviving spouse's pension—the meagre 60 percent of the deceased's pension benefits. For spouses of contributors who are not yet retired, there is also a small monthly benefit available. The calculation is rather tedious, but suffice to say the maximum benefit was $399.70 in 1996.

An "orphan's pension" is available to all children of a deceased contributor until age 18, or if they are attending school full time, until age 25. The monthly benefit was $164.17 in 1996.

Capital Cost Allowance An Income Tax Act term used to describe deductions allowed from the value of certain assets, which are then treated as expenses from an individual's or company's income.

Capital Gain A profit made on an asset when the selling price is higher than the purchase price on "capital assets," such as stocks, real estate, and bonds. To encourage investment in Canada, Revenue Canada taxes capital gains more favourably than other income. We pay tax on only 75 percent of the capital gain. We can also use any capital losses to offset taxable capital gains. Unfortunately, capital losses cannot be used to offset other types of income.

Capital Loss The opposite of a capital gain—see above.

Capitalization The total amount of all outstanding debt, common and preferred stock, contributed surplus, and retained earnings of a company. It is also sometimes shown as a percentage.

Carry-forward The difference between an individual's maximum RRSP contribution limit and the amount actually contributed. Currently, carry-forward amounts may be carried forward indefinitely, but this may not always be the case.

Cash Flow For individuals, all income received in cash (or cash value) and all expenses paid in cash (or cash value). For corporations, all earnings plus all deductions that are not paid out in cash, such as depreciation and deferred income taxes.

Certificate of Deposit (CD) More commonly called term deposit (if it matures within one year) or **Guaranteed Income Certificate (GIC)**—a deposit of funds that becomes available on a stated maturity date. See aslo **GIC**.

Class A and B Stock In most cases, class A refers to preferred stock, and class B refers to common stock. This is usually but not always the case, so it is important to ask what the difference is.

Collateral Property, securities, or assets pledged as security against a loan.

Commercial Paper Short-term (less than one year), unsecured promissory notes issued by corporations to finance short-term cash-flow requirements.

Commission The broker or agent's fee for buying or selling securities for a third party.

Commodity A product used for commerce that is traded on an exchange. Commodities include agricultural products like wheat (and pork bellies!), or natural resources like oil and gold.

Common Shares A type of stock that represents ownership or "equity" in a company. Common shares often include the right to vote in the company's affairs and entitle the shareholder to participate in a share of the company's profits, usually paid out through dividends.

Compound Returns The magic of compounding, the eighth wonder of the world! This means that interest or dividends are earned on the principal amount invested *plus any formerly earned interest or returns on the investment.* That is, if you invest $1000 at 10 percent, and set up your investment so that the interest is reinvested, in the first year you will earn $100 on $1000. In the second year, you will earn $110—because you also earn interest on the $100 paid in interest the previous year. The effects of compound returns over time is mind blowing. Unfortunately, it also works in reverse, on debt. Therefore, you pay interest not only on the amount that you initially spent or borrowed, but on the principal plus interest that has been charged to you in the past (this happens with credit-card debt).

Confirmation A printed acknowledgement of a purchase or sale of stocks, bonds, or mutual-fund units. These are normally mailed to an investor within 24 hours of a trade, and give all the details of the purchase or sale (price, number of shares or units, and commission). They are issued either by the brokerage firm or the investment dealer. Confirmations are also referred to as **contracts.**

Constrained Share Companies These are companies whose ownership is restricted to Canadian citizens. They include banks, broadcasting and communications companies, and trust and insurance companies.

Consumer Price Index A statistical measurement of increases or decreases in the cost of living. A basket of goods (housing, gas, the price of milk, etc.) is tracked on a regular basis. This is generally the way that inflation is measured.

Convertible An open-topped car that can really mess up your hair, or ...

A feature of a security (generally a bond, debenture, or preferred share) that allows the investor to "convert" or change the asset into another asset, generally a common share, according to prestated conditions.

Convertible Term Insurance Term insurance that can be converted to a permanent or "whole life" policy without evidence of insurability (medical examinations, etc.).

Coupon A bond attachment (coupon) that can be clipped and presented to a bank on or after the maturity date. The coupon entitles the bearer to an interest payment. The **coupon rate** is the rate of interest paid on the bond. A **strip bond** is a term that refers to a bond stripped of its coupons and sold separately.

Covenant A promise to do something, or not to do something, as set out in a contract or bond offering. An example might be a covenant to not issue further bond issues.

Cum Dividend A dumb term that means that the investor purchasing shares of a corporation will also receive the dividend (or profits per share for a stated time period) that is about to be paid out—the opposite of **Ex-dividend.**

Cumulative Preferred This term means that if a company misses a dividend payment to its preferred shareholder, it must make up this payment before paying dividends to common shareholders.

CUSIP An industry term used to refer to the six-digit identifying number on stock certificates.

Cyclical Stock A stock of a company that is especially sensitive to changes in economic conditions. A cyclical stock would be considered an aggressive or volatile investment, and should only be purchased with professional advice, with less than 10 percent of a balanced portfolio, and with an investment time horizon of more than 10 years.

Day Order An order to buy or sell a security that becomes void if not filled by the end of that day.

Debenture An unsecured bond, or debt instrument. At one time, bonds were always "securitized" (or backed) by the underlying assets of the corporation issuing them. A debenture is a bond that is not backed by underlying assets. This definition has become somewhat mongrelized with the advent of "junk bonds," in which the underlying assets are worth mere fractions of the value of the bond issue. When purchasing a bond, ask about the present and future values of the underlying assets.

Decreasing Term Insurance With this insurance policy, the premium remains constant while the coverage diminishes over time, decreasing the overall premium of the coverage.

Deemed Disposition A term used by Revenue Canada to refer to those circumstances that result in an asset being treated, for tax purposes, as if it has been sold. This occurs when an asset is transferred to another individual (i.e., a spouse); when an asset is contributed or swapped into an RSP; upon death; or upon emmigration from Canada.

Deferred Annuity An annuity for which income payments begin after a period of time, usually at a stated age. For instance, you might purchase an annuity with the proceeds of a pension plan on early retirement at age 55 and defer receipt of the proceeds until age 69.

Deferred Sales Charge (DSC) Deferred sales charges (or DSCs) have taken the market by storm since they became available in the 1980s. With a deferred sales charge, the fund company pays the sales commission on your behalf, but you must leave your investment with that family of funds for a stated period of time (usually seven years). If you withdraw earlier, you will be charged a fee on a declining scale (for example 6 percent in year one, 5 percent in year two, 4 percent in year three). This information is available in the fund prospectus. It's a good option if you plan to leave the funds invested at least long enough to reduce the sales charge to a range of 1 percent to 3 percent because it leaves your principal intact to work for you from day one. Be aware, though, that the DSC is often charged on the full redemption amount rather than the amount of the individual purchase (again, review the fund prospectus).

Most funds that are sold on a DSC basis allow you to redeem up to 10 percent of your investment per year without charge. It is a good idea to do this, even if you just move the redemption proceeds to the same fund's front-end equivalent because management fees may be less on front-end funds. This also provides an opportunity to **crystallize capital gains.** That is, in the eyes of Revenue Canada, although your assets may have gone up or down in value, no capital gain or loss has occurred until you create a deemed disposition (see **Deemed Disposition**). Therefore, if you have capital losses you wish to use, or if your income is lower than usual in a given year and it makes sense to declare some capital gains, it also makes sense to crystallize a capital gain. The same can be true of capital losses if you have capital gains that you would otherwise be taxed on.

Defined Benefit Plan (DBP) A company- or institution-sponsored pension plan in which retirement benefits are usually determined by a complex formula based on salary and years of service. The benefits are therefore "defined"; the pension-holder knows, or can calculate, what the payments will be in advance.

Most pension plans in Canada are defined benefit plans. DBPs may also be **contributory** (which means that both the employee and employer contribute), or (rarely) **non-contributory** (which means the employer makes all contributions on the employee's behalf).

Defined Contribution Plan See **Money Purchase Plan.**

Discount In the financial industry, "discount" generally refers to the amount a bond or debenture sells for below "par" value, its stated face value. For instance, a bond worth $100 with an interest rate of 3 percent would trade at a discount to make it attractive to potential purchasers if interest rates (for the same term) were 5 percent. Therefore, the price might be $87 for $100 of bond value, for a discount of $13/$100. The opposite of a discount is a "premium." If the bond being offered for sale paid interest of 6 percent during a period when bonds of the same maturity term generally paid 3 percent, a potential buyer would be willing to pay a premium. Therefore, a $100 bond might be sold for $107, or a premium of $7/$100.

Diversification See **Diversification** in Chapter 9.

Dividend A portion of a company's (or mutual fund's) profits paid out to shareholders (or unit-holders). May be paid in cash (usually the case with stock) or in kind (more shares or units, which is usually the case with mutual funds).

Dividend Reinvestment The term describing a process whereby dividends are paid in cash and then converted into shares or units of a company or fund (without the cash being distributed to the investor first). Some companies and most mutual funds provide this feature.

Dividend Tax Credit System A tax procedure used to encourage Canadians to invest in Canadian corporations and to reflect the fact that corporations have already paid tax on the profits they then pay out as dividends. Tax is calculated by "grossing up" (increasing) the amount of the dividend received by 25 percent. Federal tax is then calculated on this amount. Next, a tax credit of 16.67 percent of the dividend received is applied, and then provincial tax is calculated.

The result is more favourable tax treatment of dividend income than employment or interest income.

Dollar-cost Averaging This describes the process of investing a specified (unchanging) amount on a regular basis. This process mitigates volatility risk by working against natural emotional reactions—that is, when prices are down, it feels "unnatural" to purchase more, even though logically (assuming the investment is sound) we know this to be a good strategy. When prices are up, it is always tempting to buy more, although logically, we understand that this is not a good "value." Dollar-cost averaging alleviates the negative effects of both of these natural emotional reactions.

This process also lowers the average purchase price of shares or units, as the same amount buys more shares when the price is down. Market volatility then becomes a helpmate rather than an anxiety producer.

Earned Income A Revenue Canada term. Very loosely defined, this includes all income that is earned through employment or business. For most of us, "earned income" would be the amount of our gross salary. It also includes royalties, research grants, taxable alimony, maintenance and child support received, net rental income (rental income minus rental losses and costs), and disability pensions paid out under CPP/QPP. It does not include pension income, dividends, interest, capital gains, amounts received from an RSP/RRIF, or severance pay.

For a complete definition of "earned income" refer to Revenue Canada's information circular 72-22R9. These and other Revenue Canada Information and Interpretation Bulletins are available at your local Revenue Canada office.

Equities The term used to describe shares issued by a company representing ownership in that company. A mutual fund that invests largely in shares of corporations is called an equity fund. Equity also describes the right to a property or investment minus any liens against it. The equity you have in your home is (roughly) the current market value of your home minus the amount of your mortgage(s) or any loan secured by your home.

Equity, share and **stock** are generally used synonymously.

Estate All assets owned at the time of death.

Excess Contribution Any contribution made to an RSP over your maximum contribution limit. Until recently, you could overcontribute up to $8000 without penalty. That is, you could contribute an extra $8000 to your RSP without being penalized. If you overcontributed more than $8000, you were penalized 1 percent of the excess per month. Due to legislation changes, any overcontribution of more than $2000 is penalized at this rate.

If you intend to keep the funds within your RSP for a long time (more than 10 years) it can make sense to overcontribute to a maximum of $2000, even though you can't make a deduction. The benefits of tax-sheltering the growth on income can be significant. If your circumstances are such that you can't make your maximum contribution in a subsequent year, you can then deduct the overcontribution. Otherwise, plan to make the deduction in the year you turn 69, or it will be double-taxed—that is, taxed at source when you earn it, and taxed again as income when you withdraw it.

Ex-dividend Shares sold without the dividend. See also **Cum Dividend**.

Extendible Bond or Debenture A debt instrument granting the holder the right to extend the maturity date by a stated period.

Face Value The value of a bond or debenture that appears on its "face," or the front of the certificate. This is usually the amount due on maturity.

Flow-through Shares Certain losses and expenses that would normally be treated as tax deductions by a corporation or trust can be "flowed-through" or attributed to investors through these investment structures.

Front-end Load The term refers to a sales commission paid at the time of a mutual-fund purchase. Sometimes referred to as a **sales charge,** or **acquisition fee,** this fee is charged on a percentage basis ranging from 0 percent to 9 percent, with an average of 3 percent to 5 percent. There is heavy competition at the lower end, however, with many institutions selling at 1 percent to 2 percent and even lower on purchases of a minimum dollar amount.

  Shop around, negotiate, and make sure the service package you buy will meet your needs. The sales charge compensates financial advisers or planners for their services. A lower sales charge can mean warehouse-style service, or an adviser who promises (and intends to deliver) excellent personalized service but is too busy to return your calls.

  There are two alternatives to front-end load: **no-load** (no fee) and **deferred sales charge,** or **back-end load.**

Future Value The amount an investment will be worth at some point in the future at the current rate of return. A related term is **present value**—that is, the current value of an investment that will be worth a stated amount at some point in the future. For example, if I invest $1000 at 10 percent interest for one year, the present value of my investment is $1000. The future value of the investment is $1100.

Futures Contracts (traded on exchanges) that allow the holder to buy or sell commodities, currencies, etc., at a stated price on a stated date.

GIC A **Guaranteed Investment Certificate,** issued by banks, trust companies, and credit unions in Canada. The guarantee refers to insurance coverage by **CDIC** (banks and trust companies) or the **Member Protection Fund (MPF)** (credit unions). Maximum coverage under this guarantee is $60 000 per person under CDIC coverage and $100 000 under MPF coverage, subject to certain restrictions and exceptions. GICs pay a stated amount of interest to the investor. Interest can be compounded (adding to the principal on the payment date) or regular, meaning interest is paid to the investor. Terms can range from thirty days to five years.

Gross Domestic Product (GDP) The value of all goods and services produced in a country in a year. This figure does not currently recognize unpaid work, such as home caring and child rearing, but is limited to goods and services that change hands for units of value.

Gross National Product (GNP) Like the GDP (above), but includes profits and interest on endeavours by Canadians living or investing abroad as well as at home.

Growth Mutual Funds Growth mutual funds are those that invest in growth stocks.

Growth Stock A growth stock is one that is expected to grow in value more rapidly than average stocks. Growth stocks are often **small-cap stocks** (see **Blue-chip Stocks**). In addition to their potential for rapid growth, these stocks invariably have an equal potential for volatility—rapid swings in price, both high and low.

Guaranteed Income Funds A mutual fund that invests in GICs and term deposits.

Guaranteed Term The period during which annuity payments are guaranteed. If the annuitant dies during this period, payments will be made to the beneficiary. Without this guaranteed term, annuity payments would automatically cease on the annuitant's death.

Hedge A protective maneuver designed to limit losses. There are many ways of hedging, almost all of which are complex transactions that should be practised by extremely sophisticated investors or industry professionals.

Home Buyer's Plan The Home Buyer's Plan (HBP) was originally introduced in 1992 as a temporary measure to assist Canadians in buying their first homes and to kick-start the lagging residential real estate and construction industries. Originally, it was intended only for first-time home buyers and could only be used once in a lifetime—that changed with the 1998 budget. If you've completely repaid the first HBP loan from your RSP, you are now welcome to do it a second time.

Basically, it works like this. If you haven't owned a home within the past four years, you can withdraw up to $20 000 tax-free from available funds within your RSP. You can't use funds from a locked-in RSP, and if you own assets like GICs that are locked in until a specified maturity date, you will find that most institutions won't make the funds available to you just because you decided you want to nest. You'll have to wait until the maturity date. If you and your spouse are buying the house jointly, you can each withdraw up to $20 000 from your respective RSPs. Even if your legal or common-law spouse has owned a house within the past four years, you can make a home-buyer's withdrawal as long as your spouse's home was not your principal residence, so you may wish to avoid cohabitation.

This is not a tax-free withdrawal as much as it is a tax-free, interest-free loan. Beginning in the second calendar year after the withdrawal, you must repay at least 1/15 of the amount of the withdrawal per year. If you miss a payment, you must declare that amount as *income* on your tax return, meaning that you will pay tax, at whatever your current rate is, on that amount. Yikes! Of course, you will not receive a tax deduction for the repayment.

Remember, too, that 15 years of lost compound-return magic is a significant price to pay for the benefit of calling yourself a homeowner. Just because you *can* do it doesn't mean you *should* do it! A financial planner can do the calculations necessary to determine if the home-buyer's withdrawal is worthwhile for you.

Hypothecate A term used in English-speaking Canada to describe the process of pledging assets as security against a loan; *hypothèque* is actually the French word for mortgage.

Income Bond In most cases, an income bond is one that promises to repay the principal investment, but will only pay interest income when that income is earned by the issuing corporation.

Income Splitting The process of arranging income streams so that taxable income is diverted from a higher-taxed individual to a lower-taxed one.

Initial Public Offering (IPO) Another commonly used stock-market term that refers to a new issue of stock being offered to the public for the first time.

Installment Receipt A stock or equity investment that allows the investor to pay in installments rather than in one lump sum.

Inter-vivos Trust Also referred to as a **living trust,** which is what it is. A **testamentary trust** is one formed to take effect after your death, using the assets of your estate. If you create a trust while you are living, it is an inter-vivos trust. These trusts are created to minimize probate fees and allow for the direct transfer of your assets to your beneficiaries (so they are not included in your estate). Both living and testamentary trusts are advanced tax-planning tools, and should be created only with competent tax, financial-planning, and legal advice.

Intestate An awful word that describes dying without a valid will.

Joint and Last Survivor A type of annuity that provides income payments until both the annuitant and the annuitant's spouse die.

LSVCCs (or Labour-Sponsored Venture Capital Corporations) LSVCCs are a type of mutual fund sponsored by labour organizations for the purpose of funding small and medium-size businesses. As an incentive, governments offer attractive tax credits to investors. An example in British Columbia is the Working Opportunity Fund, for which the investor receives a tax credit of 30 percent on investments up to $3000. As a result of their focus on small business within a certain locale, these funds are somewhat speculative in nature.

Leverage Increasing the return (and risk) on an investment by borrowing and using the borrowed funds to invest. This is an advanced planning strategy—don't do it without advice from a competent financial adviser you trust.

Life Income Fund (LIF) A recently created alternative to an annuity upon maturity of a locked-in RSP. If you leave a corporation prior to retirement, you often have the option of receiving your pension funds; however, they can only be transferred to a locked-in RSP or used to purchase an annuity. In the past, when you wished to receive income from the holdings of the locked-in RSP, or when you reached age 69, the only option was to cash it in and purchase an annuity. In recognition of current interest-rate conditions in Canada, this legislation was recently changed to allows LIFs—essentially, a retirement income fund that has prescribed minimum withdrawals (like RRIFs) and prescribed maximum withdrawals. LIFs provide greater investment flexibility and the potential for greater returns than an interest-bearing annuity.

Liquidity An important investment term that is used to describe the ease with which an asset can be converted into cash without a significant financial penalty for doing so.

Load Sales charge or commission. See also **Front-end Load.**

Locked-in This term is used in reference to many investments and investment plans. A GIC may be referred to as locked-in if it cannot be redeemed prior to maturity.

On the stock market, investors are referred to as locked-in if they cannot sell stocks they own either because no one else wants them, or because to do so would create an onerous loss.

The term is more commonly used in reference to RSPs. Locked-in RSPs are RSP accounts created from pension-fund money. In a locked-in self-directed RSP, investments can be purchased or sold, but funds cannot be withdrawn or used to fund a mortgage on one's home.

Locked-in Retirement Account (LIRA) The equivalent of a locked-in RSP. A registered plan that can receive pension proceeds.

Long If you want to sound like a really savvy investor, instead of saying, "I **own** 100 ABC shares," you can say, "I am **long** 100 shares of ABC."

The opposite of "long" is **"short."** This means that our savvy investors have sold 100 shares of ABC that they don't own, in the hope or expectation that the price of the shares will drop before they have to buy 100 shares to cover their contracts. Savvy?

Management Expense Ratio (or MER) One of the single most important factors to be considered in the purchase of mutual funds. MER is an accounting of all of the costs of operating a mutual fund. The MER, when compared to MERs of similar funds, can sometimes give us a glimpse into the efficiency of the fund's management. In any case, even when higher MERs are justified by excellent, long-term fund performance or by unique analytical requirements, MERs reveal the price of holding a mutual fund from year to year. Higher-than-average MERs can result in thousands of dollars in lost returns over the life of an investment. As well, MERs remain relatively static (as a percentage of assets) no matter how the fund performs. If a fund is providing returns of 20 percent, an MER that is 1 percent higher than average doesn't seem significant. It can become significant when the market is in decline and the same fund provides negative returns of 4 percent—of which 3 percent are MER-related fees.

Management Fee This is a misleading term for a misleading figure. Management fees are the portion of the MER (see above) that is paid to the fund manager. It does not include the cost of administration, distribution, etc., even though those costs are paid by the fund holders. Focus on the MER.

Margin In an account where you borrow funds in order to finance a portion of your investments (a **margin account**), "margin" refers to the amount you actually own. Trading regulations determine what this amount must be (as a percentage of the account).

Marginal Tax Rate A common term that simply refers to the rate you will be taxed on the "next dollar" of income.

Market Order A stock-market term for an order to purchase or sell securities immediately, at any price.

Money Market That portion of the capital market created for the short-term borrowing and lending of funds. As opposed to being traded on an exchange, these financial instruments are traded through a network of money-market dealers, largely over the telephone. The financial instruments traded include short-term (less than three years) bonds, Canada Treasury Bills (T-Bills), and commercial paper (a term used to describe a short-term debt instrument issued by an institution or corporation).

Money-market Fund A mutual fund that invests in the money market, usually for less than one year (see **Money Market** above). These funds normally have Net Asset Values (NAVs) (see **NAV** below) set at either $1 or $10, and offer low but stable returns with low potential for volatility. There is a slight risk, however— if a very large group of investors all decided to take their money out at the same time, the fund may be forced to sell investments at below-market or par value. This is a very slight risk, but if there is some kind of future market hysteria, it is a possibility. (In the case of such hysteria, either start it and be first out, or stay put until you have a long talk with your financial adviser!)

Money Purchase Plan Another name for a **Defined Contribution Pension Plan.** Employees "purchase" future benefits through their contributions and generally have some flexibility in determining how the funds will be invested. Future pension benefits, then, are determined by the amount of contributions to the plan and the return on investment, and cannot be forecast in advance. Hence the name. The pension proceeds are not known but the contribution amount is. (Employers may or may not contribute to a Money Purchase Plan.)

Mortgage-backed Securities (MBS) (sometimes referred to as NHA Mortgage-backed Securities) These fixed-income instruments are currently sold in units of $5000, with a term of five years. They are backed by a pool of mortgages insured by the National Housing Association (NHA) (so there is no risk of default by the mortgagor). Each month, the investor receives interest and a portion of the principal. If mortgages within the pool are paid out in advance of maturity, the MBS holder will receive a lump sum in reflection of that payment.

Mortgage-backed securities trade in the bond market, at prices reflective of current interest rates. Depending on available rates and prices, these can be very attractive RRIF and retirement-income investments.

Mutual Fund A pooled group of investment funds, providing professional management and the opportunity for maximum diversification. The total value of the investment fund is divided into **units,** which are then allocated to investors at a **Net Asset Value** (see below).

There are money-market mutual funds, dividend mutual funds, equity mutual funds, growth mutual funds, sector mutual funds, foreign mutual funds, real estate mutual funds, fixed-income mutual funds—many, many different kinds of mutual funds with different underlying assets, different investment styles, and different objectives.

Unit-holders benefit from a fund's success through dividends (which are usually reinvested in new units of the funds—one of the significant benefits of owning mutual funds rather than stocks) and through the increase in the unit's value, as the value of the pool of investments grows.

Naked Writer This racy term just sounded so good I had to include it. Here's the definition provided by the Canadian Securities Institute: "A seller of an option contract who does not own an offsetting position in the underlying security or a suitable alternative. The rules for establishing whether a position is naked or uncovered are detailed in the CSI's Canadian Options Course."

Net Asset Value (NAV) In stock-market environs, net asset value is the measure of total assets of a corporation minus total liabilities. Net asset value is sometimes referred to as **shareholder's equity.**

Net Asset Value per Share (NAVPS or NAV) The valuation of mutual-fund units, net asset value is the measure of the total value of the assets of the fund, minus any liabilities of the fund, divided by the number of units outstanding.

No-load Fund A mutual fund on which no sales charge or commission is charged upon purchase or at redemption. See also **Front-end Load** and **Deferred Sales Charge.**

Offer When **bid** meets **offer,** we have a contract. An offer is the price at which a holder of securities is willing to sell them.

Offering Memorandum A legal document, reporting the pertinent aspects of an investment, for the review of potential investors. Similar to a prospectus, but released without the same degree of scrutiny by the regulatory bodies. See also **Prospectus.**

Open Order Another stock-market term that refers to an order that is "open," (or valid) until filled or until expressly cancelled by the investor.

Option A sophisticated financial instrument that allows an investor to speculate on the future prices of securities. A "put" allows an investor to sell securities at a

specified price until a specified date; a "call" option allows an investor to purchase securities at a specified price until a specified date.

Over-the-Counter The term used for the market in securities not traded on the
exchanges—generally investments best suited to sophisticated and steel-nerved
investors due to their limited liquidity (opportunity to sell the investment once
you own it).

Par Another term for face value. See **Face Value.**

Penny Stock The colloquial term for stocks that trade at less than $5. These are
generally very speculative issues traded on the resource markets (the VSE and
ASE). Although the potential gains can be astronomical, these exchanges offer
most of us (those of us who are not industry insiders) investment opportunity
approximately equivalent to that of bingo. Buyer beware!

Pension Adjustment (PA) The adjustment made to your RSP maximum contribution limit, based on the combined value of your employer's contribution to
your pension plan and your own. Although this calculation is complex, you
should never have to do it—your PA is provided on your T4 at the end of the
year and is also provided on your Statement of Assessment from Revenue
Canada.

Present Value See **Future Value.**

Price-earnings Ratio (also referred to as P/E ratio or P/E multiple) This is a
calculation used to determine whether a stock is expensive in relation to its
underlying profitability. If you purchase stocks from a broker, you will probably hear this term. It is, quite simply, a company's earnings per share divided by
its share price.

Prospectus A prospectus is a legal document, required by law, that discloses everything you need to know about a particular investment. If you cannot bear to
read it all, read the sections entitled "Risk Factors" and "Summary of Investor
Expenses" plus every section that sounds as if it might relate to risks or fees.
Essential reading for every investor.

Real Rate of Return A figure you should always know as it applies to your
investments—real return is the stated return on your investment, minus tax
considerations, minus the rate of inflation.

Registered Education Savings Plan (RESP) A registered savings/investment
program that allows you to accumulate funds in a tax-sheltered environment to
pay for secondary education for your children, nieces, nephews, grandchildren,
etc.

      Contributions are not deductible, but returns on the funds are tax-
sheltered, and are then taxed in the hands of the student, who presumably will
have little other income.

Registered Pension Plan (RPP) A pension plan, generally established by an
employer on behalf of its employees to provide pension income in retirement.
See **Defined Benefit Plan** and **Money Purchase.**

Registered Retirement Income Fund (RRIF) In the year you turn 69, you must close your RSP. Your options are as follows:

You may cash the entire amount in. This is usually a terrible idea, as the entire amount will be treated as income for that year and will be taxed at the highest rate for your tax bracket.

You can use the funds to purchase an annuity. In times of high interest rates, this can be a very attractive option. In times of low interest rates, an annuity still provides a predictable income stream, but may not provide adequate returns to fund a long retirement.

You can convert the RSP into a **RRIF**. RRIFs are like RSPs in that there are a variety of different options available. A RRIF can be "managed" (the kind you buy at the bank that pays interest) or it can be a mutual-fund RRIF (in which your funds are invested in one mutual-fund family). You can also have a self-directed RRIF (in which you can invest in any qualified investment). A self-directed RRIF works best for anyone who had a self-directed RSP, as you don't have to redeem your investments simply to convert to a RRIF.

Like RSPs, you can have as many RRIFs as you like, but it makes sense to have as few as will meet your needs.

Registered Retirement Savings Plan Very simply, a tax-deferral plan. To encourage us to prepare for retirement, RSPs allow us to defer paying income tax on a portion of our income until we withdraw the funds. When we contribute (within prescribed limits), Revenue Canada will refund the amount of tax we have already paid on that amount, or will use the deduction to offset any tax we owe.

An RSP is not an investment in itself. Funds contributed to an RSP can be invested in a vast range of assets, from the mortgage on your own home, to Canada Savings Bonds, to term deposits. However, the account that holds these investments must be "registered." When you fill out your application (actually a registration contract), the plan trustee notifies Revenue Canada that the plan exists and that you are contributing to it. This process ensures that Revenue Canada gets its piece of the action at withdrawal time and that any RSP deduction is legitimate. See also **RRIF**.

Renewable Insurance A feature on some term-insurance policies that allows the insured to renew the policy without "evidence of insurability" (medical information, etc.) at the premium rate applicable according to age. Without this feature, it is probable that some people with health challenges would not be reinsured when their term insurance matured.

Return The amount of income you receive from an investment.

Reverse Mortgage A loan against your home (mortgage) that is used to purchase an annuity, which then provides monthly income. This is an option for those seniors who have very limited cash flow but own their homes outright—however, because compound interest works against you here, a reverse mortgage should only be arranged after consulting a competent financial planner.

Right Another stock-market term. A right is a privilege granted to existing shareholders that allows them to buy more shares at a stated price. These rights are often sold as part of a share package, enhancing the value of the shares.

Risk Risk is one of those words that has a different meaning for everyone. In the investment industry, risk is defined as the possibility that a particular investment will not do what we expect it to do, or hope it will do. **The principle of investment risk is universal and operates without exception the higher the expectation of return, the higher the probability the investment will not perform as expected.** At the risk of being redundant, I'll say it again. There are no exceptions, no matter what you hear, no matter what you are told. Higher potential returns equal greater risk.

Self-directed RSP An RSP in which the plan-holder pays an administration fee to a trustee in order to have the privilege of holding any qualified investment within one plan. The plan-holder gets to decide which investments are held.

Speculation "Speculators" often don't realize that's what they are. In fact, speculation can be defined as purchasing an investment in the hope that it will increase in price within a defined (usually short) period of time. Conversely, an investor is someone who purchases an investment with the desire to participate in that company's success (or asset's increase in value) over an extended period of time.

Spousal RSP Contribution An RSP contribution that is made (and deducted) by one spouse on behalf of the other. This is an effective income-splitting device, and is especially valuable when one spouse gives up career earnings and pension opportunities to stay home with the children.

If spousal contributions are withdrawn, they are taxed in the hands of the contributing spouse for the first three calendar years. Therefore, it is a good idea to make spousal contributions in December rather than RSP season (January or February). For instance, if you make a spousal RSP contribution in December 1997, 1997 is counted as the first year, and withdrawals made in the year 2000 would be taxed in the hands of the receiving spouse.

If you are in a lower income-tax bracket, earning substantially less income, and your spouse is not making contributions on your behalf, it could be worth asking why not.

Stocks A stock certificate is a kind of "currency" that serves as evidence of ownership in a business. The company (or business) can range in size, from a mom-and-pop craft shop in the basement, to global conglomerates. In the case of M&P Enterprise, it is likely that the shareholders (the owners of the stock, and therefore the business) would be Mom and Pop themselves, perhaps their offspring, and perhaps a relative or friend who has given them start-up funds in exchange for partial ownership. In the case of the global conglomerate, millions of shares might be in circulation, trading on one or more stock exchanges, and owned by both private investors and institutions, such as banks, mutual funds, and insurance companies.

When we refer to "stocks and bonds," or the "stock" market, we are generally referring to stocks of publicly traded companies. In order to trade its stocks on an exchange, a company must meet certain regulatory criteria. This affords the investor a very limited degree of protection. Largely, this protection is limited to the assurance that the company will publicly disclose relevant information.

Strip Bonds If held to maturity, strip bonds provide a predictable rate of return. However, if not held to maturity, they can be quite speculative, depending on the volatility of the bond market. It is important that they be purchased only with professional advice, and preferably with the intent to hold them until maturity. See also **Coupon.**

Tax Deferral The process of postponing payment of taxes for as long as legally possible. The longer you have your money, the longer it can work for you.

Tax Shelter Any investment vehicle that allows funds to be "sheltered" from taxation for a period of time. As it is usually used, the term "tax shelter" refers to rather speculative investments for which the major selling benefit is a tax advantage. In some cases, tax credits or deductions are provided as part of the investment structure. In other cases, certain "losses" or expenses are "flowed through" (attributed to) the investor. The investor can then use these losses to offset income and/or gains from other sources.

Tax shelters are not all risky, speculative investments—an RSP is a tax shelter. However, a decision to invest in a tax-sheltered investment should always be made on its investment merits, not on its ability to avoid tax. Losing a dollar to save 50 cents never makes sense. Advice from a trusted, competent financial adviser is crucial.

Term Insurance A type of insurance policy that provides coverage for a stated term. Term insurance is much less expensive than whole (or universal) life insurance, as coverage is applicable only to the term for which it is purchased. Term life is granted on the presumption of certain odds about the number of people who will die in any given year.

Term insurance is a great option for short-term insurance needs (to provide for our children, for instance, or to pay off a mortgage). However, most of us will live a good many years. If we want insurance to supplement or provide an estate for our heirs, we need whole or universal life.

Testamentary Trust A trust that is designed to come into effect after the death of the contributor. See also **Inter-vivos Trust.**

Treasury Bill (or T-Bill) These are short-term government debt instruments that are issued in denominations of $100 000 to $1 million. Investors can participate by owning a T-Bill "position" through a bank or brokerage firm; that is, they own a portion of a T-Bill and receive a stated rate of return as provided by the underlying T-Bill.

T-Bills are very liquid as they have short maturity periods (usually 90 and 180 days) and can also be bought and sold between maturity dates. They are fully "government backed," which means they are extremely secure.

T-Bills do not pay interest, per se. Rather, they are purchased at a discount (i.e., a $100 000 T-Bill is purchased for $97 000; therefore, the yield to maturity is 3 percent).

Trust A legal instrument placing property or assets in the hands of a "trustee," a person, persons, or an institution elected to manage assets or property and over-see its distribution to another person or persons. An RSP is a "trust," but the "trusts" we normally hear about when we're talking about investments are either inter-vivos (living) trusts or testamentary (after-death) trusts. See also **Inter-vivos Trust.**

Unit A term used in reference to mutual-fund holdings.

Universal Life A form of whole life insurance that provides life-insurance cover-age and an insurance component that is indexed to money-market yields. Universal life is very popular when interest rates are high.

Variable Life Another form of whole life insurance in which the investment por-tion of the plan is invested in mutual funds. These plans are more flexible and may provide higher returns than universal life policies, but are not as pre-dictable.

Whole Life See **Universal Life, Variable Life,** and **Term Insurance.**

Yield The return on an investment, normally expressed as a percentage.

INDEX

abundance mentality, 37-40, 46-47
acquisition fee, 161
action steps, 118-20
advertisements, 111
allowances, children's, 188-90
alternate beneficiary, 185
asset, allocation, 148; types, 148-50
asset allocation funds, 152
assets, hard, 150

baby boom generation, 131
balanced funds, 152
Balancing Act (Yaccato), 10
bank accounts, 57
bear market, 140
beliefs, 9-10, 18-35, 40-42, 205;
    reframing old, 43-47. *See also* abun-
    dance mentality; poverty mentality
beneficiary, 185
bill paying, 61
blue-chip companies, 140, 144
bond funds, 149, 180
bond offering, 137
bonds, 2, 140-43, 164
books, 11, 74
book value, 170
bottom-up investment style, 153-54
Breathnach, Sarah Ban, 74
Bre-X, 8, 9
Buffet, Warren, 19
buy-and-hold strategy, 180

Cameron, Julia, 114
Canada Mortgage Insurance
    Corporation (CMHC), 194
Canada Savings Bonds (CSBs), 132,
    156, 180
Canadian Depositary Insurance
    Corporation (CDIC), 141
Canadian Education Savings Grant
    (CESG), 191-94
Canadian equity, 151
capital gains, 162, 180, 182
career, 1-6, 126

Carry-forwards, 176
cash, asset type, 148; mutual funds, 148
cash-flow statement, 69, 99-102
children, 67; education planning,
    191-94; responsibility of rearing,
    125-26; teaching money matters to,
    188-90
clothes, 52-53
commission, sales, 161
common-share offering, 142
Conran, Shirley, 41
conscious/subconscious mind, 17, 18
contribution room, maximum, 176
Cork, David, 131
costs, 119-20
creative power, 81
credit counsellor, 63-64
credit management, 58-60
current reality, 82, 108-9

debit, direct, 61
debt securities. *See* fixed-income
    investments
deemed disposition, 162, 173
deferred sales charges (DSC), 162
derivative-based mutual funds, 180
details, 55-57, 81
disability insurance, 105
discretionary spending, 69-70
dissatisfaction, 86
diversification, 137, 140; bonds and,
    140-43; mutual funds, 153, 156;
    strategy, 143-44
dividend and capital gains-bearing
    investments, 179-80
dividend funds. *See* equity funds
divine indulgence, 49-52, 74
domestic work, unpaid, 175
donations, charitable, 77-76, 168-69,
    182, 205
dream book, 115-17
dreams, dreaming, 83-88, 110-17. *See*
    also vision
Dworkin, Andre, 9

eating out, 51
education planning, 191-94
End of Work, The (Rifkin), 6
equalization payment, 68-69
equities, 136-40, 141, 150
equity funds, 149, 180
estate planning, 183-87
Excellent Advisor, The (Murray), 64
executor, 184-85
expenditures. *See* recordkeeping; spending
Eynon, Ann, 147

faith, 56
fear, 37, 42-43, 46, 124
financial advisers, 19, 123, 134-36, 145, 147, 156, 160, 198-203
financial net-worth statement, 90, 91-93
financial planning, and investing, 135; point of departure, 90; teaching children about, 188-90. *See also* bank accounts; bill paying; credit; money management; order; pre-cohabitation discussion
Financial Pursuit, 122
fixed-income investments, 149-50, 156
Fox, Emmet, 114
freedom, financial, 7, 120
free units, 162
Fritz, Robert, 80, 82
fund managers, 145, 158

gender bias, 124-25
gendered differences, 9, 48, 76-78
gender roles, 9
GICs, 132-34, 148, 156, 164, 170, 171, 180
goal-setting, 81
Gratitude Journal, 113
growth managers, 154
guardianship, 184

hard assets, 150
heart (subconscious). *See* beliefs; conscious/subconscious mind

high-ratio mortgages, 194
Home-based business. *See* self-employment
Home Buyers Plan, 194
home ownership, 194-96. *See also* real estate prices
hybrid diversified mutual funds, 180

income, 177; bonus, 182
income splitting, 175
index funds, 153
inflation, 132, 150
Initial Public Offering (IPO), 142
"in kind" contributions, 172, 173
insurance, 104-8
interest rates, 133-34, 141
international equity, 152
international funds, 180
in-trust account, 193, 194
investment, diversification in, 143-44; in equity markets, 133-34; estate planning, 185-86; fundamentals of planning, 135; individual control, 69-70; risk, 138-40, 146; styles, 153-54; and taxation, 179-82; time horizons, 137-40

journal, 113
Jubinville, Paula, 179

Labour-Sponsored Venture Capital funds, 181-82
living expenses, 175
Living Will, 186
long-term care insurance, 186
Lynch, Peter, 19

managed RSPs, 171
Management Expense Ratios (MERs), 148, 149
management expenses, 148
maturity dates, 144
meditation, 82-84, 90, 114
momentum managers, 154
money, 15, 64, 90, 118
money management, 70-75. *See also* financial planning

money-market account, 170
money-market funds, 180
Money Market funds, 148
monthly contributions, 155, 173
mortgage, 194-96
mortgage funds, 149, 180
Murray, Nick, 64
mutual funds, 145-65, 170; buying,
    154-55; equity funds, 151-53; fees
    and commissions, 160-62; fund
    companies, 158-59; management
    fees, 148; management styles,
    153-54; pooling of resources, 151;
    recommended, 133; RSPs, 171;
    segregated, 163-65; selling decision,
    159-60; short- and long-term cash
    flow needs, 156-57; "turnover" rate,
    180; types, 148-50; units, 146

needs analysis, 107
Net Asset Value (NAV), 146
no-load funds, 161-62

order, 55-57, 63, 75
overcontributions, 176

Path of Least Resistance (Fritz), 80
pay-yourself-first program, 70-71, 205
Peck, Scott, 103
Pension Adjustment (PA), 176
Pension Adjustment Reversal (PAR),
    176
permanent insurance, 108
Pig and the Python, The (Cork), 131
positive people, 46, 47
Potuzak, Rob, 158
poverty, 37
poverty mentality, 15
power, 15
Power of Attorney, 186
pre-cohabitation discussion, 46-70
preferred shareholders, 142
prospectus, 148
Pulos, Lee, 82
purchased insurance, 106

quality of life, 93-98, 120

Raising Your Business (Yaccato and
    Jubinville), 179
real estate investment fund (REIF),
    170
real estate investment trust (REIT),
    170
real estate prices, 131-32. *See also*
    homeownership
realtors, 195
receipts, 73-74
recordkeeping, 60, 69-70, 73-74
references, 203
Registered Education Savings Plans
    (RESPs), 191-94
Registered Retirement Savings Plan
    (RRSP), 169, 176
Registered Savings Plan (RSP),
    beneficiary, 185; borrowing to
    contribute, 174-75; compound
    returns, 172; contributions, 124, 170,
    172-74; GICs, 133; investments,
    179-80; spousal contributions,
    175-76; tax-deferred device, 169-70,
    172; types, 170-74, 171-72
retirement planning, 120-23, 157
rewards, 74
Rifkin, Jeremy, 6
risk, 133, 135, 146
risk management, 103-8
risk tolerance, 157-58
Road Less Travelled, The (Peck), 103
RRSP index participation mutual
    funds, 180

St. James, Elaine, 51
Savage, Cara, 59
savings accounts, 170, 171
saving. *See* pay-yourself-first program
sector equity, 152
segregated funds, 163-65
self-directed RSPs, 171-72
self-employment, 6, 6-7, 177-79;
    status, 178; tax deductions, 178-79
self-fulfillment, 113
self-insurance, 106-7
self-reliance, 19
self-worth, 44-46

service fees, 57
shares, common, 142, 149; preferred, 149. *See also* equities
shopping, 48-49, 74
Simplify Your Life, (St. James), 51
small cap equity, 152
small cap managers, 154
social programs, 188
special equity, 152
spending, keeping track of, 73-74; miscellaneous, 99; understanding where money goes, 69-70, 71-73
spending patterns, 51-52
standard deviation, 146
Statement of Assessment, 176
stock market, 134, 135, 137-40, 150-51
stock picking, 140, 147
stocks. *See* equities
strategic asset allocation, 153
subconscious mind. *See* conscious/subconscious mind
Superwoman (Conran), 41

tax audit, 179
tax credit, 168-69
tax deductions, 179, 182
taxes, 71, 141, 167-68; investment income, 179-82
tax refunds, 174-75
tax returns, 182
tax shelters, 169, 181-82, 192
Templeton Growth, 147-48
tension, and creative power, 81
term insurance, 108

time horizon, 137-40, 143-44
time management, 63
time, quiet, 113
top-down investment style, 154
trading (high-turnover) strategy, 180
Treasury Bills (T-Bills), 148, 156; funds, 148

unexpected bills, 61
U.S equity, 151

value managers, 154
vision, 19, 80, 81-88, 119-20, 122-23. *See also* dreams, dreaming
vision statement, 98
voting rights, 142

Watters, Graydon, 122
wealth creation, 19
whole life insurance. *See* permanent insurance
wills, 183-87
Winfrey, Oprah, 42, 114
Winning the Tax Game (Cestnick), 179
women, balancing responsibilities, 1-6, 77-78; financial responsibility, 126-29; inexperience in money matters, 10, 16-17; life-cycle stages, 123-24; money matters, and cohabitation, 46-70; traits of financially successful, 39-40

Yaccato, Joanne Thomas, 10, 129, 179
Young, Duff, 133